CONFESSION

CONFESSION
Studies in Deviance and Religion

Mike Hepworth and
Bryan S. Turner

Routledge & Kegan Paul
London, Boston, Melbourne and Henley

First published in 1982
by Routledge & Kegan Paul Ltd
39 Store Street, London WC1E 7DD,
9 Park Street, Boston, Mass. 02108, USA,
296 Beaconsfield Parade, Middle Park,
Melbourne, 3206, Australia, and
Broadway House, Newtown Road,
Henley-on-Thames, Oxon RG9 1EN
Set in 10/12 pt Press Roman by
Thames Typesetting, Abingdon, Oxon
and printed in Great Britain by
Redwood Burn Ltd
Trowbridge, Wiltshire

Library of Congress Cataloging in Publication Data

Hepworth, Mike.
Confession : studies in deviance and society.
Includes bibliographical references.
1. Deviant behavior. 2. Criminal psychology.
3. Confession (Law) I. Turner, Brian S. II. Title.
HM291. H522 302.5'42 82–7624

ISBN 0 7100 9198 2 AACR2

Anyone writing confessions is
in peril of becoming lamentable

Contents

Acknowledgments

We have derived considerable benefit from conversations with many colleagues at conferences where previous versions of these essays on confession first saw the light of day. Associates in the Department of Sociology at Aberdeen have also, over the last eight years, made many valuable contributions to our research. In particular, however, Rod Watson, on the basis of his own studies of police practice, has been generous in providing criticism and support. Dr Bryan Wilson offered many valuable suggestions for improving an early version of 'Confession and social structure'. Similarly, Peter McCaffery contributed significantly to our understanding of the theology of penance. Jim Teele and Ellis Thorpe have, at various times, cast refreshing doubt on the whole enterprise. We would finally extend our thanks to Ruby Heath whose patience and precision were invaluable in sorting out a consistently untidy manuscript.

Three chapters of the present volume originally appeared as the following: M. Hepworth and B.S. Turner, 'Confessing to murder, critical notes on the sociology of motivation', *British Journal of Law and Society,* vol.1 (1974), pp. 31-49; Bryan S. Turner, 'Confession and social structure', *The Annual Review of the Social Sciences of Religion,* vol. 1 (1977), pp.29-58; M. Hepworth and B. Turner, 'Confession, guilt and responsibility', *British Journal of Law and Society,* vol. 6 (1979), pp. 219-34. We are grateful to the editors for permission to reprint these existing articles. Finally, we would like to offer our thanks to various editors of Routledge & Kegan Paul for the tolerance with which they have awaited the birth of this book.

Introduction

> Then a sheep confessed to having urinated in the drinking pool . . . and two other sheep confessed to having murdered an old ram, an especially devoted follower of Napoleon by chasing him round and round a bonfire when he was suffering from a cough. They were slain on the spot. And so the tale of confessions and executions went on, until there was a pile of corpses lying before Napoleon's feet. (George Orwell, *Animal Farm*, Penguin, 1951, pp. 73–4)

George Orwell's *Animal Farm*, first published in 1945, followed in the wake of public concern in Europe and America over show trials and public confessions in Stalin's Russia. The popularity of *Animal Farm* and its political setting underline the typical response to confessions. They are seen to be interesting and unusual because they are the false and abnormal statements of otherwise rational men subjected to clever but inhuman practices. They are regarded as a breach of normal political practice or infractions of proper codes for the use of prisoners. The ability to get rational men to confess to imaginary crimes or to 'false' thoughts appears to have been reduced to a mere set of techniques which could be followed in any society. The victim is isolated and deprived of normal and familiar social contacts; he is persuaded to make a voluntary admission of guilt; co-operation is rewarded by certain desired privileges; he is caught between the cross-pressure of friendly and menacing interrogators; his family is threatened. While in the Russian show trials confessions had often been achieved by physical brutality, 'indirect methods' of psychological pressure were much preferred by the NKVD.[1] It was precisely this feature of confession – the ability to make apparently rational men confess to anything without violence – which appeared threatening to Western observers, particularly during the Korean War.

The Chinese interrogators of American POW's during the Korean War deliberately employed a lenient, *laissez-faire* technique for achieving what in the West became known as 'thought reform', 'ideological remoulding' or simple 'brainwashing'. The latter term appears to have been first employed in 1951 by Edward Hunter in *Brain-Washing in Red China*, as a translation of the term 'hsi nao'. While the Chinese do not favour this term themselves, they did in that period frequently refer to self-criticism as a form of 'cleansing oneself'.[2] Following the repatriation of American prisoners in 1953, a rash of psychological commentaries on Chinese interrogation methods and their implications followed in academic publications.[3] These reports showed that, with the right combination of social isolation, inducement, persuasion and deprivation, prisoners of war could be made to condemn themselves, their government and the whole ethos of Western liberal democracy and to espouse the values of world communism. It was in this context that the new techniques of confession were seen as a threat, not only to the institution of the Western world, but also to its most prized possession – the self-activated rational individual. The extraction or eliciting of confession was now regarded as simply one aspect of a new phase of political indoctrination within the broader political perspective of the Cold War. Confession was a strategy for the macabre 'battle for the mind'; an element within the scientific battery of 'techniques of persuasion'.[4] We are, therefore, more familiar in contemporary society with confession in the pejorative sense – nefarious practices by the communists and possibly the Gestapo – than with its use in everyday police practice since, until quite recently, we have automatically assumed that our police act fairly. We assume that confessions given to the police tend to be spontaneous rather than the product of undue pressure. This is reflected in general public ignorance concerning the interrogation of murder suspects in Britain and this is further supported by the inaccessibility of police manuals – a situation very different from that pertaining in the United States. Cruel and unfair pressures, we assume, were abandoned with the Catholic Inquisition or the collapse of fascism.

The psychologists and social scientists who became interested in confession in the 1950s and 1960s were not slow, however, to point out the affinities between the modern methods of criminal and political interrogation and such phenomena as religious conversion, religious proselytisation and witchcraft trials. William Sargant has been particularly influential in bringing the apparent dangers of brainwashing before the public. His early work on the psychiatric problems associated with shell-shock and battle fatigue was followed by *Battle for the Mind* which sold over 250,000 copies. Describing his work during the war, he wrote,[5]

> Having linked up Pavlov's findings with our studies of acute war neuroses, with Wesley's mass-conversion techniques and with some

> aspects of the Freudian couch technique, I began to wonder whether the same principles must also hold good for political techniques of brain-washing, and also for the illegal eliciting of criminal confessions from suspects by police forces all over the world. Many prisoners from Brixton jail, sent to us under police guard to be given brainwave tests for possible epilepsy, had, we found, somehow been persuaded by the police to make full and detailed confessions of crimes which would assure them savage sentences in court, hanging included, and which some of them had subsequently wished to withdraw. I examined the all but universal police techniques of eliciting such confessions, some of which, such as Evans's later confessions in the Christie murders, seemed so false; and searched for examples of the 'equivalent', 'paradoxical' and 'ultra-paradoxical' phases of brain reaction occurring under psychological and physiological stress by police questioning. Wesley, Pavlov, battle-shocked soldiers, the police, MI5, or the Russian Ogpu – here was material for an overall psychological thesis.

Sargant's thesis continues to have public and political relevance. As a potential defence witness in the recent Patty Hearst trial in San Francisco, Sargant was called to the proceedings by the defence lawyer on account of his expertise in brainwashing techniques. He examined Patty for five days in jail and then destroyed his legal acceptability by appearing on television before the trial was over, and before he had appeared in court, to assert 'she had definitely been brainwashed by the Symbionese Liberation Front.'[6]

More disquietingly, perhaps, the psychiatric approach to murder in terms of a mechanistic view of the confessional has recently revealed an interesting dichotomy:

> psychiatrists in America have suddenly begun to treat ex-servicemen, who served in Vietnam, as patients. They are consulting psychiatrists to confess their part in atrocities committed in Vietnam. None of the men has confessed before and their visits to psychiatrists are because they are now breaking down and need help to live with their feelings of horror developed after as long as five years. One psychiatrist in Boston has already seen 40 such patients.

Whilst the above confirms the traditional belief in the 'burden of guilt' leading to an overriding 'impulse to confess', the same report also suggests that not all men can be so categorised. 'Some men', it seems, 'are more prone to kill indiscriminately than others', and the current trend appears to be to attempt to screen out those who reveal this tendency in specially constructed attitude questionnaires.[7] The distinction is further elaborated in an article almost a year later in the same newspaper. It now appears that psychological tests, such as the Minnesota Multiphasic Personality Inventory, are being used by the US government in a context reminiscent of *A Clockwork Orange*. The trick is to separate out those men who reveal above average aggressive/hostile responses and to expose them to 'stress reduction training' to prepare them as professional killers. 'The Pentagon in Washington last night denied categorically that the US navy had ever "engaged in psychological training or other types of training of personnel as assassins".'[8] Both pieces confirm the notion that taking human life is only likely in certain predictable circumstances or by people with distinctively aggressive/hostile and often depressive personalities. The secular practice of confession as a clinical technique geared to the demands of the state thus has clear historical antecedents in the pioneering work of therapeutic psychiatry as practised by Sargant.

Against a background of psychological research into the techniques of brainwashing and growing public disquiet about its contemporary political utility, it was not particularly difficult for social scientists to trace an historical lineage connecting confession with the brutalities of medieval torture and the apparent irrationality of witchcraft and sorcery. Witchcraft confessions were treated as the outcome of fantasy and cruelty. In more recent times, confession has been linked in popular literature with the new vogue for the occult and the bizarre. Whereas in the aftermath of the Russian purge, political confessions were seen as a threat to democracy, confessions of satanic possession in the contemporary period are seen as a threat to order and rationality, as an intrusion of a medieval, dark mentality into a stable, industrial society. This fear of the bizarre dimensions of confession was particularly marked in the press coverage of the Ossett murder case of 1974. Michael Taylor murdered his wife by tearing out her eyes and tongue in October 1974 after an all-night exorcism conducted by two Yorkshire clergymen. During this exorcism, forty devils were cast out after Taylor's long confession of satanic possession. Many features of the case struck the police and legal authorities as problematical and disturbing. Michael Taylor, prior to a short period of instability leading up to the murder, was apparently happily married, well adjusted and peaceable. What stands out in the law report on the case is the sense of an abnormal intrusion into the community by some anti-rational force. At the Leeds Crown Court, Mr Geoffrey Baker, QC, prosecuting, said of the nocturnal exorcism and confession of possession that it 'is difficult for those who read it and for those who listen not to believe that they are back in the Middle Ages.'[9] The trial served to bring to light the fact that many ministers of religion have a special interest in the field of demonic possession and are called upon to hear confessions of the possessed as part of the ministry of exorcism.

In this collection of essays, we are specifically concerned with the complex relationship between criminal and religious confessions. We consider this relationship within the context of law and religion as mechanisms of social control. There is, in these studies, a particular concentration on confession to murder. This focus on murder and religion might suggest that this study is also based on the premise that confession is about the abnormal, unusual and sensational. To link confession with murder might be to suggest that confession points to phenomena which intrude on social reality from outside in such a way as to threaten the normal bases of social behaviour. Our orientation to the issue is in fact the reverse of this assumption. Above all, our intention is to emphasise the striking domesticity of English murder in a society where revolutionary turmoil and civil disturbance have been relatively absent from modern English history. In English society, one is more likely to kill or to be murdered by one's immediate kin than by strangers. Furthermore, we shall be looking at confession to crime in law and confession to sin in religion as routine, common and 'natural' procedures. Our aim is to explore society and deviance from the point of view of confession as a routine feature of social relationships. Before proceeding with this task, it is important to provide, at least initially, a working definition of confession.

There is a scene in *Barchester Towers* where, after the Reverend Slope's attempted flirtation with Eleanor Bold, Trollope makes the observation that there are many occasions in which[10]

> both men and women feel themselves imperatively called on to make a confidence; in which not to do so requires a disagreeable resolution and also a disagreeable suspicion. There are people of both sexes who never make confidences.

In daily conversation, the verb 'to confess' appears in numerous contexts. It typically means to declare intimately a minor personal weakness or failing ('a confidence'). 'To confess' means 'to acknowledge or own, to admit'.[11] In its most general form, we use the verb 'to confess' in order to make a statement. While these every day interpersonal meanings of confession are of clear sociological interest, our use of confession is restricted to acknowledgment of major, actionable crimes and religiously defined sins of theological importance. In part, our selection of confession to murder is an attempt to limit the field of the sociology of confession which otherwise would be without boundaries. Such a decision to concentrate on crimes of murder has an arbitrary element to it in the sense that one could equally well select confession to homosexuality or to rape as an object of study. Furthermore, what will count in any society or epoch as a major crime is not an irreducible, objective fact, but rather the outcome of social practices. What will count as something worth confessing is a socially constructed reality – the product of social processes of definition within specific social contexts. This epistemological problem leads directly to the second criterion which defines what will count as a confession.

In this study, we are not specifically concerned with those confessions which take place within formal settings and contexts. Confessions may occur as statements within every day conversations, as chance remarks, as elements within the normal flow of day-to-day conversations. Our focus, however, will be on confessions which are the product of institutionalised, controlled and regularised investigations or interrogations of officially defined suspects and penitents. In short, the confessions which are the subject matter of this study are the products of routinised settings – confessional boxes, police interrogation centres, religious rituals and law courts. Such confessions are deliberately constructed by trained personnel out of the rich and complex verbal out-pourings of suspects. By contrast with the informal confidences of every day language, confessions which are to be officially validated as 'proper confessions', have to be made to persons in authority. A confession[12] 'consists in accusing ourselves of our sins to a priest who has received authority to give absolution.' Only priests have the 'power of the keys' of absolution and hence only priests are authorised to hear valid religious confession. Most definitions of 'confession' typically point to the importance of a 'person in authority'. Thus,[13]

> *Confess*: to acknowledge fully (especially something wrong); to own or admit; to make known, as sins to a priest. (Fr. confessor – L. confiteri, confessus – *con* – signifying completeness, and *fateri*, to confess – fari, to speak).

To confess is to speak fully of one's sins to a person with authority to hear.

Another aspect of confession as a structured situation and as a routine occurrence is the existence of confessional theories, that is, official viewpoints of what causes a person to confess, why the confession is important and what attitudes are appropriate for the confessant. In Catholicism, confession belongs to the sacrament of penance which is fully articulated in various theologies of sin, penance and reconciliation. Over the centuries in which Christians have practised the rite of penance, systematic codes have been developed for the guidance of confessors. These theological codes specify certain appropriate attitudes for the penitent. As the patron saint of canon lawyers Raymond de Peñaforte expressed it, confession must be 'bitter, speedy, complete and frequent'. One's complete statement of guilt had to be accompanied by outward symbols – humility, bitterness, effacement – of inner contrition.

Our final criterion for a confession is that, while the act itself may be private (within the confessional box of the Church) or secluded (within a police station), it must have some public consequences. In particular, we are concerned with confessions which were initially made 'in private' (to a police officer or to a priest), but subsequently come to play a major part in legal trials as admissible evidence. This concern with the public consequences and social dimensions of a private or secluded activity extends to a concern for published or written confessions over verbal statements. In its written form, the confession became a public restatement of social order, of the normality of the criminal, and ultimately came to play a part in popular entertainment as a special genre of crime writing. At present, this distinction between the private and the public dimension of the confession is necessarily crude. It is clearly the case that an action does not have to be performed before another person or a large group in order to be public or at least to have public implications. As Durkheim noted, suicide is fundamentally public and social. Our distinction draws attention to the fact that we (as a public, as readers, as sociologists) do not know or are unlikely to discover what takes place within a religious confessional, a political interrogation or a police interrogation of a suspect. Only rarely is the confessional bugged.[14] Our approach to confession must be necessarily indirect since we, like judges, are trying to make sense of publicised confessions, of confessions that have already been processed and socially manufactured after the event. There are, as it were, no 'pure' data on confession. Even the testimony of a person who has confessed is a testimony of a past event. At this stage, we merely want to lay down certain guidelines which indicate the range of phenomena in which we are interested. We use the term 'guideline' deliberately in order to avoid suggesting the spurious coherence of a social science typology. Our guideline is that we are conerned with confessions about (1) actions which are considered by law, theology or public opinion as serious crimes or sins or misdemeanours (2) which are confessed in a structured setting to a person in authority to hear (3) which are hedged around by articulated theories of human psychology and (4) which become public in the sense of having public consequences (within a trial) or in the sense of being published.

A guideline is not a watertight criterion. Pepys's diaries, Boswell's *Life of Johnson* or de Quincey's *Confessions of An Opium Eater* have a bearing on our chosen topic without fully meeting our requirements of a public, structured confession of major crime. Clearly a work like George B. Mair's *Confessions of A Surgeon* bears on our subject matter. These particular confessions have attracted the attention of the police, containing the claim that euthanasia is more common in hospitals than we believe. It appears that the police could not prosecute since Mair had had the foresight not to provide concrete evidence against which a charge could be sustained. It is a book which medical sociologists must take seriously, since euthanasia is an informal medical practice bordering ambiguously on the area of manslaughter and murder. In a different field of investigation, we can profit considerably from anthropological research into confessions in pre-industrial society.[15] We are, however, primarily concerned with confession within western, literate society. A more important objection might be that, in restricting our primary attention to cases of confession to murder in modern England, we have robbed ourselves of useful comparison with police practice in Russia or group confessions within China or to some other non-European context. While some aspects of the universality of confession are considered in Chapters 1 and 3 our focus is primarily restricted to western societies in the belief that, while there might be important parallels between, for example, European and Chinese confessional practice, confession is an institution peculiar to western society, because it grew out of the traditional Christian sacrament of penance. Confession is part of a moral-legal syndrome of practices and beliefs which includes certain key concepts (the conscience, the self, interior guilt, sin) and which has played a major part in shaping contemporary western culture. Russian confessions during the purge would, of course, be a borderline case. It is beyond the scope of this study to decide to what extent the existence of public confession within the Russian orthodox Church prepared the way or contributed to confessions which took place under Stalinism.

Confession, whether it takes place within the Christian confessional, the police station or within a court of law, typically presupposes a constellation of notions about the private self tormented by guilt and the private conscience exposed to self-criticism. This constellation is a specific product of Christian history. Of course, it is possible to trace these Christian assumptions back to a Jewish origin, but their full development depended on centuries of cultural and institutional development within a Christian context.[16] Similarly, there are elements of a confessional within Islam, especially within Sufism. In the Egyptian Sufi brotherhood studied by Michael Gilsenan, the brothers confess (*'itiraf'*) their sins to their Sheikh, but the[17]

> essential point of distinction is that there is no forgiveness given or absolution promised by the Sheikh, nor is it within his power to do so. This is linked with the notion of the Absolute Transcendence of the Omnipotent God, and with the nature of Islam. . . . Certainly the sense of sin, of the fall from grace, of spiritual guilt and the whole theodicy of suffering are virtually absent from Islam by comparison with most of the Christian Churches.

Where quasi-confessional practices arose in Islam, such as among the Bektashi Order of Dervishes, there is reason to believe that these arose from specific Christian influences.[18] No other religion seems to have an institution of private confession and an obligation to confess controlled by an official priesthood which alone has the power of absolution and reconciliation. The existence of confession in Christianity is the product of 'human failure' in a community of believers who have already been saved by the redemptive sacrifice of Christ as the suffering God. Confession is thus the resolution of the paradox of unfaithfulness of the Faithful. The other resolution of this tension lay in excommunication, but, by comparison with excommunication, confession has the advantage of being an act of charity in restoring and reconciling the sinful within a sinless community. Confession in principle is a remedial institution. Confession[19]

> is the receiving back by God's family into the Father's home of a brother who is conscious of having sinned not only against the Father's love but also against the peace and unity of the whole household.

That the Christian confessional had a more sinister aspect than the charitable restoration of prodigal sons will become evident later.

Within Christianity, it is possible to make a distinction between confessions of that which is publicly known (consciousness) in the confession of faith and that which is interior and private (conscience) in the confession of sin. St Augustine, for example, made a distinction between confession of faith, of praise and of sin. The Augustinian emphasis was on praise by which Augustine hoped 'to unlock the riddle of evil'.[20] Indeed, Augustine's emphasis on praise was an attempt to restore the theological balance since[21]

> there are some of the faithful who are so little informed that, when they hear the Scripture speaking of confession, they immediately beat their breasts as if there could be no confession other than of sins, and as if they had been warned to confess them.

Confession thus is linked primarily with the notion of 'conscience' as a practical exercise, as an accusation, a trial of the interior self. 'Conscience' has a juridical sense, as in the 'Court of Conscience', where the self is exposed to the internal counsel for the prosecution. The notion of 'consciousness' came to denote the ethical, theoretical sphere of knowledge in the sense of awareness of something. Paul Tillich notes that the Roman language[22]

> following popular Greek usage, unites the theoretical and practical emphasis in the word *conscientia*, while philosophers like Cicero and Seneca admit it to the ethical sphere and interpret it as the trial of one's self, in accusation as well as in defence. In modern languages the theoretical and the practical side are usually expressed by different words. English distinguishes *consciousness* from *conscience*, German *Bewusstsein* from *Gewissen*, French *connaissance* from *conscience*.

'Conscience' is the practical action of moral inquiry, while 'consciousness' implies theoretical knowledge of morals. Thus, Aquinas distinguished between *synderesis* as the habitual knowledge of moral principles and *conscientia* as the act of applying moral principles. Confession can thus be seen as 'speaking fully' (*confiteri*) about the trial of the self through the active principle of the interior conscience. The notion of the subjective, personal conscience, however, did not begin to develop until the twelfth and thirteenth centuries.

In his study of the awakening of the 'conscience', Father Chenu treats the twelfth century as a pivotal period which prepared the way for a mature development of a new psychology of human nature and morals in the thirteenth century.[23] Pierre Abélard (1079–1142) played a major philosophical role in shifting attention away from morality as conformity of actions to external laws to morality as intention and will. In consequence,[24] 'c'était ruiner à la base la discipline morale et pénitentielle en cours, qui était établie sur la loi objective et les contraintes de la coutume.' Abélardian subjectivism had a direct impact on the traditional confessional which had weighed actions by reference to exterior standards. The three major components of the religious confessional are contrition, satisfaction and absolution. Before the development of a subjective theory of 'conscience', the confession had been dominated by absolution as an ecclesiastical and objective event. For the followers of Abélard, contrition as the subjective element of the rite of confession became paramount. Contrition as a moral intention removed sin, thereby reducing the priest's absolution to a formal declaration. This new theological position enhanced the importance of private and personal confession and contributed significantly to the *summas* of the next century. This emphasis on man as the subject rather than on external nature had a wide-reaching impact on law, religion and art. In addition to Abélard, Chenu argued that the tradition of the troubadours and the culture of 'courtly love' contributed to the emergence of the 'conscience'.

The romance literature of the period produced a more refined and subtle notion of love which was categorised in terms of *amour céleste, amour naturel, amour charnel* and *amour pur*. Platonic affection as a value meant respect for *the person* rather than mere sexual attraction to the body as a sexual object. Personal love once more strengthened the focus on the subjective rather than on external codes.

The morality of the conscience was associated with a new emphasis on intention, subjectivity, the person and grace. This new ethic was the consequence of the rise of the market, the development of urban culture and the emergence of new social strata which challenged the existing feudal order. The main locations of the new philosophy were the guilds, the universities and the urban communities. Life in the towns was incompatible with feudal restrictions on travel and exchange and hence it was in the towns that one finds the first glimmerings of the doctrine of individualism. The traditional axiom that 'There is freedom in town air' is certainly true of the development of confession based on an interior conscience. Chenu comments that[25]

> L'adaption de l'examen de conscience, non seulement à la personalité de chacun, mais aux divers états de vie et professions, représente un remarquable effort d'intériorization, y compris dans la manière de juger les fonctions de la vie sociale, dans l'objectivité des relations humaines transformées par la société marchande nouvelle.

The transition from a society based on use-values to exchange-values on an open market is clearly fundamental for the emergence of the notions of a subjective self, an interior conscience and personal responsibility for actions and intentions. Urbanisation and commercialisation provide two important themes for our study of confession. The market and the city were fundamentally important for the main philosophical constituents (contract, equality and individualism) of the Enlightenment. As Lucien Goldmann has pointed out, the most significant[26]

> consequence of the development of a market economy is that the individual, who previously constituted a mere partial element within the total social process of production and distribution, now becomes, both in his own consciousness and in that of his fellow men, an independent element, a sort of monad, a *point of departure*.

The unique development of European cities against the cultural background of Christianity seems, therefore, to be connected fundamentally with the growth of an interior conscience and hence with the specific form in which confession of sins was expressed. The occidental city was an autonomous association of individuals rather than clans. As Weber pointed out, it was Christianity that had robbed 'the clan of its last ritualistic importance' since the Christian community 'was a confessional association of believing individuals rather than a ritualistic association of clans.'[27] If there is, in Weberian terms, a relationship between the emergence of an exchange economy, individualism and conscience as necessary conditions for the confessional as a court of personal inquiry, then it might seem somewhat problematic for our thesis that Protestantism appears to have no institutionalised confession. Against the casuistical view of sin as a collection of discrete actions, Protestantism adhered to a view of man as inherently and totally sinful. Jansenism had, of course, a similar viewpoint. The solution of total human sin was not the confession, but the birth of a new man through conversion to Jesus Christ. Nevertheless, there was in Protestantism a confessional exploration of the conscience through the Protestant diary as a devotional form, through the Wesleyan class meeting and penitential band, and through the Quaker testimony.

If the confessional inquiry into conscience in some way prepares the historical basis of modern individualism in urban society, then it is also connected with contemporary, secular self-analysis, namely psychoanalysis and psychotherapy. While in our study of confession we are mainly concerned with law and religion as interrelated aspects of social control, we cannot ignore the role of psychology and psychoanalysis in contemporary law and police practice. Although psychoanalysts and religious confessors seem to have much in common, they also devote much of their professional time to explaining the differences between religion and psychotherapy. In one of his lectures, Freud sets up an imaginary conversation between a psychoanalyst and an Impartial Person. The latter observes that allowing people to talk out their own neuroses 'is the principle of Confession, which the Catholic Church has used from time immemorial.' The analyst (Freud) gives the following reply:[28]

> Confession no doubt plays a part in analysis – as an introduction to it, we might say. But it is very far from constituting the essence of analysis or from explaining its effects. In Confession the sinner tells what he knows; in analysis the neurotic has to tell more.

By 'to tell more', Freud means of course that psychoanalysis attempts to explore the unconscious whereas confession is only an exploration of the conscious. Freud complains that the Impartial Person cannot escape from the conceptual apparatus of existing religious confession to perceive psychoanalysis and the concept of the unconscious as something new and revolutionary. Whether or not Freud's science of psychoanalysis did break with existing religious ideas or with neurology is not part of our immediate concern. What is evident is that Freud's division between the confession and 'talking therapy' was too neat and too sharp. While much of traditional religious confession had become a routine statement of conscious sins, many spiritual directors did operate at a level of much greater depth and sophistication. The problem is, however, complicated by the fact that contemporary religious practice has (often deliberately) been influenced by psychotherapy in that at least some clergy have borrowed and adopted the methods of secular psychotherapy in the confessional, in counselling and in pastoral work generally. Many clergy refer their penitents to psychologists. More infrequently, psychologists refer their patients to clergy as was reported in the Osset exorcism debate in the press. Many of these issues will occur in various arguments within this study of the confession. At this stage we are merely pointing to the fact that a concern for understanding confessions to murder leads out to far wider problems of the relationship between law, religion and psychoanalysis, and hence to the historical and social roots of concepts like 'conscience', 'consciousness' or the 'self'.

What might explain the ubiquity of confession? Psychologists have occasionally referred to a universal 'compulsion to confess' or they have regarded confession as a general escape mechanism for resolving psychological tensions or they have regarded it as a standard aspect of child socialisation.[29] As sociologists, we are interested in confession as a social practice, in the social relationships between analysts and analysands, between confessors and confessants, between suspects and interrogators, and in the social contexts within which confessions occur. Confession is part of every-day interaction and conversation.

Confession is also part of major public events in law courts, in churches, in police stations. Confession, therefore, is not something that obtrudes from 'outside' the normal routine of society, but part of its normal processes. We do not conceive confession in terms of drives, compulsions or needs, because we are interested in how a meaningful confession is socially constructed by actors in a context. Above all, we wish to focus on social motives of crime, that is, on what array of 'motives' are seen as 'reasonable' causes of murder and how these 'motives' are established within the process of confessing to crime. However, to understand the social context of confession we need to examine confession as a social ideology which has a social history. Since we believe that confession is specific to certain types of culture, we are reluctant to accept the notion of a universal psychology of confession that is somehow detached from any social location. Confession is ubiquitous in the sense of being omnipresent within social relations, but the private, institutionalised confession which entails concepts of 'conscience', 'the guilty self' and 'absolution' is peculiar to Christian/European cultures. We would seek to explain the ubiquity of confession in western religio-legal practice by claiming that confession serves certain fundamental functions within a society. For example, the confession of the guilty absolves judges of responsibility for the administration of their punishment; confession is a method of asserting fundamental values of a society which at the same time restores the guilty to the boundaries of normal society; confession defines what it is to be 'human' in that the guilty show 'normal' psychological reactions of humility, shame and repentance; confession is an important aspect of social control since it is a method of linking the interior conscience with the exterior public order. It is along these lines that, in these essays, we want to establish both the importance for sociology of the analysis of confession and the importance for society of a ubiquitous remedial institution, a ritual of social inclusion. In arguing that confession has important social consequences or functions, we are not necessarily arguing that confession uniformly has positive, congenial, remedial functions. Confession may symbolically restore men to society while at the same time committing them to mental institutions, prison or the gallows. Confessions may also be false or extorted. The 'compulsion to confess' may be not the outcome of an isolated, guilty self, but of subtle social pressures brought to bear on a suspect. As the recent Royal Commission on Criminal Procedure demonstrates, it is in practice extremely difficult for suspects to exercise their legal 'right to silence'.[30] Even the innocent under the pressure of determined interrogation when police officers play upon the weaker points of character will talk volubly. Confession lies at the sensitive intersection between the interior freedom of individual conscience and the exterior requirements of public order. Confession is a social activity shot through by contradictions between spontaneity and compulsion, between disinterested confessions and confessions as part of 'bargain justice', between moral consensus and political force.

Chapter 1
Rituals of social closure

Classical criminology was dominated by the theoretical search for a set of discrete and finite causes of crime which were thought to lie primarily in the biological or psychological constitution of criminals. These physical and psychological constituents of criminal behaviour were conceived independently of the social context within which criminals operated and without reference to the social processes by which laws were modified or enforced. One of the most influential representatives of this positivist trend in criminology was Cesare Lombroso who attempted to isolate a number of distinctive physical characteristics of the criminal type. Although Lombroso's biological typologies of the criminal are now largely discredited, theoretical attempts to explain criminal behaviour in terms of physical defects or low intelligence continued into the twentieth century. In reply to biological positivism, sociological theories of criminal behaviour have extended the range of behaviour to be explained by considering all forms of deviant behaviour in society and have focused on the social processes by which social actors become labelled as 'deviant'. More significantly, the sociology of deviance has, often implicitly, come to regard the search for primary causes of deviant behaviour as a theoretically fruitless exercise. Contemporary deviancy theory has been predominantly interested, not in the immediate causes of deviant actions, but in the social reaction of social groups to the presence of deviant behaviour and in the social effects of legal enforcement and public response on the self-conception and social identity of the deviant. Theoretical interest has, in short, shifted from the causes of crime to societal response to criminality. The principal component of modern deviancy theory have been the so-called 'societal reaction' school. The implication of this theoretical trend in sociology is that law and legal enforcement has come to be viewed in a critical or negative perspective. The deviant is perceived as the victim of legal procedures or moral condemnation whose identity is stigmatised by socially imposed labels. Deviance is no longer seen as the consequence of human biology, but as the complex outcome of a labelling process which has the effect of isolating and excluding the deviant from conventional roles and activities.

These shifts in the explanation and description of deviancy can be summarised under the general notion of 'secondary deviation' which was developed by Edwin Lemert in the early 1950s.[1] If primary deviation refers to initial acts of criminal or deviant nature, secondary deviation includes deviant behaviour which is a consequence of new roles and deviant identities forced upon the deviant by societal reaction to detected deviance by the moral indignation and legal reaction of society. The importance of secondary deviation is that it involves the acquisition of a deviant career, new social labels and a reorganisation of self-conceptions. The development of a deviant identity was conceptualised in terms of various processes of social stigmatisation brought about by the impact of degradation ceremonies. Lemert's theory of secondary deviation, therefore, incorporated much of the sociology of Erving Goffman on stigma[2] and Harold Garfinkel on degradation ceremonies.[3] These developments in deviancy theory resulted in a conception of law (and more generally of conventional social norms) as a coercive apparatus which paradoxically generated secondary deviation and stable criminal careers by forcefully excluding the deviant from the non-deviant community. This conception of law as a system of social exclusion is indicated by the title of Howard Becker's influential study *Outsiders*. In this perspective, deviance or criminality is no longer the product of individuals with specific biological or psychological attributes since[4] 'social groups create deviance by making rules whose infraction constitutes deviance, and by applying those rules to particular people and labelling them as outsiders.'

We can summarise this particular perspective on deviance as one which treats forms of social control as a system of rituals of exclusion and which explains social order in terms of the consensual imposition of deviant labels on actions or persons threatening the existing moral order. It is important to bear in mind, however, that deviancy theory recognises that the imposition of deviant labels is ambiguous and uncertain in industrial society where the dominant system of values is pluralistic. While deviancy theory thus acknowledges the existence of diverse and contradictory values in urban, secular society, it has retained a strong notion of the importance of stigmatisation which ritually excludes deviants from the central moral community. The importance of normative exclusion of deviants is particularly marked in Garfinkel's concept of 'degradation ceremony' which is now routinely referred to in deviancy literature. These ceremonies refer to the ensemble of routine processes in law courts, prisons, borstals or other 'total institutions'[5] whereby the existing identity of an individual is replaced by another morally degrading social status. Like other forms of ritual activity, a degradation ceremony can only be successful where certain fixed procedures are routinely applied and adhered to. Degradation and stigmatisation as admission procedures to total institutions involve both an exclusion from conventional society and a mortification of persons assuming the new identity of an inmate.[6]

Deviancy theory, however, does not treat the deviant as merely the supine object of social reaction, labelling and degradation, since the deviant actor is subjectively aware of and responds to social labels. The deviant may define his social situation in ways which limit, reject or transform the negative identity which the legal system attempts to impose. Labelling is conceived as a process of definition and counter-definition between legal agencies and the deviant subculture. The inspiration of this approach to counter-definitions came originally from the philosophy of language of J.L. Austin in *How To Do Things With Words* (1962). Austin was particularly interested in the role of 'excuses' in every-day situations where individuals attempt to avoid accusations of responsibility for untoward actions which have been challenged by another speaker. An excuse is thus an important and routine counter-definition of a situation which is aimed at the avoidance of responsibility. Austin's treatment of the language of excuses came into the sociology of deviance through the work of C. Wright Mills on 'vocabularies of motive',[7] Scott and Lyman on 'accounts',[8] and Hewitt and Stokes on 'disclaimers'.[9] The argument of these various approaches to linguistic accounts is that deviant subcultures develop powerful cultural techniques by which the impact of deviant labels can be mitigated or removed. These linguistic devices for avoiding accusations of criminal responsibility are particularly well illustrated by the 'techniques of neutralisation'[10] which are available within the deviant community. These techniques include attempts to deny responsibility, to redefine the nature of the injury, to justify the action by questioning the innocence of the victim or to legitimate the action by a 'condemnation of the condemners'.

The theoretical perspective of modern deviancy theory may, at the risk of massive over-simplification, be summarised under two headings. First, it is concerned to analyse the nature of those labelling processes by which deviant persons are physically and symbolically separated from the community. In order for such a person to be successfully degraded,[11]

> the denounced person must be ritually separated from a place in

> the legitimate order, i.e., he must be defined as standing at a place opposed to it. He must be placed 'outside', he must be made 'strange'.

Second, deviancy theory attempts to understand the techniques by which the denounced deviant copes with this new identity and how the full impact of stigmatisation is limited by the processes of counter-definition and neutralisation. The image of society implied by deviancy theory is that the dominant social group which controls the legal and moral apparatus attempts to defend a central core of values against certain peripheral subgroups.[12] Successful degradation of the periphery simultaneously has the effect of legitimising the power of the dominant group as the custodian of moral values. While this theory of social control bears some superficial similarity to Marxist theories of the state as a system of repressive and ideological mechanisms[13] and to Marxist theories of the criminal law as an aspect of class struggle,[14] in practice much of the inspiration of deviancy theory has been implicitly derived from Emile Durkheim's studies of law and religion. For Durkheim, in societies with a low division of labour, the effect of participation in religious rituals was to reinforce and recreate the bonds of social solidarity and communal fellowship. In a similar fashion, punishment of legal offences had the unintended consequences or latent function of demarcating and strengthening the *conscience collective* or common culture of the group. The view of law in deviancy theory as a system of rituals of exclusion can be seen as an attempt to bring out the radical implications of Durkheim's view of the moral order as a set of protective ritual practices. Deviation is not necessarily a feature of anomic social situations, but on the contrary[15] 'can often be understood as a normal product of stable institutions, an important resource which is guarded and preserved by forces found in all human organizations'. Saints and deviants are thus both products of the normal functioning of society's moral code and ritual apparatus.

The existence of a network of rituals of social exclusion defining the boundaries of the normative order of society would imply the presence of a complementary set of rituals of inclusion which also define membership and social incorporation. It is interesting to note, for example, that Garfinkel thought there was a structural resemblance between degradation ceremonies and ceremonies of 'investiture and elevation'.[16] It would be possible, therefore, to think of all societies as possessing complementary rituals of inclusion and exclusion which together specify the conditions for social membership. This discussion of society as a system of ritual in-put and out-put does not, however, imply a purely mechanistic analogy with society smoothly sucking in and spewing out equal quantities of social members. The central thrust of these studies of confession and murder is that, in practice, the operation of these rituals of inclusion and exclusion is typically ambiguous and contradictory. Our criticism of deviancy theory is, however, that in emphasising stigmatisation and victimisation as effects of socio-legal reaction to crime and deviance, deviancy theory fails to take seriously the nature of law as a system of rituals of social inclusion. Deviancy theory assumes (1) that societal reaction to deviance is uniformly negative and derogatory (2) that the repressive apparatus of the law as a system of social, if not class, control will be systematically and uniformly employed and (3) that deviants will invariably appeal to techniques of neutralisation to avoid societal reaction and legal degradation. These three assumptions in deviancy theory have consequently neglected the importance of legal pardon, mercy and sanctuary in the history of, particularly English, legal institutions and of confession to crime in the treatment of offenders. Before illustrating this argument by reference to pardon and confession, it is important to consider in greater detail the ambiguities of deviancy, moral pollution and rituals of exclusion and inclusion. For the sake of brevity, these complementary rituals will be referred to as rituals of social closure since they, as it were, open and close moral gateways.

Much of the theoretical framework for the analysis of pardon and confession as rituals of inclusion has been brilliantly outlined by Sasha Weitman in 'Intimacies: notes towards a theory of social inclusion and exclusion'.[17] Weitman starts with the obvious and trivial observation that personal intimacies – kissing, embracing, handshaking, touching – between friends in public places may be employed implicitly or explicitly as an act of social exclusion of bystanders. These little acts of gratifying personal emotions are public signs of exclusion. These mundane activities have, therefore, important implications for the preservation of public order since the social bond is 'created and perpetuated by repeated acts of generosity, by sacrificial acts.'[18] Weitman goes on to argue that all social relationships can be understood as complementary acts of exclusion and inclusion by which human emotions are given expression, direction and control. Acts of expulsion, obstruction, hospitality, and salutation are illustrative of these categories of inclusion and exclusion. Since public displays of intimate inclusion between friends may generate intense feelings of annoyance, anger and hostility in those excluded from such pleasures, there are compensatory norms and practices which are aimed at controlling these adverse responses to intimacies.

While Weitman draws upon a diverse set of sources in sociology and anthropology to provide examples of these ritual practices, the basic idea of sacrificial acts of generosity is taken from Lévi-Strauss's discussion of sacrifice. The groundwork for nineteenth-century theories of ritual sacrifice was established by William Robertson Smith in his *Lectures on the Religion of the Semites* (1889). These lectures became the starting-point for Durkheim's discussion of piacular rituals and for the general theory of sacrifice in Henri Hubert and Marcel Mauss's *Sacrifice: Its Nature and Function* (1898). Smith's argument was that sacrifices create a social bond between the human group and the god where both engage in a common meal and that sacrificial rituals create fellowship between men. These ritual meals are, like all forms of secular, communal feasts, forms of intimacy between man and god which bring the sacred into proximity with the profane. Sacrificial meals are consequently threatening and hazardous events because they bring about a close contiguity between the sacred which, in Durkheim's terminology, is forbidden and set apart and the profane which is familiar and commonplace. In short, the analysis of primitive sacrifices was connected with anthropological debates about the relationships between holiness and cleanliness, ritual purity and physical contamination. In sacrifice, the two worlds of sacred and profane become intermingled by rituals of inclusion which create intimacy within the social group and between the social group and its sacred totem. Objects, animals and plants which are in the normal course of events regarded as taboo become, through ritualised acts of inclusion, accessible to the social group through sacrifice. To employ a rather different terminology, acts which are regarded as deviant (such as eating a sacred animal) in every day circumstances are made normal by the use of correct ritual and ceremony. Rituals make possible the conjunction of otherwise socially and conceptually separate and distinct categories.

The idea that rituals of purity are intimately connected with conceptual categories of symbolic order and hence with the integration of the social group became the subject of a famous study by Mary Douglas in *Purity and Danger: An Analysis of Concepts of Pollution and Taboo* (1966). For Professor Douglas, the symbolic conceptions of the sacred universe are also expressions of the moral and social unity of the group. To explain the list of forbidden foods in Leviticus, for example, by reference to notions of hygiene is to impose our conceptual divisions between religion and medicine onto a culture where these conceptual divisions were either absent or underdeveloped. Although in these essays on confession we do not draw extensively on the anthropological literature relating to confessions in primitive witchcraft, sorcery and shamanism, we do not want to argue that sharp distinctions between sin, crime and sickness are the product of social and intellectual specialisation in the eighteenth and nineteenth centuries. One theme of our study is concerned with the historical and institutional separation which took place between the confession of sin and the confession of secular crimes. By contrast, in traditional society, sin, crime and disease were all forms of deviation from a sacred reality. Just as Becker employs the notion of 'outsider' to describe the world of the deviant in contemporary society, so in traditional society disease and sin were treated as signs of an individual's departure from social norms and social membership. Frequently the presence of disease in an individual resulted in moral condemnation and social ostracism. Most traditional societies possessed a plethora of rituals which gave clear expression to these pathological departures from the normal. Religious rituals of excommunication and anathematisation are particularly prominent examples of what Garfinkel has termed 'ceremonies of degradation' in which the social and personal status of individuals was totally transformed.

However, if we accept Erikson's argument that deviation is the normal product of stable institutions, then we also want to claim that all social groups also provide mechanisms by which deviant individuals can be restored to group membership. The rituals of exclusion are complemented by rituals of inclusion. While social groups are equipped with procedures for degrading and mortifying those who are deemed to have transgressed sacred and secular norms, they also possess rituals of restoration, healing, forgiveness and return. In more graphic terms, while deviancy theory has taken as its province the imagery of one 'cast into outer darkness' by stigmatisation and negative labelling, it has paid insufficient attention to the figure of the Prodigal Son who, after suitable temptation and tribulation, is returned to high status and his father's favours. These symbols of return and restoration are institutionalised in legal pardon and pre-eminently in such religious practices as pilgrimage, penance and confession. The sacrament of penance, of which confession was a central element, can be regarded as a ritual of inclusion by which deviant members of the community are restored to their normal roles and status through ritualised expressions of guilt, sorrow, self-criticism and remorse. These emotions of self-accusation, unlike disclaimers and accounts, reaffirm the central moral code of society because they require unqualified admissions of responsibility for offences against the community.

The starting-point of our treatment of confessions is the notion that, at least in pre-industrial society, the dominant social group adheres to common notions of moral value, health, civility and sacredness. We do not argue that this dominant ideology is necessarily shared by all members of the society, but merely that the dominant group, by virtue of its political and economic location, is able to enforce some acceptance, however minimal, of these values.[19] Deviation from this moral order is indicated by the presence of sickness, criminality, madness and sin. These transitions and deviations from the moral core can be conceptualised as a human traffic from centre to periphery, from inside to outside, but the traffic is a two-way process. Those who are degraded by rituals of exclusion may also be provided with ritual opportunities of return and inclusion. The presence of these complementary rituals provide, at least in principle, the possibility of a double-confirmation of the authority of those in power and the validity of their moral universe. The original exclusion of deviants and offenders is evidence of the power and effectivity of the apparatus of social control, while subsequent confession and pardon of deviancy attests to the humanity and mercy of those social groups which exercise legal and political authority. Although this particular perspective provides our initial understanding of confession, it is obvious that, especially with the development of a professional police force, forensic science, psychological techniques for the interrogation of suspects and so forth, the sociological interpretation of confessions to crime in a secular society will have to be a good deal more complex than we have as yet indicated. At this point, it will be sufficient to comment that part of our general argument is that in modern societies there develops a gap between legal ideology which requires 'true' confessions to be free and spontaneous and the legal apparatus which acknowledges the importance of skilful interrogation of suspects in the detection of crime. It is also important to recognise that, even in pre-industrial societies, the actual operation of public reaction to deviance, the employment of rituals of exclusion and the effect of sanctuary and pardon were often paradoxical, if not contradictory.

In this study of confession, we have selected a particularly serious offence, namely homicide, to illustrate the argument that even the most extreme forms of deviance do not lead automatically or inevitably to social exclusion, because compensatory rituals or mechanisms may provide, as it were, a way back from the outside. However, in order to provide further illustration of this theme from a different form of 'deviance', we want to examine social reactions in medieval times to forms of physical disease which were simultaneously regarded as socially dangerous and the product of personal deviance. One extreme case of such response to disease is provided by the case of leprosy.

In medieval Christendom, physical health was closely associated with spiritual well-being and the verbs 'to save' the soul and 'to salve' the body have a common root. The doctrine of the resurrection of the body on the Day of Judgment meant that spiritual existence was also a corporal event. Conversely, the causes of sickness and disease were often sought in the moral and religious character of the afflicted. For example, epilepsy in both Greek and Christian civilisations was popularly regarded as a form of diabolic possession.[20] It was not uncommon to regard diseases with moral causes as requiring secular punishment under the law. The history of attitudes to leprosy provides one clear illustration of moral and legal reaction to disease. In medieval times, the term leprosy (from *lepra* or scaly) was used to cover a wide range of skin diseases including, not only leprosy proper, but also eczema, scrofula and skin cancer. More importantly, little distinction was made between leprosy and venereal disease. This implicit equation of leprosy and sexually transmitted diseases may partly explain why both diseases were often regarded as evidence of moral failure, especially adultery and promiscuity. It was also thought that leprosy actually increased sexual desire so that lepers were regarded as lascivious and given to debauchery. In the popular imagination, lepers were thought to take their revenge on society by raping young virgins who, given the contagious nature of the disease, would be forced to join leper houses or colonies.

True leprosy first appeared in England around the seventh century having initially spread to Europe from Asia. Spreading steadily northwards from the southern coast, leprosy was most prevalent from the eleventh to the thirteenth century after which the disease became relatively uncommon. The importance of the disease and its distribution can be to some extent measured by the building of leprosaria or lazar houses. A few leper houses were built under royal and ecclesiastical patronage in the eleventh century in Rochester, Lincoln and Cambridge, but by the thirteenth century when the disease was spreading rapidly many old almshouses had to be converted to lazar houses. It may be that famine and bubonic plague in the fourteenth century had a devastating effect on lepers who, because of their weak condition, were especially prone to additional disease and infection. One indication of the sudden decline in leprosy in the population is that there was very little legislation relating to the control of lepers after 1349.

The location, activities and status of lepers were strictly controlled by religious ritual and secular legislation. Since leprosy was held to be the result of immorality and was regarded as a major threat to society, the presence of repressive legislation and ritual should not be surprising. Civil restrictions on lepers were particularly extensive and bear all the marks of a ceremony of degradation. Lepers, for example, were forbidden to inherit property and to be judged leprous had, therefore, profound consequences for the distribution of wealth. Lepers were precluded from sexual intercourse with anyone except their wives; they were forbidden ordinary social intercourse with children and strangers. Lepers were forced to wear special uniforms, including the clapper and begging bowl. They were forced to leave their villages and had to stand down wind from strangers. These norms of social exclusion were dramatically enacted by the religious 'office at the seclusion of lepers'. Clergy were summoned to judge, often with the aid of a lay jury, whether a person was leprous. Once labelled as a leper, a special rite was held in which the leprous individual was driven from his home and buried to the neck in a grave. These rites were symbolic of the social death of lepers who were henceforth required to abandon their premises to live the life of a beggar. These procedures for making all lepers into social outcasts were summarised in England under the statute *De Leproso Amovendo*. On the continent, the regulations controlling lepers were often more rigorous. For example, in 1318, the French King Philip V proposed to burn alive all lepers in order to purge their bodies and their souls.

We can initially regard the rite for the seclusion of lepers as a clear illustration of a rite of exclusion which, by witnessing the social death of lepers, produced a total transformation and mortification of the social status of the leper as a physical and moral pervert. There is, however, ample evidence to suggest that these rituals were infrequently and ineffectually employed to remove lepers from conventional society. It is interesting to note, at the outset, that, while leprosy was regarded as the consequence of moral failure, leprosy was also referred to as the 'sacred malady' and the 'sacred disease'. Leprosy was ambiguously regarded as either the product of a lascivious nature or the sign of divine favour. Taking the biblical story of Lazarus as their basis, religious authorities could also argue that disease of the body was a sign of divine grace and that illness had to be patiently borne in this world. For the faithful, this-worldly tribulation would be compensated in the next world where the rich would be consumed by heavenly fires. It was not uncommon, therefore, for lepers to be referred to as *pauperes Christi* or Christ's poor.[21] In addition, many lazar houses were built by rich patrons as an act of religious charity to gain religious merit. The idea that leprosy was a sign of supernatural grace became especially potent in the period following the early crusades. It was thought that soldiers who fought in the crusades would be certain of heavenly reward. It was difficult to reconcile this belief with the fact that many soldiers returning from the crusades were suffering from venereal disease and leprosy. If leprosy was caused by sexual immorality, then it was not possible to believe that leprous soldiers were destined to heavenly election. The solution was to emphasise the Lazarus story and to regard leprosy as a sign of God's favour.

Leprosy was a hideously disfiguring disease in the Middle Ages when diagnosis and treatment were primitive. Untreated leprosy can result in paralysis, destruction of tissue and bone, and loss of limbs. Medieval paintings of lepers typically portrayed their missing limbs and physical deformity. Since leprosy was highly contagious and affected all social ranks in society, the existence of stringent legal and religious rules governing the exclusion and segregation of lepers is perfectly understandable. However, these rules were difficult to enforce and there is evidence to show that relatives were often prepared to harbour and protect kin suffering from leprosy. This willingness to support leprous kin and protect them from the law appears to have been especially common in medieval London where the civil authorities constantly complained about the persistent evasion of the leprosy regulations. Furthermore, the wording of documents like the *De Leproso Amovendo* suggested that restrictions on lepers could only apply in cases where lepers proved to be an 'annoyance and disturbance' to the local community. While there was legislation to remove individual rights from lepers such as preventing them from entering churches, markets or other public places, or from burial in common churchyards, there was also compensatory rulings which gave lepers special privileges. The lepers of Shrewsbury in the thirteenth century had the right to a proportion of the flour in the market and similar privileges existed at Chester and Southampton. King John built a leper settlement at Bristol where the lepers enjoyed his protection and were permitted to beg in safety. In short, societal reaction to a disease which was often regarded as the consequence of immoral behaviour was highly ambiguous and variable. On the one hand, there is the case of Aelfweard, bishop of London and abbot of Evesham, who was forced to leave his London post by the monks who were reluctant to tolerate his presence. On the other, there is the story of Gerard by two monks of Canterbury who, because of his local popularity, remained in his home town despite his obviously leprous condition.

This brief account of leprosy has been introduced to illustrate two arguments which are important in subsequent chapters on confession.

First, we cannot assume that, even in the case of serious crime, disease or moral offence, societal reaction will be entirely negative and uniform. This variability and ambiguity in public reactions to crime have important implications for the theory of stigmatisation and degradation. Second, although societies may possess powerful legal machinery for dealing with offenders, it does not automatically follow that the law will be consistently employed against deviants. There may exist widespread public tolerance of or sympathy for the offender. Furthermore, as the case of leprosy shows, many offences have paradoxical implications in terms of stigma. Leprosy was both a moral offence and a 'sacred malady'. In this respect, leprosy is not a unique case. Our argument might be equally supported by public reaction to and official definitions of lunacy. The problem of madness has been of interest to deviancy theory because the history of social response to lunatics appears to provide perfect support for the theory of labelling and social control. The proposition that lunacy is a stigmatising label which is employed to control social deviants has been extensively developed in the research of Szasz and Scheff.[22] Not only does the successful application of the label 'mad' bring about a profound loss of social and moral status, but the incarceration of lunatics also involves a substantial loss of constitutional and other legal rights. The institutionalisation of unwilling patients is thus regarded by Szasz as a form of 'psychiatric slavery', while Scheff treats institutionalisation of lunatics as a clear illustration of the general features of 'deviancy-amplification'.

While not wishing to criticise the general validity of approaching madness as a social label within a deviancy perspective, it can be argued that madness, like leprosy, is an ambiguous label and that societal reaction to madness is not as uniform as writers like Szasz and Scheff have implied. While Szasz correctly concentrates on the impact of the definition of insanity on minority groups, marginal people and underprivileged classes, the application of labels of insanity to privileged classes did not necessarily carry a stigmatic implication. Not all forms of mental illness were regarded as socially degrading. On the contrary, they conferred a morally prestigious status. Vieda Skultans[23] has shown how prevalent were 'vapours', 'spleen' and 'melancholy' among the British aristocracy and intelligentsia in the seventeenth century. While 'spleen' among serving women was regarded as lowness of spirit, 'melancholy' among the privileged was treated as evidence of superior intelligence and sensitivity. Indeed, melancholy had become a fashionable complaint towards the end of the sixteenth century and came to be regarded as a mark of moral distinction. Thus, David Hume was flattered to discover that he had contracted the 'vapours' which George Cheyne informed him was 'the disease of the learned'. Just as leprosy could be regarded as a 'sacred malady', so mental illness, at least among the well-placed, could be regarded as an indication of sophistication and intelligence. In terms of societal reaction to lunacy, it was not the case that institutionalisation of the insane had the whole-hearted support of the middle class throughout the nineteenth century. Investigations of asylums clearly showed that recovery rates among inmates were very low and there was a vigorous campaign for the abolition of restraint among such groups as the Quaker reformers. There is some evidence, therefore, that there was a reluctance to utilise fully the existing apparatus to control lunacy. It was also the case that ratepayers were increasingly reluctant to support a system of asylums which was obviously failing to produce the intended moral reform of inmates.

We have argued, therefore, that, although societal reaction to deviants may involve degradation and stigmatisation, there are institutions and rituals which permit deviants to return to conventional society. Rituals of inclusion, especially confession, can be regarded as remedial devices or restitutive institutions. One obvious objection to this theoretical approach is that it rests upon a form of functionalist anthropology and that most of our illustrative material is taken from traditional, pre-industrial society. While the notion of 'rituals of social closure' may have some relevance to societies with relatively coherent cultures and simple social structures, the notion is not pertinent to modern society. While we quote sociologists and anthropologists who have been interested in the importance of rituals of social closure in pre-industrial society, we do not derive theoretical inspiration from sociologists whose work is focused on societies where social control is not characteristically achieved by ritual means. In short, the theory of ritual closure cannot apply to societies which are organised in terms of class relationships, secular law and professionalised police force.

As an initial response to this form of criticism, it is interesting to note that Max Weber developed a particularly explicit theory of social closure to explain conflictual power relationships between social groups. The notion of social closure occurs in Weber's analysis of 'pariah-groups', his analysis of professions and finally in his conception of class relations within a competitive market situation. In his analysis of 'the economic relationships of organized groups' in *Economy and Society*, Weber argues that where there is an increase in the number of individual competitors in search of inelastic profits, there will arise a strong interest to curb competition by limiting access to market rewards. The curbing of competition will take the form of social closure in which some prominent social characteristic (such as religion, ethnicity, language or social origin) is employed as the basis of excluding outsiders. Membership of privileged interest groups in the market will be further reinforced by the development of formal regulations, formal processes of socialisation into the group and eventually by legal and political arrangements. In this case,[24]

> the interest group has developed into a 'legally privileged group' (*Rechtsgemeinschaft*) and the participants have become 'privileged members' (*Rechtsgenossen*). Such closure, as we want to call it, is an ever-recurring process; it is the source of property in land as well as of all guild and other group monopolies.

This monopolisation of the supply of goods and services on the market always involves the closure of social opportunities to other groups which, on the basis of positive or negative characteristics, are converted into outsiders or 'negatively privileged status groups'. While this notion of social closure provides Weber with an explanation of the social stratification of groups within economic relations, it is also employed by Weber in his discussion of the concept of pollution in caste hierarchies and in his analysis of the historical dynamics of the Jews as a 'pariah-group'. The exclusion of religio-ethnic groups on the basis of cultural characteristics becomes the basis for the development of radical ideologies of revenge which may also be the foundation of subcultural solidarity against privileged groups.

While privileged groups attempt to legitimate practices of social closure in terms of theodicy, negative status groups are more likely to adopt a radical millenarian doctrine. This contrast formed the starting-point of Karl Mannheim's discussion of utopian and ideological perspectives and, more recently, of Frank Parkin's discussion of 'social closure as exclusion'.[25] Briefly, Parkin argues that economically privileged groups maintain their dominance by practices of social exclusion and disprivileged groups adopt alternative practices of social usurpation which are directed at weakening and eventually undermining the exploitative advantages provided by exclusionary monopoly of resources. Historically, the basis of class power has been derived from economic rights to property. The criterion of birth, adherence to primogeniture and dynastic marriage settlements were the principal methods of maintaining privileged access to land as an exclusive right. By contrast, the bourgeoisie are more likely to favour credentialism (educational certificates, professional qualification, membership of elite associations and so forth) as the basic form of membership to the group. Paradoxically, however, credentialism is also associated with norms of open access to education regardless of birth, with ideals of social mobility based on achievement, with the importance of merit and with a commitment to liberal, democratic procedures. There is a tension between the need to legitimate privilege by reference to open access and the need to reproduce privileged class positions by social closure. The rituals of social inclusion and exclusion are not, therefore, uniquely characteristic of pre-industrial society; they are a permanent feature of the social dynamics of group conflict over resources. Legality, health and religion can be regarded as 'social resources' for defining group membership in the same way that Weber treats market opportunities as the basis of economic membership. Leprosy, like religion, language and birth, is a perfectly suitable characteristic for allocating social actors to negatively privileged status groups. We would merely add to Weber's notion of 'social closure' and to Parkin's version of 'exclusion' the fact that social groups also possess various rituals by which deviant members can be reinstated to social membership. Legal pardon, moral forgiveness and ritual purification serve to reinforce sentiments of social solidarity while legitimating dominant groups and general social values.

What arises from this discussion is the claim that law plays a central – perhaps the central – part in institutionalising practices of social closure between antagonistic groups in a situation where resources are in short supply. To develop this perspective on law does, however, raise an obvious difficulty of sociological interpretation. We can treat law as a coercive apparatus through which the dominant class exercises power over subordinate classes. In this case, the law is merely an instrument of the dominant class. Alternatively, we can think of law as relatively independent of economic and political power so that law is the embodiment of values and interests which are common to society as a whole. In this case, the law is a general requirement for the reproduction of society as such and not merely of class relations narrowly defined. The attempt to locate legal relationships within a theory of social closure leads into the traditional debate over the relative autonomy of the superstructure of society from the economic base. A discussion of the role of confession is not the proper context in which to raise systematically the question of the relative autonomy of legal forms in relation to the economic mode of production.[26] It is pertinent to our argument, however, to consider the more specific problem of criminal law in the context of class relations in English history.

In general, Marxist theories of law have been concerned with two separate, but related, features of law in capitalist societies. First, law is a condition for securing the stability of contractual relationships between economic subjects in a society dominated by the production of commodities by wage labour for market exchange. In this respect, law does not appear as a coercive system of imperatives backed up by state power. Rather law appears as the umpire between formally free and equal parties to exchanges in that law guarantees rights of possession, regulates contracts and proscribes 'unfair' practice in the market place. In capitalist society, therefore, law is not a collection of arbitrary, *ad hoc* decisions overtly supportive of sectional and class interests. Under capitalism, law takes the form of an abstract, universal and objective system of regulations. The form of law as an abstract system of relations between legal subjects is thus derived from the form of commodity production in which economic subjects, who are formally free and autonomous, are linked together by economic exchange. The object of materialist analysis is to penetrate the ideological form of law to expose the actual subordination of wage labour to owners of productive property. The second focus of Marxist legal theory has been on law as an overt form of class control. Although law in general may assume the character of a neutral umpire of social rights, criminal law is typically regarded as the direct expression of the class interest of property owners. Thus, Evgeny Pashukanis regards the form of law as an outgrowth of the commodity form, but treats criminal law as the undisguised and direct instrument of class rule:[27]

> the bourgeoisie maintains its class rule and suppresses the exploited classes by means of its system of criminal law . . . . Criminal justice in the bourgeois state is organised class terror, which differs only in degree from the so-called emergency measures taken in civil war.

While there are clearly important theoretical differences between Marxist writers on law,[28] we can summarise the Marxist position by noting that law is regarded as a system for regulating property rights and as a form of coercive control. These two features are, for Marxism, closely connected.

It is conventionally assumed that sociological theories of law, which take their lead from Max Weber, can be clearly distinguished from Marxist theory in that sociologists treat legal relations as largely independent of economic, or more specifically class, relations. It will be convenient here to separate Weber's general commentary on law and economy from his specific discussion of English criminal law. The essence of Weber's sociology of law is that the character and social role of law are determined by the interests of clients, by the institutional forms in which law is produced and finally by the nature of legal administration. While Marxists give prominence to legal clients (owners of land and capital), Weber was more concerned with the question of legal professionalisation. In terms of law-making, the training of lawyers in the university system or in a guild organisation had far-reaching implications for legal rationalisation. Systems of law which developed within a guild system of legal-training and which were determined by practical problems of legal decision-making lacked rigorous systematisation and deductive rigour. Legal norms which were tied to every day professional problems of lawyers organised on a guild basis were pragmatic, *ad hoc* and unstable. By contrast, when lawyers were trained in the universities away from the immediate pressures of legal practice, law developed on a more formal, objective and systematic basis. Because of the conjunction of a number of contingent circumstances, continental legal systems, drawing heavily upon the formalism of Roman jurisprudence, developed very abstract principles of codification and elaboration. The isolation of university-trained legal theorists from the day-to-day requirements of legal practice contributed to the development of a gapless, formal system of rational law. Although rational law is partly a consequence of professional organisation of lawyers who utilise professional legal qualifications as a principle of social exclusion, a formally rational legal system is a necessary requirement of capitalist economic relations. Weber regarded rational law as a condition of capitalist economies because legal stability facilitated rational economic calculation and guaranteed economic contracts. For contingent historical reasons, the professional interests of lawyers and the market requirements of capitalists converged to stimulate legal systematisation.

The main difficulty for Weber's argument that rational and formal law is a condition of existence of the capitalist mode of production was that the English system of judge-made law was anything but stable, deductive, universal and abstract. In fact, Weber treated English legal arrangements as the virtual antithesis of formally rational law. He frequently compared English case-law with Islamic qadi-justice which he regarded as thoroughly arbitrary and inconsistent. The various theoretical strategies which Weber adopted to resolve this apparent contradiction in 'the England problem'[29] need not concern us. In terms of the arguments we present about the legal importance of confession, it is interesting to realise that Weber thought that the arbitrary character of English judge-made law perfectly suited the class interests of the bourgeoisie. Weber thought that English law was riddled by overt class bias in favour of property-owning classes. In particular, he felt that the centralisation of legal administration in London and the high cost of litigation meant that in practice the English working class had no legal franchise. There is, therefore, an important area of theoretical overlap between Marxist and Weberian sociologies of law. While Weber admitted that English case-law lacked the rationality of Roman law as it developed on the continent, he argued that the guild structure of law-training and the expense of litigation perfectly suited the economic and political interests of the dominant class.

Although the argument that English law, especially laws relating to property and criminal offences, is a direct expression of class interest has been frequently asserted,[30] recent studies of eighteenth-century England suggest a more complex relationship between class interest, property and law. The analysis of crime and society in *Albion's Fatal Tree* has been especially influential in this respect. One oddity of the period is that, by comparison with earlier centuries, 'the eighteenth-century criminal law claimed few lives.'[31] In spite of the growth of the English population, the increase in convictions for theft and the expansion of capital statutes, the actual number of hangings for crimes against property remained relatively stable. The immediate explanation for this stability is that there was a corresponding increase in the use of royal pardon by which transportation was substituted for public execution. Why did transportation appear preferable to public hanging? The explanation provided by Douglas Hay in *Albion's Fatal Tree* is framed in terms of an argument about 'legal mercy' as an ideology which legitimated the authority of the legal process and ultimately justified the existing inequality in property relations. Because only half of those condemned to death actually went to the gallows in the eighteenth century, it appeared that the law did not rest on arbitrary power and capricious violence. The legal decisions were not merely the result of imperfect human judgment, but rather rested on common moral notions which had divine sanction. The legal sentence provided ample opportunity to remind the court that the ultimate judge of human actions was not the secular court but God himself since 'execution was a fate decreed not by men, but by God and Justice.'[32] Like the priest in the confessional, the judge could appear as merely the neutral vehicle of divine will. The royal prerogative of pardon was thus part of a greater sacred drama in which divine mercy was continuously poured out in favour of sinful subjects. Pardon was thus part of the scheme of secular and religious deference. Just as working men sought pardon through the patronage of their social superiors, so sinful man sought either through the Church as the treasury of merit or directly through Christ the forgiveness of their Maker. Men who failed to ask for pardon and who, remaining unrepentant, were in contempt of court, alienated from their fellow men and from God.

From a Weberian perspective, the institution of pardon which interfered with the formal operation of the law as a machine-like system of judgments must appear as an example of the substantive irrationality of English criminal justice. The discretionary powers of the Court for Crown Cases Reserved might be regarded in a similar light.[33] From another perspective, the institution of the royal pardon, in a society where deference and patronage were still central features of the social structure, was a crucial feature of legal and religious ideology which legitimated power by encouraging the view that all English men were equal subjects under the law. In particular, pardon demonstrated publicly the reality of legal mercy.

It is difficult to discuss the ideological importance of pardon without also considering the sociological significance of repentance and confession. It is odd, therefore, that confession has been largely neglected by criminology, sociology of law and deviancy theory.[34] We have suggested that, because deviancy theory has emphasised the importance of degradation ceremonies and criminal accounts, sociological perspectives on the law have not taken rituals of inclusion particularly seriously. When the institutions of sanctuary, pardon and confession are taken seriously, they are typically regarded as aspects of an ideological system which legitimates power and inequality. To regard confession as simply a form of social control, however subtle, is not entirely satisfactory. To start with, it is important to make a distinction between the motives of an action and its social consequences. Obviously very few individuals consciously confess their crimes in order to legitimise the social system. However, a confession may be given for conscious, instrumental ends to avoid further torture, for example, or to protect relatives. In modern legal theory and police practice, the evidence obtained from confessions can only be admitted when a confession has been obtained without 'undue pressure'. In attempting to isolate the many sociological difficulties which arise in understanding confessions, we have largely concentrated on the question of confessions to murder. Since in England we are faced with 'domestic murder' between kin, it is often found that offenders, not only freely admit responsibility, but often call the police to the scene of the crime. Interrogation of the confessed offender is often minimal and the motives of the crime appear to be obvious – revenge, jealousy or gain. In this situation, there is an apparent agreement between common sense and legal theory. According to both, criminal men suffer from 'the burden of guilt' for their offences and confession thereby provides an escape from these psychological pains. Through confession and contrition in which 'normal' emotions of guilt, despair and remorse are given expression, the deviant can return symbolically, if not physically, to the every day world.

From a sociological perspective, it is not possible to accept the concept of 'the burden of guilt' as a universal human motive which will conveniently explain the motivation producing confession. In a rather humorous discussion of this issue, Kant noted the dangers which attend the just man who imputes a conscience to the unjust:[35]

> The virtuous man lends to the vicious one his own character: he supposes that the vicious man has a fully-developed conscience which cries against the least over-sight of the moral law, all the more vigorously the more the man is virtuous. . . . As long as he can escape public punishments for his crimes, the vicious man laughs at the fear of those inner reproaches which plague honest people.

The fact that men and women confess to their crimes is not incontrovertible evidence for the existence of a universal compulsion to confess as an escape from a burden of guilt. One of the central arguments of this collection of essays is that confessions are constructed and not discovered. In other words, they are the products of social encounters between suspects and police in which, from the total array of 'facts' surrounding the case, a statement is finally agreed upon which is recognisable as a 'confession'. Confessions are constructed in this sense because what is relevant as evidence in a court of law is not necessarily relevant from the offender's point of view. The problem of confession must be approached, not in terms of given psychological motives, but in terms of social processes of disclosure and legal processes of conviction. The motives of confession must be examined in the specific situational and interactional contexts in which they emerge in terms of their relevance to the parties concerned. In crude terms, if the police operate with the assumption that offenders are plagued by guilt, then they will be looking for statements which suggest the presence of guilt. In turn, evidence of a 'burden of guilt' is also evidence that the confession is voluntary and spontaneous rather than the product of 'oppression'. Although we want to make a distinction between the motives of confession and the ideological effects of confession, these two are closely related. The idea that men are punished by their own consciences rather than by a repressive social environment (the ideology) may be written into or form part of the language by which offenders are expected to describe their actions (the motivation). However, the problem of how confessions take the form they do, that is, how they are constructed, is separate from the problem of why people voluntarily offer confessions or provide other forms of self-disclosure.

Rather than attempting to provide some general theory of unsolicited self-criticism, accusation or confession, we have attempted to illuminate the problem by looking at specific forms of confession, namely confession to domestic murder. Unlike the habitual offender, such as prostitutes, the murderer does not typically have a deviant career. Murder is typically an unpremeditated, 'one-off' offence against a known victim; it is not necessarily associated with a criminal background, a deviant subculture or exposure to deviant definitions of the situation. In short, Becker's discussion of the deviant process in the analysis of marihuana use in *Outsiders* has very little relevance to understanding English domestic murder which is characteristically the unintended outcome of violent domestic conflict. In this sense, the domestic murderer lacks the deviant occupational training which is often part of a career in prostitution or theft. The typical English murderer, especially of the last century, is perceptively described by George Orwell as a suburban professional man who, overcome by a guilty passion for his secretary or neighbour's wife, commits murder after a long struggle with his conscience.[36] In this sense, there is a close parallel between the sociological dynamics of 'naive check forgery' and 'naive murder'. Lemert's research on cheque forgers suggests that they have higher social status, better education, less previous criminal involvement and are generally older than other criminal groups. The three situational requirements of systematic cheque forgery are pseudonymity, mobility and seclusiveness. Because the forger has constantly to assume new identities, to limit primary contacts with others and to move residence regularly, the interpersonal relationships of the cheque forger are shallow, irregular and fleeting. The requirements of this form of crime mean that the self-image of the forger cannot be validated by close, supportive interaction with others. Because police detection of forgery is almost inevitable and because the cheque forger does not have the social support of a deviant subgroup or subculture, the forger is ultimately driven into an isolated social cul-de-sac. The solution to this isolation is either to abandon this form of deviance or to instigate their own arrest. The first solution is difficult because cheque forgers typically acquire an expensive life-style which cannot be supported without continuous cheque forgery. The second solution is relatively easy. Although many forgers are caught by chance or as the result of police activity,[37]

> an impressive number of others engineer their own downfalls. For example, some phone the police or parole officer and tell them where they can be found. Closely akin are those who foreclose their current criminal careers rather simply by remaining where they are, knowing full well that police or detectives will soon catch up with them, to find them in a resigned mood awaiting their arrival.

The self-disclosure of the cheque forger presents a social solution to his criminal activity which, by its very requirements, produces a 'cumulative state of apathy or sense of psychic exhaustion'.

These studies by Lemert provide a model for examining the processes by which criminals may disclose themselves to the police as a result of situational continencies rather than as the result of a guilty conscience. The forger rarely feels a sense of guilt about his activitiies or toward his victims. In so far as there is a feeling of guilt it 'remains largely retrospective and remote for the forger, without social reinforcement.'[38] The apparent relief which forgers feel on being apprehended by the police is the result, not of a 'burden of guilt', but of the resolution of the social and psychological ambiguities of their deviant activity.

Our study of confession is, therefore, based on a number of central distinctions. First, we approach confession, both in the religious and the legal context, as a ritual of inclusion. Confession is part of a symbolic system in which, after suitable expiation, the repentant sinner may return to the community. Thus, in medieval times, after some form of penance, such as pilgrimage, the offender could physically return to the social group and to the sacramental life of the Church. It is important to stress the importance of these symbolic restorations since deviancy theory has one-sidedly emphasised the role of law as an apparatus of personal and social degradation. Second, we recognise that, despite these inclusive functions, confession also has important ideological consequences in legitimating the moral order and legal force. A confessional system reinforces the notion that deviance is essentially individualistic. Sin, crime and disease can be treated as the personal failure of the individual who is forced, in order to receive pardon, to admit his responsibility for the offence. Through confession, the offender accepts, or at least appears to accept, the legitimacy of the accusation against him and the correctness of the moral world which he has challenged. A confession is, in this respect, unlike the techniques of neutralisation by which offenders deny responsibility for their untoward activities. Third, we suggest that the problem of the motivation to confess and its meaning for the confessant is separate from the social functions and ideological consequences of institutionalised confession. The motivation of the offender becomes visible, so to speak, during the process of investigation or interrogation. Because confession of crimes can play a strategic role in the conviction of criminals, the police have an obvious interest in securing admissions of responsibility under specified conditions. In this situation, there often emerges a clear conflict of interests between police and offenders. Although suspects have traditionally enjoyed the 'right of silence', there is also the assumption that an innocent man 'has nothing to hide'. In this collection of studies of confession in religion and law, we do not pretend to offer an unambiguous and definitive answer to the common sense question – Why do people confess? A number of answers suggest themselves. People confess because of duress or because they have, like the cheque forger, reached a social dead-end, or because they expect to receive a reduced sentence, or because they wish to draw attention to themselves for notorious crimes they have not in fact committed, or because they are the victims of 'brain-washing' techniques. In our view, these plausible explanations miss the real issue. The crucial problem is not so much why people confess, but how do they remain silent? As we show in subsequent chapters, there are innumerable legal, situational and ultimately linguistic factors which frequently coerce suspects into making statements which may incriminate them. Confession is a double-bind. If I confess, or at least make a statement, then I may directly or indirectly accept responsibility for an action. If I do not confess, I may by implication suggest that I am not entirely innocent. Given the appropriate social circumstances, it is not that we all suffer from a compulsion to confess, but rather that we are subject to powerful norms not to remain silent.

Chapter 2
Confession and social structure

The sacrament of penance and, more specifically, the confession of sins played a major part in the devotional life of both Catholic and Protestant Christianity. While historians have provided fairly detailed studies of Christian confession, especially in the medieval period, there are few important sociological analyses of penance, indulgence and confessions.[1] The sociological neglect of the sacrament of penance represents a significant gap within the sociology of religion, since confession is of critical importance in the relationship between organised religion and its social environment. The study of confession can illuminate a number of interesting aspects of the place of religion in society. Despite their neglect of the sacrament of penance, sociologists have undertaken research into witchcraft trials and accusations and have provided an understanding of the general social functions of confession to demonic possession. In his study of African child-witches, for example, Robert Brain argues that the confession of children reaffirms in a clear, direct manner the somewhat vague beliefs of adults; confessions also serve as a channel for aggression whereby the confession of guilt feelings can achieve a cathartic effect.[2] Similarly, I.M. Lewis notes that in simple, uncentralised societies a confession during a seance has the function of ventilating and solving social conflicts.[3] Public confession of smouldering tensions can help restore social harmony in a ceremony where the village shaman gives expression to the consensus of the local community. The research of social anthropologists into the confessional rites of simple societies provides a number of suggestive theoretical guidelines for developing sociological theories about the Christian sacrament of penance.

In this study of Christian confession, my argument falls into three sections. Following a brief account of some of the historically interesting features of the sacrament of penance, the first section will outline what appear to be the central social functions of the confession of sin. Since there are well-known theoretical problems associated with functionalist theories in sociology, it will be necessary to provide a critical commentary of the general assumption that confession is uniformly cathartic. My reservations concerning functionalism lead directly into the second section of this paper which examines confession as a form of social control in relation to changes in social stratification. While functionalist theories of confession appear to be based on the problematical notion that some form of public confession is functionally indispensable for social consensus, the existing literature on the psychology of confession is also wedded to the idea that there is universal compulsion to confess. Everyone, according to O. Hobart Mowrer, has 'an intuitive compulsion to admit, or confess, his guilt to others.'[4] These psychological assumptions depend on certain undeclared theories about universal human nature which largely ignore the extent to which guilt, conscience, and confession are socio-culturally determined. There is, for example, only sparse evidence for the existence of an institutionalised confession in Islam.[5] The concluding section of my argument examines the relationship between the traditional sacrament of penance and Freudian psychoanalysis. The development of the Freudian 'talking cure' may be regarded in part as a secularised form of the cure of souls which raises interesting sociological questions about the professional competence of ministers of religion in their pastoral role.

The functions of confession

It is important to make a distinction between a confession of beliefs that are publicly known (consciousness) as in a confession of faith and a confession of interior, private affairs (conscience) as in a confession of sin. In Christian theology, a variety of confessions have been recognised. St Augustine distinguished between confession of faith, praise and sin. In this discussion of confession, I shall be exclusively concerned with the sociology of confession of sin. In the Christian tradition, confession of sin has been closely associated with the idea of a private conscience which came to be regarded as a practical, ethical exercise, as an accusation or trial of the interior self. 'Conscience. has a juridical sense, as in the expression 'the Court of Conscience' where the self is exposed to an internal prosecution. C.S. Lewis reminds us that *conscientia* (knowledge of, or privy to) underwent a remarkable development in the English language eventually acquiring the meaning of an active ethical principle; thus, in Milton, God declares 'I will place within them as a guide My umpire conscience.'[6] A confession involves speaking fully (*confateri*) about the trial of the self under the active guidance of the interior conscience. Thus an elementary definition of confession refers to 'accusing ourselves of our sins to a priest who has received authority to give absolution.'[7] The institutionalised sacrament of penance in the Roman Catholic tradition involves a series of actions, namely contrition, confession, satisfaction and absolution. The historical development of this sacrament involved a number of crucial social changes in the relationship between priests and laity, Church and society.

Spontaneous confession was uncommon in the early Church and confessionals were not provided until after the Council of Trent. Furthermore, only certain sins could be absolved; absolution of such sins as fornication, homicide and idolatry was impossible. The history of confession in Christianity involved a process from infrequent, voluntary, public acts of contrition to confession as regular, obligatory and private. In the early Church, confession was offered only once in a person's lifetime but by the eighth century Christians were expected to confess their grave sins regularly and confessions became fixed for certain times of the ecclesiastical year. In the year 760, Chrodegang of Metz ordered his canons and the poor who were supported by the Church to confess twice every year at Lent and in the autumn; the subsequent Rule of Chrodegang stipulated that monks should confess every Saturday. By the end of the twelfth century, regular confession at appointed times throughout the year, confession before the Eucharist and confession of all major sins had become a legally enforced requirement, replacing the early practice of single, spontaneous confession in a lifetime.

One other major development in the sacrament of penance in the medieval period must be referred to, namely the establishment of a priestly monopoly for the hearing of lay confessions. Before the thirteenth century, laymen were by custom entitled to hear the confessions of other laymen and, while laymen had no power of absolution, a confession to a layman was held to be an adequate substitute for a confession to a priest. A division of labour evolved permitting laymen to hear the confession of venial sins, but reserving to priests the task of hearing obligatory confession of mortal sins. The Lateran Canon of 1216 gave a formal, legal backing to practices that had become accepted procedure in hearing confessions. It increased the importance and extent of ecclesiastically controlled penance by making compulsory the act of confession to a priest. The Canon gave priests the sole right to hear confessions of their flock and, with the creation of this jurisdiction over confession, a lay penitent who wanted to confess to a different priest had to obtain permission from his parish priest. The Canon gave a bureaucratic stamp to the traditional view of the 'power of the keys', that is the power to bind and loose which had been handed down from Peter and the Apostles to bishops and priests of the Church. These 'keys' were a set of judicial rights through which certain members of the Church, namely the priestly hierarchy, had control of penance and absolution. In this respect, the parish priests enjoyed a delegated authority from their bishops to hear confession and pronounce absolution, but bishops reserved the right to hear confession for certain major sins. These mortal sins came to be known as 'reserved cases'. The judicial character of the keys, the reserved cases and the delegated rights of priests pervades the medieval sacrament of penance so that, for example, the Celtic penitentials refer to the penances meted out to sinners as *iudicia paenitentiae*.

To complete this preliminary sketch of the sacrament of penance it is necessary to discuss indulgences. Indulgences first arose as a form of relief for laymen where the penances prescribed for sins were so heavy that they could not be adequately completed. Where the penance involved some separation from the life of the community, the indulgence provided a form of support for lay people who were temporarily excluded from society. With the commercialisation of penitential relief, the spread of indulgences needed some overt theological justification since, in practice, it became increasingly difficult to distinguish between absolution and indulgence. The primary legitimation of the system of medieval indulgences was found in the theory of the 'treasury of the Church', originating with Cardinal Hugh of St Cher in 1230, which asserted that the blood of Christ and the martyrs had produced a store of merit over which the Church held a spiritual monopoly. From this store or treasury, the Church distributed aid to sinners in the form of indulgences. From St Thomas onwards, the jurisdiction of indulgences was regarded as the exclusive privilege of bishops who controlled this store of merit for the benefit of lay people. In turn, the bishops enjoyed this right by way of papal authorisation. Thus, the public, infrequent, voluntary confession of the early Church had been transformed into a bureaucratically controlled system of penance in which confession had become private, frequent, and obligatory.

On the basis of this historical outline of the early development of the sacrament of penance, there appears to be some *prima facie* evidence for the idea that the social functions attributed by social anthropologists to witchcraft confessions and confessions in primitive societies may also be characteristic of ecclesiastical confession and penance.

Four social functions are fulfilled by the institution of confession of sins. There is first the therapeutic or cathartic function of confession which has been widely commented on by anthropologists and psychologists.[8] From the earliest times, the Church regarded confessions as a method of restoring the individual's health. Thus in the New Testament, we find James recommending confession for anyone who is ill – 'confess your sins to one another, and pray for one another, and then you will be healed.' This view of confession is, of course, closely associated with the fact that physical health and spiritual salvation were hardly distinguished. A direct analogy was made between the healing work of doctors and priests. Origen recommends confession for those who are 'choked by their peccant humours' and Augustine urges us to 'admit the healing hand, make your confession'. The Irish penitentials also dwelt on this medical dimension of confession and the penitential of St. Columbanus observed that the 'spiritual doctors' of the Church, like 'doctors of the body', are able to provide 'diverse kinds of cures for the wounds of souls, their sickness (offences), pains, ailments and infirmities.'[9]

The sacrament of penance served to bring about the cure of souls, the restoration of individuals to spiritual health, by releasing them from their sins. This cure of the conscience, however, involved a second function – the reconciliation with the Church as a social community by lifting those prohibitions which barred the individual from the altar and the Eucharist. Thus, confession may be regarded as an institution that served a remedial function in restoring 'deviant' individuals to the religious community. A recent publication on confession refers to attendance at the confessional as 'a homecoming',[10] while Evelyn Underhill regards confession as the restoration of a sinner to the 'family' of the Church.[11] Confession and the fiduciary issue of indulgences were social processes whereby the spiritually deviant could be symbolically restored to the community. Confession is thereby a ritual of inclusion that forms a counterpart to the rituals of exclusion, that is, anathematisation and excommunication. The Celtic system of penance clearly illustrates these processes of exclusion and inclusion. In the case of murder, for example, a pilgrimage in which the offender was cut off from his home and family in order to devote himself to the service of God was commonly prescribed. The penitential of St Columbanus punished murderers with a ten-year period of exile in which the murderer, like Cain, should be 'a wanderer and fugitive upon the earth'. Alternative forms of exclusion from the every day life of family and society included entry into a monastery or service in the Crusades. Successful completion of confession and penance resulted eventually in the restoration of the individual to the sacramental life of the Church and inclusion in the routine life of family and community.

It is interesting to note, therefore, that the confession of sins is frequently associated with conversion to faith so that sociologically confession and conversion represent aspects of social inclusion processes. There is an important etymological relationship between the Vulgate's *poenitentia* ('contrite repentance') and Tertullian's use of *agere poenitentiam* to signify a 'change of mind'. Erik Berggren has drawn together a wealth of evidence to show how, even in Protestant Christianity, evangelical conversionist movements resulted in the establishment of confession and absolution.[12]

In consequence of this remedial aspect of confession, the sacrament of penance plays an important role – its third function – in justifying and maintaining social values by legitimating current concepts of proper behaviour and belief. According to the research of historians and anthropologists, witchcraft confessions by demonstrating the widespread and consistent design of the devil to corrupt men gave evidence of the existence of God's divine intervention in reality. This aspect of confession appears to be culturally universal. Thus, referring once more to Robert Brain's study of African child-witches, it seems to be that the confessions of European and Bangwa children 'add logic to beliefs that need constant buttressing' and that a full confession of guilt 'is more effective than persistent protestations of innocence.'[13] Similarly, confessions of treason and witchcraft from the scaffold have the effect of confirming the values held by magistrates.[14] Etienne Delcambre has shown how magistrates and victims shared the same religious definition of witchcraft trials as a sacramental event. By helping the accused, through torture if necessary, to confess themselves guilty of witchcraft, the magistrates thought of themselves as fulfilling a 'priestly function and contributing to the eternal salvation of the accused.'[15] Confession not only provided proof (however dubious the methods for obtaining confession) of guilt, but also, in Macfarlane's words, demonstrated publicly and unambiguously 'an acceptance of society's verdict'.[16] The regular confession of lay people in the Church had a similar, although less dramatic, consequence. The penitential handbooks and *summa* for confessors throughout the medieval period provided great compendia of the dominant values of Christian society. These handbooks provided priests with a routine guide for classifying and codifying human sin. With the aid of 'confession mirrors', questionnaires drawn up for the purpose of self-examination, priests were able to reinforce orthodox beliefs through the contrition of the sinner.

Finally, confession was not only important for maintaining orthodox belief, but also for defining appropriate attitudes and character. The final social function of confession to be considered here is the part confession of sin plays in the definition of what counts as 'human character' in a society. Demonstrations of guilt, remorse, and repentance provide evidence that the penitent, no matter how gross the sin, is also capable of human feeling, capable of responding to his confessor in a manner characteristic of ordinary human beings. Contrition is evidence that a person is worthy of restoration not only to his particular family, but to humanity as such. A full and sincere repentance – as de Penaforte recommends 'amara, festina, integra et frequens' – was taken by confessors as an outward sign of an inward preparation for a true homecoming to normal human intercourse. The spontaneous confession is the most valuable form of human restoration since, unlike the forced confession, the penitent returns himself to society by a voluntary change of character. A French magistrate of the seventeenth century, reflecting on the relative merits of free and forced confessions from a religious point of view, commented that confessions of witchcraft acquired by means of torture 'are never so agreeable to God as voluntary ones accompanied by humility, contrition and repentance.'[17] The attitude of contemporary British jurisprudence continues to display a similar respect for voluntary confession as evidence of a change of heart and character development – a voluntary confession, according to the Warickshall case which provides the legal basis for contemporary interpretations of confession in relation to evidence, 'is deserving of the highest credit, because it is presumed to flow from the strongest sense of guilt.'[18] It is for this reason that confessors and lawyers have been exercised by the critical problem of testing genuine contrition in order to guard against fake repentance. In practice, confessors have often found it difficult to distinguish between 'real' human remorse for past sins and what Frank Lake has called mere 'self-righteousness and perfectionism.'[19] Since theologians and psychologists have assumed that the compulsion to confess is a universal human mechanism for releasing the psyche from the burden of guilt, a person who does not exhibit such a desire to confess is typically regarded as odd, if not inhuman. In literature, the fictional character Meursault in Camus's *The Outsider* remains outside human society precisely because he is not motivated to confess to the murder of an Arab worker. This humanising and therapeutic feature of confession is possible only where the penitent voluntarily returns to society. The brutal, de-humanising consequences of the forced confessions which take place with 'brain-washing' have been amply illustrated in the psychological research of William Sargant and J.A.C. Brown.[20]

The foregoing represent four eufunctional features of confession, the effect of which is to integrate the social system around a common set of values by inducing certain cathartic changes in the character of apparently deviant social actors. This functionalist treatment of confession is not entirely satisfactory for reasons that are endemic to sociological functionalism as a whole. To accept an uncritical view of confession as a primarily therapeutic institution is to adhere to the dominant ideology of confession as held by religious and legal authorities. It is equally important to examine situations in which the institution of confession played a part in disrupting social relations. To recognise the fact that confession may be sociologically significant in social conflict is not, of course, to offer an alternative to functionalism, since in this instance we are merely alluding to a range of possible dysfunctions. However, by developing our interpretation of the sociological importance of confession in this direction, we are specifying more precisely the conditions under which the therapeutic consequences of the institution of confession can obtain. For example, it appears to be the case that confession performs integrative functions only where a common set of social values is already well established. Where a society is disrupted by conflicts of class and ideology, confession may become a focus of social conflict in which the confessional exacerbates existing tensions. For example, following the collapse of the feudal system in Europe, it becomes increasingly difficult to assert that religious confession continued to produce positive, functional effects for society. The conflicts over confession in French society in the eighteenth and nineteenth centuries provide a clear illustration of this issue.

The conflict between Jansenists and Jesuits over the nature of confession illustrates certain aspects of the general breakdown of the Church's monopoly of moral values and the growing pluralism of beliefs in society as a whole. The gradual disintegration of the existing consensus over the relevance and importance of the traditional confessional is simply one dimension of secularisation in European society. The Jansenist theology of God, man and sin was in some respects an attempt to defend a traditional world-view and system of authority which was being challenged by emergent social groups. In opposition to Jansenist traditionalism, it was left to the Jesuits to attempt to liberalise the Catholic world-view in the expectation of retaining the enlightened bourgeoisie within the Catholic Church. In intellectual terms, the Jesuits claimed that the Jansenist view of man as an utterly depraved creature was either morally unjust or logically incoherent. According to Jansenist theology, God had made man corrupt only to punish him eternally for sins which were inherited from the Fall. Jesuits detected a further difficulty in Jansenist ethics – if all actions which are not God-centred are sins, then all men live in perpetual sin even when they are performing otherwise commendable actions, such as being loving parents, respectable citizens or honest traders. To overcome these problems, the Jesuits developed a casuistic moral philosophy which distinguished not only different degrees of sin but also between sin and moral failing. There thus developed an indeterminate moral area in which actions were neither sins nor positive virtues. The Jesuits created a complex moral territory within which the middle classes could live with untroubled consciences. Within the new situation created by Jesuitical casuistry, the confessors were preoccupied with complex problems of classification – did the confessant's description of apparent misdemeanour constitute a real religious sin or simply a socially inappropriate action? For the wealthy bourgeois, the complexities of the Jesuitical view of man had a direct appeal, since the bourgeoisie was constantly involved in the world of trade where the threat of sinful behaviour in the Jansenist view was omnipresent. In any case, the Jansenist emphasis on total depravity was hardly consistent with the bourgeois ideal of the honest man. Those who opposed the Jesuitical casuistry complained that Christians had been turned into a 'people of philosophers' for whom the traditional virtues could now be summarised in terms of 'public weal, the properties of civil life, law and order, social tranquility'.[21]

This is not to suggest that the Jesuits merely manufactured a morality of convenience for the bourgeoisie; indeed, there were many sections within the middle class which held that the Jesuits had gone too far on the road towards permissiveness and laxity. The ideological struggle between the clergy and the anti-clerical party, Jesuits and Jansenists involved a running battle over the question of moral laxity. The anti-clerical party, regarding the confessional as a major institution of priestly power at the local, village level, brought a number of arguments forward to demonstrate the pernicious, anti-social consequences of confession. In particular, they saw confession as a threat to family life since the priest came between husband and wife thereby undermining the authority of the head of the family. It was also thought that the confessor corrupted the innocent by suggesting sins to confessants of which they would otherwise be ignorant. Attitudes between and within the various contending parties in France in the nineteenth century were very divided. Protestants, anticlericals and Jansenists shared the assumption that confession tended to corrupt morality because inadequate penance was imposed on sinners: recurrent absolution on demand encouraged recidivism. Those clerics who defended the traditional system of penance regarded the confessors of the Church as, in Mgr de Segur's words, 'the Good God's police'. By contrast, the moderate party within the Church, the Jesuits and ironically the secularists rejected the punitive regimentation by confession of women and children. The Jesuits believed that the austerity of the Jansenist position was driving people from the Church who were not prepared to accept the confessor's scrutiny of private lives.

This account of what Theodor Zeldin has called the 'conflict of moralities' in eighteenth- and nineteenth-century France raises a number of issues for the functionalist analysis of confession. The first is that confession may in fact sustain and generate psychological anxieties about personal sin by institutionalising the 'compulsion to confess' rather than simply acting as a therapeutic ritual. This problem is reminiscent of the debate between Malinowski and Radcliffe-Brown over the anxiety-reducing potential of magical practices.[22] For Radcliffe-Brown, the possibility that magical rituals could be inadequately performed was an anxiety-generating feature of their cultural environment. Similarly, one might argue that, by rephrasing an academic joke about Freudian psychoanalysis, confession is the sickness of which it purports to be the cure. Confession trains or socialises people into a set of culturally defined sins for which it also provides recognised cure or absolution. If this is too strong a claim, it is certainly the case that theologians and confessors have been alive to the dangerous side-effects of confession. The psychological disturbance known as 'scrupulosity' is apparently most common in Roman Catholic populations.[23] Like the scrupulous natives discussed by Radcliffe-Brown, religious scrupulosity is manifest in obsessive fears that past sins have not been properly confessed or were not understood by the confessor. In their study of obsessive Catholic children, Weisner and Riffel reported that those children suffering from scrupulosity were characterised by 'endless ruminations and repetitions of the same sin, and of all the trivial circumstances surrounding their actions'.[24] In such circumstances, confession may well exacerbate rather than solve guilt-feelings. The other potential 'dysfunction' in psychological terms of confession is that it will, as an unintended consequence, train the innocent in otherwise unknown sins. Catholic confessors have been well aware of this danger. The *Rituale romanum* (1757) warns confessors to avoid 'imprudently questioning the young. . . lest they be scandalised and learn thereby to sin.'[25] This lenient position, however, came under attack in the nineteenth century over the tacit acceptance of 'the wicked crime of Onan' in France. From the 1880s onwards, a much tougher line was advocated and the French clergy were criticised for their tolerant 'mutisme' in matters relating to sexual ethics. The confession was to be used as a method for ensuring that the laity adhered to the Catholic ideal of large families, providing the offspring could be raised as committed Catholics. The dangers of 'imprudently questioning the young' were apparently a risk worth taking since onanism was a sin closely associated with relative affluence among the Catholic middle class and with the secular idea that sex was a pleasure which could be separated from the duty of procreation.

A further problem of functionalist theories of confession is their circularity. We have already noted that when consensus over central social values is shattered by the conflict of interests of social classes and social groups, as, for example, in nineteenth-century France, religious institutions like the sacrament of penance can no longer contribute directly and unambiguously to social integration. This conclusion can serve to illustrate the circularity of functionalist accounts of the remedial nature of confession. In a society where there is relative agreement over certain crucial social values, confession may serve to reinforce and underline those values by confirming the beliefs of persons in authority, symbolically restoring 'deviant' individuals to the community and by socialising individuals in terms of anxieties about certain types of misconduct. Confession thus serves to buttress social values, but changes in social values – the development of Jesuitical casuistry, for example – bring about changes in the nature and role of confession in a society. Consequently an integrated system of social values is crucial for the maintenance and operation of the institution of confession. Without that common value system, there could be little agreement between confessant and priest over the nature of sin and the appropriateness of certain penances. A minimal requirement of confession is a shared set of moral standards for categorising actions as sinful or not sinful. Such an argument is clearly circular since confession functions to endorse shared values, while shared values are necessary for the continuation of confession. My argument is not that the circularity of functionalist theories of confession renders such theories inappropriate or worthless. It implies rather that such functionalist theories of confession are limited unless we can discover some event, social institution, or structure which will explain the presence of confessional rituals in a society without recourse to 'a shared value system'. In short, we can break the circularity of the theory by positing a cause which, as it were, triggers off the processes connecting the sacrament of penance with a common set of beliefs. A number of historical studies of confession, referred to below, suggest that an explanation of changes in the social function of confession might be located in changes in the class structure of society and thereby in changes in the relations of production. This possibility indicates that an alternative perspective on confession can be found within a Marxist orientation to sociological issues. In such a perspective, confession would be viewed not so much as an institution which reinforces commonly held values but as an institution of social control which enables the ruling class to dominate subordinate classes through the psychological mechanism of a 'compulsion to confess'. This Marxist interpretation of the social nature of confession forms the subject of the middle section of my analysis, but, before coming to that subject, it is important to make a crucial observation on the relationship between functionalist and Marxist theories. While Marxists and functionalists may differ significantly in their evaluation of societies, they may not, as Merton observed, 'differ materially in their analytical framework'.[26] It is frequently possible to render Marxist explanations in functionalist terms and vice versa without logical misrepresentation of either position. For example, it would be perfectly intelligible for a Marxist sociologist to argue that the institution of confession has the social effect of reinforcing social values in such a way as to provide a religious legitimation for the class structure of society, regardless of the intentions or beliefs of the actors involved. The purpose of this comment is to suggest that the analysis of the social functions of confession from a functionalist perspective is not analytically incompatible with a Marxist approach to confession as an 'instrument of social control'. Indeed, an analysis of the class structure of societies may provide an explanation of confession which will break the circularity involved in a functionalist perspective.

It is possible to read Marx's commentary on 'ruling ideas' in *The German Ideology* in a variety of ways. One might take his view to be that those who rule politically deliberately manipulate the ruled by controlling the means of indoctrination. In our particular study, through their control of the institution of confession, the ruling class also enjoyed power over subordinate classes by controlling the means by which theological beliefs and religious attitudes were disseminated. In this view, ideological control involves a dominant group doing something to a subordinate group. This particular interpretation ignores the fact that it is equally important for any ruling class or group to control itself ideologically with the same set of beliefs which are held, or at least partly held, by a subordinate group. Significant ideological beliefs must be shared as a common belief system by dominant and subordinate classes so that an ideology will be distributed, as it were, horizontally and vertically through the class structure. Confession is important for the Marxist analysis of ideology since confession linked classes together in a common system of belief and practice. Peasants confessed to priests, but so did knights. Confession served as an institution of social control in societies where there was a shared value system uniting social classes within a common culture. From this point of view, Marxist and functionalist interpretations of the institution of confession may be regarded as analytically compatible.

Confession, social control and social stratification

Let us now consider certain aspects of confession in relation to social stratification. First, the confessional itself was based on status inequality between penitent and priest and this status inequality formed part of a spiritual hierarchy connecting the penitent to God. The canon of 1216 required that to be true, a confession must be made to someone in authority, normally a priest. Berggren has argued that it is the very authority of the priest to absolve sins that induces sinners to seek priests rather than laymen as confessors. While the penitent is impure, the priest in his role as priest is fully competent to hear a confession regardless of his moral standing as a man. The purity of the priest is ritually given as a social fact. Thomas Tentler comments that the priest 'may even be immoral. But if he holds the key of power he may forgive sins.'[27] In Weberian terms, the priest enjoyed a charisma of office which guaranteed the purity of his role and the authority of his pronouncements regardless of his personal failings. The penitent therefore stood at the bottom of a status hierarchy constituted by 'spiritual estates' – the saints, angels and God – which were the sacred counterpart of feudal estates within secular society.

The penitent was also differentiated from his confessor in terms of knowledge and skill. While in the medieval period parish priests had a reputation for their lack of education and training, they at least had the support of the penitential manuals which in principle allowed them to deal with all cases of conscience however complex and involved they might be. The summas made the conduct of confession a matter of routine application of codified knowledge which enabled the priest to master and control the confessional by simply following written instructions. The status of the confessor was futher buttressed by the fact that he was a 'father' in charge of a flock of sinners. Where these symbols of status appeared to fail in inducing an attitude of respect towards the clergy, the Church could, as a last resort, always turn towards gimmickry and popular superstition. One example of such practices was the *confessional à surprise* in which, by use of concealed switches, a painting of Christ was transformed into an image of the devil to the accompaniment of loud noises from whistles and pipes. The priest's insignia, the use of confessional boxes and grilles, and the requirement that the confession must flow from humility and bitter self-accusation all contributed to emphasising the social and spiritual gap separating penitent and priest. We can claim, therefore, that confessions were made to status superiors whose authority was buttressed by a variety of social and religious credentials.

This status hierarchy within the confessional mirrors the secular status order within feudal society itself. The confessional recreated the hierarchy of honour and personal worth of the secular order in religious terms. While the members of the cominant secular estates enjoyed personal worth by virtue of their location within the social stratification of society, the confessor was guaranteed a spiritual 'honour' which flowed from the objective merit of the Church. It was a microcosm of the social realm that the confessional was, in Tentler's terms, a powerful 'instrument of social control'.

In the period following the Lateran canon, confession was used as a device for discovering and eradicating heresy. One of the primary aims of confession was, therefore, to protect and enforce orthodox belief and practice. Public adherence to orthodox norms and practices was achieved by internalised, private guilt and by the methodical searching of conscience under the careful scrutiny of the priest. The mechanism for the maintenance of the external social order was the internal 'court of conscience'. The Church, of course, possessed a battery of institutions for bringing about adherence to orthodox belief – excommunication, public expiation, ecclesiastical courts – but in the sacrament of penance, these institutions become 'subsidiary to, and at the same time are incorporated into, a culture of guilt'.[28] The extent to which confession was an efficient method of social control is difficult to assess. The opinion of historians of the sacrament of penance is divided over a range of issues, for example, while Henry Lea argues that there was considerable lay resistance to the imposition of confession after 1216, Bernhard Poschmann believes that there was virtually no opposition to this canon. The bishops of the Church were, however, constantly issuing threats to their laity about the dire consequences of irregular confession and absenteeism and blacklists of laity who failed to provide adequate confession were drawn up. Roberto da Lecci complained that the multitudes who had not confessed for twenty years or more constituted 'a venomous synagogue of hell'.[29] The complaints of bishops about the behaviour of their laity are very inadequate data of the effect of confession on social behaviour. The attempts by Lea and others to quantify the impact of the confessional on moral behaviour by comparing, for example, incidence of prostitution and illegitimacy rates among different religious and non-religious groups are far from convincing. What does appear to be clear is the existence of a widespread belief that without some form of confession of sin by the laity on a regular basis the moral control of Christianity would have been greatly impaired. The most direct affirmation of this viewpoint came from writers like Abbé Laurichesse who, noting that Christianity is 'law, rule, restraint', asserted that, for Christianity, confession is 'the severest form of repressive force' since it is by confession that Christianity 'captures man and dominates him'.[30] Many Protestant authors looked back on the confessional as an effective means of moral control and John Aubrey commented that in Catholic England 'Then were the consciences of the people kept in so great awe by confession that just dealing and virtue were habitual.'[31] Keith Thomas, in assessing the somewhat slight and heterogeneous pieces of evidence, concludes that personal confession was a strong element of public order: 'The personal confession and interrogation of every single layman was potentially an altogether more comprehensive system of social discipline than the isolated prosecution of relatively notorious offenders.'[32] The confessional performed this social service primarily by providing a bridge between the internal prosecution of the guilty self by the private conscience with the external public order of society.

In addition to this surveillance of the conscience, confession produced politically important information about treasons and plots; information gathered among subordinate groups could become available to ruling groups through the mediation of the priest. The confession was a method of uncovering crimes because the confessor normally encouraged penitents to reveal the names of accomplices in criminal activities. According to Lea, this practice gave priests considerable opportunities for blackmail, and in the middle of the eighteenth century Benedict XIV brought in various rules to guard against blackmail. In principle, the seal of the confession prevented knowledge of crimes confessed in the privacy of the confessional becoming publicly available. The first formal recognition of an obligation on the priest to protect the secrecy of confessions occurs in 813 and this recognition was further endorsed by the canon of 1216. There was, of course, considerable pressure from the courts for priests to break the seal of confession and various devices were used to bring this about. Lea refers to situations where priests would not break the seal as priests, but would divulge information in their role as citizen. It was widely believed that information concerning crimes which had been confessed was frequently passed on to the authorities. The sixteenth-century catchphrase, 'he hath been at shrift!' (Tynedale, *The Obedience of a Christian Man*, 1528), was applied to someone who had been betrayed as a result of confessing to a priest. The use of the category of 'reserved cases' also meant that important crimes came to the notice of higher ecclesiastics; the 'reserved cases' typically included such crimes as homicide, forgery, witchcraft, and arson. Since these cases could not be heard by a parish priest, grave crimes detected in the local parish were confessed upwards before higher authorities. In certain exceptional circumstances, the protection offered the laity by the seal has been directly removed by civil authorities. The Spiritual Regulation of Peter the Great in 1712 instructed priests to violate the seal if they discovered anything that might be seditious. While confession was primarily a means of ensuring that adherence to the regulations of the Church was a matter of conscience, confession also acted as a spiritual arm of the State's legal apparatus.

Functionalist accounts of religion have been frequently couched in terms of, to use Merton's terms, 'large, spaceless and timeless generalisations'. In recognising the role of confession as an instrument of social control, it is important to take notice of the fact that the confessional and confessional beliefs were subject to changes which were brought about by the conflicting interests and needs of contending social classes. In an important study of mendicant orders, Rosenwein and Little trace the development of two different types of spirituality which they demonstrate were connected with changing social relations. Cluniac spirituality was a response to the growth of violence and the emergence of the professional man of war in ninth- and tenth-century Frankish society. The Church came to terms with the new level of violence by attempting to ensure that organised violence was carried out only by properly constituted authorities under specified conditions. The penitentials of this period worked out the exact penance required for certain instances of legitimated violence against communal enemies. Cluniac spirituality offered vicarious expiation for sins committed by the knightly class who were not members of the monastic order. Cluniac liturgy thereby provided[33]

> an important link between the sinner and God in the tenth – and eleventh – century penitential system. Men who joined a confraternity with Cluny, or simply made a donation there, were assured of prayers on behalf of their souls.

In this period, the confessional was very much concerned with the practical moral solution of problems generated by violence and by a new class of violent men. By contrast, the penitential practice and theory of the Franciscans and Dominicans were focused on problems created by new forms of commerce in the city life of later European society. Concern for the moral value of wealth earned on the market was closely associated with the development of the concept of an internal, subjective conscience. The twelfth century was a pivotal period in the creation of a new psychology of man and morality in which attention switched from viewing moral activity as conformity with external laws to interpreting morals in terms of intention and will. This reorientation of moral theory had a direct impact on the sacrament of penance. Whereas confession had been traditionally dominated by the act of absolution as an ecclesiastical and objective event, for the followers of Abélard, contrition as a subjective act of self-accusation became paramount.[34] The legitimation of knightly violence had been in terms of external, behavioural conformity to objective laws; the morality of the city market place was concerned with inner intentions. Christian morality changed its location from 'the open field of bad actions and penitential counteractions to the private chamber of intention and contrition.'[35] In their protest against wealth, the friars espoused a life of poverty and rejection of worldly status and yet, paradoxically, the confessional came to reflect the market place as a system of transaction and negotiation. For a certain fee, the penitent could exchange his debt of sin against the store of virtue built up by Christ and the saints. The notion of a Treasury of Merit was particularly apt in characterising the relationship between the Church and men. In opposition to wealth which had been acquired by a process of calculation, the begging of the friars was 'irregular, unplanned and indiscriminate'.[36] On the other hand, the new doctrine of penance helped to legitimate economic behaviour by showing that, provided a merchant had good intentions in providing a necessary social service, his behaviour was religiously acceptable. The consequence of these religious practices was to 'work out for the ruling classes an acceptable version of the previously objectionable activities.'[37] Rosenwein and Little conclude their analysis by noting that, once these religious orders had performed these important functions of legitimating first organised violence and then wealth, they went into social decline.

These examples from Franciscan and Benedictine spirituality serve to illustrate my contention that the confessional is a sort of mirror image of the total secular class structure. They also point to a further feature of confession as an instrument of social control in that confession worked to police the behaviour of subordinate classes while legitimating actions and beliefs among emergent groups within the ruling classes. The sacrament of penance, therefore, linked classes together in a set of common practices. While the confessional was an important feature, to use a spatial analogy, in the vertical organisation of the social structure of Christendom, it was also crucial for the horizontal linkages between status groups. Although as we have seen the penitent was in certain important respects the social and religious inferior of the confessor, in the regulation of confession an attempt was made to match the rank of confessants within feudal estates with the ecclesiastical status of the confessor. These regulations ensured that members of superior secular estates did not confess downwards to priests of inferior ecclesiastical rank. A lengthy quotation from Lea provides a good indication of the nature of these arrangements:[38]

> in the compilations for the guidance of confessors, we find elaborate enumerations of all the grades of society, with designations as to whom they are to seek for their shrift, and long lists of their habitual sins which are to be enquired for. Thus we are told that dukes confess to the bishops of their capitals; there are various directions as to marquises and counts, whose rank and possessions were by no means uniform; a baron confesses to the parish priest of his chief town, while knights, merchants, peasants and their children confess to the priests of their parishes.

Kings were expected to confess to the bishop or archbishop of the city of their coronation, but they frequently obtained papal permission to select their own confessor. A similar set of arrangements also existed for ecclesiastics who did not confess downwards below their rank. Thus the confessor is the status superior of the confessant within the confessional in the sense that the priest possessed purity of office, but confession is generally made to status equals within the social and ecclesiastical hierarchy. It was presumably a matter of some dishonour for a baron to confess to a parish priest. These status regulations ensured that the sacrament of penance did not endanger or sabotage the hierarchy of feudal estates by requesting the nobility to confess to poor priests. The idea that a parish priest was competent to hear the sins and to be privy to the secrets of the ruling classes would have implied that in practice all men are equal before God and his representatives on earth. These status arrangements prevented the nobility entering the confessional stall with lower clergy; once inside the confessional, the penitent was subject to the power of the priest by virtue of the Church's Treasury of Merit. The full force of the Church's monopoly of spiritual power was felt mainly by peasants since the nobility could always curtail the Church's control by, for example, selecting their own confessors. These observations do not imply that confession was, as it were, forced down the throats of unwilling peasants. The confessional in principle embraced all levels of society within a common practice and to some extent each stratum in society controlled itself internally rather than externally by priests from superior social strata. The confession was not just an instrument for disciplining subordinate social strata or for controlling the lower levels of the ecclesiastical hierarchy. Confession was a much more comprehensive instrument of control working both within and between social classes.

In feudal society, the sacrament of penance was a key mechanism for maintaining and enforcing certain commonly held beliefs about appropriate and inappropriate social behaviour. At the same time, the successful operation of this mechanism depended on the existence of a relatively homogeneous culture. The apparent circularity of this form of explanation can be avoided by noting that changes in the social structure, such as the development of a new form of organised violence and a military class, transforms the nature of that mutually dependent relationship. Although confession was a major social institution of social conformity and control in a society where religious beliefs and values held primacy in social organisation, the extension of market relations, the development of the city and the relative autonomy of the urban class of burghers radically transformed the confessional. The transition from a society based on use-values to exchange-values on an open market contributed to the emergence of such notions as the subjective self, the interior conscience and personal responsibility for intentions and actions. The market and the autonomous city were also important in the development of the major concepts (contract, equality and individualism) of the Enlightenment. As Lucien Goldmann has demonstrated, the development of a market economy had a fundamental consequence for the individual who now became 'both in his own consciousness and in that of his fellow men, an independent element, a sort of monad, a *point of departure*.'[39] Jansenism and Jesuit casuistry represent two responses to the new social situation in which the commercial and industrial bourgeoisie began to play a decisive part. Jansenism was an attempt to defend traditional values in a rapidly changing world; Jesuitical Catholicism represented a more liberal accommodation to the needs of the honest man of business. Whether or not Christianity in any meaningful sense survived the industrialisation of European societies in the nineteenth century is obviously a matter of lively and unsettled sociological debate. What is clear and uncontroversial is that Christianity no longer enjoyed a monopoly in the field of moral pronouncement and psychological guidance. While the conflicts between Abélard and his opponents, Jansenists and Jesuits, had been conflicts within an accepted religious framework, the emergence of secular psychoanalysis represented an alternative to the traditional theories of the cure of souls which, however ambiguously, fell outside the framework of theism.

Secularisation and psychoanalysis

The precise relationship between Freudianism, religion and secularisation has been for many decades the subject of a complex and often acrimonious debate. Benjamin Nelson has noted that, while the Protestant emphasis on guilt and individual responsibility is compatible with certain psychoanalytic assumptions about the nature of the individual, Protestantism was hostile to any form of institutionalised, regular confession and to any attempt at external psychic direction of the individual penitent.[40] Nelson observed that psychoanalysis, originating in Catholic Vienna among Jewish intellectuals, had its maximum impact in secular, Protestant America. Many of the early psychoanalysts felt that the Catholic confessional was an important prescientific model for the development of secular therapy, but Protestantism was necessary for breaking the monopolist position of the Church. Theodor Reik claimed that the Catholic Church had provided an objective institutionalised confessional for the 'compulsion to confess', while Protestantism had turned men inwards towards the subjective self.[41] By demolishing the objective structure of the Catholic confessional, Protestantism had set the scene in which secular therapy could replace the religious cure of souls. Ironically, C.G. Jung discovered that the overwhelming majority of his patients were Protestants; this situation was explained, Jung concluded, by the fact that mentally ill Catholics had recourse to their confessors, whereas Protestants had to turn to secular analysis.[42] Philip Rieff goes further by suggesting that it was the failure of Christianity as a system of morality to 'compensate men satisfactorily for the necessary deprivations imposed upon their impulse lives' which provided the social and psychological conditions for the rise of Freudian therapy.[43]

Freud was aware of what he regarded as superficial similarities between religious confession and his therapeutic, talking technique.[44] There was an important analogy between the penitential features of compulsive behaviour in neurotics and its solution through Freudian analysis and the Catholic confessional and its cathartic consequences. Talking ('giving utterance to a tormenting secret, e.g. confession') was a basic plank in Freudian therapy. While Freud recognised the similarities between religion and psychoanalysis, he was at pains to stress the differences. While therapy as a method might be useful for pastors, there was an analytic incompatibility between theological metaphysics and scientific theories of mental illness. Confession might be an introduction to analysis, but in the religious confessional the penitent 'tells what he knows; in analysis the neurotic has to tell more.'[45] In the confessional, the penitent enumerates 'conscious sins' which are publicly recognised by the Church, but in analysis the neurotic must uncover and acknowledge his unconscious secrets. The neurotic person behaves as if he were overwhelmed by a feeling of guilt 'of which, however, he knows nothing, so that we must call it an unconscious sense of guilt, in spite of the apparent contradiction in terms.'[46] In the view of a number of contemporary French 'structuralists', Freudianism represents a scientific break with existing ideological thought about illness and the essence of this scientific break or 'epistemological rupture' is Freud's discovery of the 'unconscious' which enabled Freud to conceptualise the science of psychoanalysis on an entirely new theoretical 'terrain'.[47] According to this interpretation, although Freud may have initially approached therapy in terms of existing concepts, some of which were undeniably religious concepts, Freud's mature scientific thought owes nothing to the traditional approach of the Church.

Although the 'structuralist' interpretation of Freudian thought has much to commend it, in practice Freud was unable to indemnify his thought and practice against the encroachment of religious beliefs. Freud bitterly criticised those analysts who tuned psychoanalysis into a form of religious therapy. In particular, Freud rejected Jung for turning analysis into a cure of souls. In an important sense, Freud offered no cure; psychoanalysis simply revealed psychic problems by uncovering hidden features of the unconscious which only the patients could resolve. It can be claimed, however, that the Jungian emphasis on the cure and salvation became the dominant aspect of contemporary analysis so that the modern analyst has 'succeeded to the preaching functions of the pastors'.[48] The importance of analysis for traditional Christian pastoral work was certainly not lost on Freud's contemporaries, especially Pastor Pfister. According to Pfister psychoanalysis and Christianity both aimed at removing the burden of guilt and treated suffering as a punishment for breaking the injunctions of authority (either God or the super-ego). In both analysis and confession, there was a regression during therapy to an infantile dependent state which was preparatory to full maturity. While Jung converted Freud's science of psychoanalysis back into his own peculiar brand of anthropological religion, Pfister was much closer to Freud's orientation to therapy as a neutral tool in the hands of doctors, priests or secular analysts. Pfister wrote to Freud that, 'Just as Protestantism abolished the difference between laity and clergy, so must the cure of souls be laicised and secularised' (Meng and Freud).[49] It was along these lines that Pfister attempted to insert Freudian analysis as a neutral tool of therapy into the traditional Christian fields of pastoral work and pedagogy.

The failure of Christianity to provide an adequate system of moral control for human psychology in an industrial civilisation resulted in the secularisation of the confessional, by which I mean, to use Klempt's formula, 'the transformation of conceptions and modes of thought which were originally developed by the Christian salvation belief and its theology into ones of a world-based outlook.'[50] The result of this transformation has been that Freudian analysis came to perform social functions which had been once exercised by the Christian cure of souls. To consider this possibility involves an examination of the sociological parallels between analysis and confession. In both situations, there is an important status inequality between analyst (confessor) and patient (penitent). In the psychoanalytic interview, the analyst acts as the status superior of the analysand in knowledge, skill, self-mastery and typically in social status. Just as the authority of the priest rested on an objective merit delegated to him by the bishop, so the analyst's authority rests upon the collective authority of professional bodies. In the Catholic confessional, the grille and stall symbolised the authority of the priest and emphasised the social distance which separated his priestly office from the world of the penitent. The priest was in this respect the anonymous voice of ecclesiastical authority. Similarly, Freud insisted on an attitude of respect towards himself and his method on the part of the patient. Casual or careless behaviour implied a lack of appropriate respect for the efficacy of the 'talking cure'. As the medieval pardoner asked his fee, so the modern analyst has a contractual relationship with the patient; the fee is a token of the patient's commitment to recovery. Of course, the relationship between analyst and analysand must be one of trust and friendship but this does nothing to change the status relationship between them, since the contractual nature of the 'friendship' cannot be easily concealed. The contractual fee acts to ensure the impersonality 'behind the ostensibly intensely personal character of the psychoanalytic relationship'.[51]

The medieval confessional was a sociological mirror reflecting the organisation of hierarchical estates and status honour of feudal society. In noting the social distance which separates the analyst and his patient in Freudian analysis, I have suggested that the Freudian 'confessional' might also reflect the general class structure of industrial societies. However, it might be argued that my attempt at drawing out a parallel between confession and analysis will not work, since modern industrial societies are characterised by egalitarian ideologies, political pluralism and social mobility. I would suggest that the demand for various types of co-therapy and equality between analyst and analysand reflects a general pressure towards social democratisation. Priests and analysts can no longer simply ignore lay opinion and 'consumer interests'. However, the existence of socially mobile people does not mean that classes no longer exist and the widespread belief in greater equality between classes should not blind us to the massive continuity of class inequality.[52] The apparent democratisation of industrial society exists alongside the class inequality. This relationship between superficial democratisation and class stratification is reflected in Freudian psychoanalysis. Regardless of the movement towards equality in Freudian therapy, inequalities within the therapy session remain, because the contractual element and the professional status of the analyst are not easily eliminated. Inequalities in the type of therapy which are available to patients from different social classes are also fundamental. In their study of social stratification and mental illness, Hollingshead and Redlich distinguished between three types of therapy – psychotherapy, organic therapy and custodial care.[53] The use of psychotherapy was heavily concentrated in social classes one to three, while custodial care was associated with classes four and five. Of the various psychotherapeutic treatments, psychoanalysis was limited to classes one and two. Myers and Schaffer found that the middle class share a common set of beliefs, language and attitudes with professional psychotherapists which facilitates the process of 'talking therapy' and, in order that lower class patients can use the services of psychoanalysts, these patients must 'acquire new symbols and values to participate in expressive psychotherapy.'[54]

There is, however, a much more fundamental relationship between the middle class and psychoanalysis than merely a common culture between analyst and analysand. The neuroses of the middle class seem to be an effect of its location in the social structure. In class terms, the middle class fears that it will be sucked into the working class, while at the same time it aspires to rise into the upper classes. Hence, the middle classes are typically associated with the norms of self-control, achievement motivation and self-discipline. The position of the middle class is one of uncertainty and anxiety. The build up of neurotic anxiety over the sexuality of the self and its bearing on class mobility created massive psychological tensions. While Freud's theories were potentially radical and subversive from the point of view of the Viennese *status quo*, Erich Fromm has drawn attention to the conformist character of institutionalised post-Freudian analysis. In his reinterpretation of the 'case of Little Hans', Fromm pointed to certain blind spots in Freud's approach to incest whereby the emphasis ascribed to the incestuous inclinations of the child functions as 'a defence of the parents, who are thus absolved of their own incestuous fantasies and the actions that are known to occur.'[55] The consequence of Freud's position is to affirm the authority of parents over children and the dominance of men over women. In Freudian analysis, the woman appears as 'a crippled, castrated man'.[56] Institutionalised Freudianism allowed the normal individual, once he had come to terms with the demands of the superego, to be safely incorporated within the nuclear family of the middle class. Once the problems of guilt and sexuality had been resolved by the analyst, the middle class could settle down to the routine demands of business and family life. The connection between psychoanalysis and economics is conceived by Fromm as an analogy between the *homo economicus* of classical political economy and the *homo sexualis* of Freudian analysis since both are characterised by anxiety over the satisfaction of needs in a market where scarcity prevails.

In Freudian theory, 'all human strivings for lust result from the need to rid oneself from unpleasant tensions rather than that lust is a phenomenon of abundance aiming at a greater intensity and depth of human experience.'[57] Utilitarian political economy was similarly founded on assumptions about scarcity and anxieties about the satisfaction of human needs in a situation of uncertain supply. In these terms, Freud is the Malthus of human sexuality.

There appears, therefore, to be an interesting parallel between the medieval confessional and contemporary psychoanalysis. Just as the Benedictine and Franciscan spirituality were responses to certain crucial transitions in feudal society and just as Jesuit casuistry was an attempt to come to terms with the psychology of the early, commercial bourgeoisie, so Freudianism has itself represented a cultural response to modern social conditions, especially the location of the middle class in contemporary society. Psychoanalysis attempts to solve certain problems created by the accommodation of the middle class to the conditions set by industrial society. In Fromm's view, the basic categories of Freudian analysis were merely the products of a specific form of social and economic organisation, namely capitalist society. For example, anal repression was merely the psychological counterpart of capitalist rationality and Keynesian hoarding. Other members of the Frankfurt School, notably Max Horkheimer, argued that the apparent weakness of Freud's theory – its instinctualism and its blindness to the social role of the family – was in fact its strength. The supposed one-sidedness of Freudianism was an adequte description of the psychological one-sidedness of bourgeois culture. Freud's psychoanalysis thus represents a sociological mirror of the tensions of the industrial bourgeoisie.

Theologians might be tempted to assume that the transposition of Christian beliefs and practices into contemporary psychoanalysis and the parallel between confession and analysis provide evidence for the belief that all men have a profound need for salvation, or at least for relief from a tormented conscience.[58] It is certainly the case that Catholic priests and Protestant ministers, especially in the United States, followed the lead given by Pfister in regarding psychoanalysis not as a secular threat, but as a potentially useful discipline in relation to their traditional pastoral concerns and therefore as an appropriate addition to college curricula.[59] With the development of pastoral counselling, clinical theology and confessional theology, the new ideas of psychiatry, psychology and psychoanalysis were grafted onto the existing beliefs and practices of traditional pastoralia in such a way that ministers of religion could define themselves as professional practitioners on a par with social workers, doctors and psychiatrists. Very few theologians have, however, been aware of the cost involved in the purchase of this role definition. The interpretation of the modern minister of religion as a sort of Freudian analyst with a Christian vocation to serve the neurotics of industrial society has in practice involved a diminution of the sacramental aspects of the confessional, namely the priest's spiritual power of absolution. The co-optation of secular therapy by ministers of religion involves a profound redefinition of Christian belief so that sin, confession, and absolution are replaced by the new concepts of guilt feeling, free association, and freedom from neurosis. Psychology replaces both morality and theology. Crucial differences between the spiritual claims of theology and the scientific status of psychoanalysis are blurred. Mowrer comments that secular psychotherapy 'does not really believe in guilt, only guilt feelings (or a "guilt sense"); and the aim of the type of "confession" which it encourages, i.e. free association, is "insight" rather than repentance and restitution.'[60] While the adoption of secular psychotherapy might imply a subtle secularisation of the traditional salvational beliefs of

Christianity, the definition of the priest's role in terms of Freudian psychoanalysis has a definite appeal for the modern clergy. Bryan Wilson has argued that, in a society where the traditional claims of ministers of religion have lost coherence and authority, the clergy have attempted to develop an area of unique professional competence in matters of ritual practice.[61] The technical division of labour, the professionalisation of work and the growth of specialisation of labour have undermined the traditional role definitions of the clergy. While becoming 'liturgical specialists' might be one possible solution for a vocation under attack, 'pastoral analysis' might be an equally appealing occupational label. The theological cost which is required by such a strategy has already been discussed. Whether such an occupational label will prove successful seems uncertain since the pastoral analyst is laying claim to a professional competence and to a lay audience which is disputed by associated professional workers in the field of social work, medicine and psychiatry.

Conclusion

In *The Sociology of Religion*, Max Weber argued that the confessional was a relatively ineffectual or uncertain system of moral control and that the confession as a form of institutionalised grace inhibited the comprehensive rationalisation of ethics because the absolution of sins retained a quasi-magical dimension. In Catholicism, the sinner can always expect to receive absolution by balancing certain discrete ritual actions (penances) against sins which are conceptualised as 'discrete actions'.[62] The ability of confessors and spiritual directors to exercise moral control over their flock was weakened by 'the circumstance that there was always grace remaining to be distributed anew.'[63] In short, for Weber, the doctrine of the Treasury of Merit encouraged recidivism among sinners. This form of institutionalised grace is contrasted in *The Sociology of Religion* with ascetic Protestantism which developed a theory of sin as a total, comprehensive condition of man, not just a collection of 'discrete actions'. In Protestantism, sin cannot be removed by mechanical absolution by priests who mediate between God and man; sin can only be obliterated by a total conversion of man to Christ who redeems man from his fallen state. The centrality of this salvational belief in Protestantism resulted in an anti-magical rationalisation of ethics and life. While Weber recognised that a form of confessional ritual was not unknown in Protestantism – Wesley's penitential bands, for example – in various periods, he argued that the action of the individual conscience on the whole man in the absence of priestly mediation was crucial, not only for the development of ascetic religion, but also for rational capitalism.

By arguing that institutionalised confession tended to encourage recidivism, Weber is, probably unintentionally, not unlike those Protestant critics of Catholicism who condemned casuistry for its leniency towards sinners. A similar critical attitude is also found among certain moral philosophers; Henry Sidgwick believed that the quasi-legal conception of morality which was originally developed in the penitential manuals 'would have a tendency to weaken the moral sensibilities of ordinary minds.'[64] We have already seen that the radical secularists of nineteenth-century France thought that confession, rather than operating as an instrument of moral control, actually undermined moral authority. In this discussion of confession, I have attempted to show that it is impossible to arrive at an adequate sociological understanding of the confessional without locating it within the context of definite social structures. Weber ignores the dynamic relationship between the sacrament of penance and the class structure so that, at best, his implicit moral evaluation of confession might have relevance to the confessional at a specific point in its historical development. The Catholic confessional changed fundamentally at certain periods in response to the economic and moral interests of social classes and groups. Thus, the emergence of a subjective interior conscience with Abélard's theology constituted a profound break with the conceptual basis of the early penitential system. Rather than engage in moral evaluation of confession, my discussion has centred on the social functions of the confessional as a mechanism of social integration and social control. In this respect, confession is most adequately understood as simply one instance of a ritual of social inclusion which continuously demarcates the moral boundaries of a social group. It was, however, precisely the failure of confession to provide a system of moral control under the conditions which were established by industrial capitalism that created the conditions for the growth of secular psychoanalysis. While post-Freudian analysis might represent a form of secularised confessional, the adoption of psychoanalytic concepts and practices by Christian pastors threatens to bring about a further erosion of Christian belief.

Chapter 3
On the universality of confession: compulsion, constraint and conscience

Our argument so far has been that the institution of confession, if not unique to western Christianity, is at least a peculiar, persistent and ubiquitous feature of western culture. Any claim about the uniqueness of any institution may, of course, be merely the product of definitional fiat. We have defined confession as any full admission of personal guilt for misdemeanours (religious, legal or customary) to an individual in authority in a private setting. This definition is not an arbitrary selection of features since this meaning of confession is deeply embedded in both historical and contemporary usage. The definition, however, has to assume that the initial Catholic conception of confession has been, as it were, redistributed within legal and psychoanalytical theory. This dispersion has been demonstrated in our analysis of the history of confession in Chapter 2 and in the study of Michel Foucault in Chapter 4. To recap, the Christian confession was originally part of the sacrament of penance, involving contrition, confession, satisfaction and absolution. The institution of confession presupposes, therefore: (1) a theory of individual guilt (2) a moral order against which individual sins are committed (3) a system of authority which can receive and absolve sins, and (4) a variety of techniques for speaking about, hearing and interpreting confessional statements. Because confession involves, on the one hand, the notion of individual responsibility for personal misdemeanours and, on the other, the idea of a public morality binding on all, the Western confessional is closely connected with individualism and with a cosmology based on a clear sacred/profane dichotomy. Guilt and anxiety are thus the products of a world-view in which complete conformity to a set of ideal norms is, by definition, uncertain. In other words, our argument about the peculiarity of the western confessional is closely related to Max Weber's view of the sociological importance of Christianity for the development of an urban, individualist, capitalist society.

Two aspects of Weber's characterisation of Christianity are important for our analysis of the confessional. In his discussion of theodicy in *The Sociology of Religion*, Weber claimed that the prophetic monotheism of the Christian tradition created a chasm between the secular order, especially in relation to the existence of force and sexuality, and sacred reality. Because human beings cannot exist outside this secular order, the problem of human sinfulness occupied a central place in Christian theology and ritual. The implication of this discussion of theodicy is that Christianity developed two basic solutions to the paradox of sin. First, it was possible to create a religious elite who, by receiving alms and tribute from lay people, could partially isolate themselves from the world of violence and sexuality. This elite lived a life of holiness on behalf of the laity. This was the traditional Catholic solution which institutionalised grace through the monastery and the priesthood. Second, it was possible to legitimate secular life provided it was engaged with in terms of a religious calling. The secular activities of husband, worker and citizen were subordinated to strict religious norms and were motivated by religious conceptions. This attempt to master the world was regarded by Weber as a revolutionary consequence of the Protestant concept of *beruf*. In both Catholicism and Protestantism, there is a fundamental profane/sacred distinction, but the solution of this dichotomy took radically different directions in these two separate forms of Christianity. As we have seen, Weber treated the confessional as an institution which reduced the separation of sacred and secular by allowing the individual to cope with sin on a piecemeal basis. There are two strong objections to Weber's view of the confessional. It is not the case that pietist Protestant groups entirely abandoned the confessional; confessional practices merely reasserted themselves in the form of penitential bands, devotional diaries and religious testimonies. Weber's interpretation of confession also assumes that confession and absolution actually worked, in the sense of removing subjective guilt. Persistent anxieties about the fullness and regularity of confession, that is, the problem of scrupulosity, suggests that the confessional does not work as, so to speak, a moral vacuum cleaner. Despite these two criticisms, from Weber we derive the view that any religious tradition, which has a strong distinction between this world and a sacred reality, will generate a set of religious practices for coping with human sinfulness. It is not important to this basic assertion whether religious traditions have a monotheistic or dualistic theology. On these grounds, both Christianity and Zoroastrianism would be conducive to the growth of confessional rituals.

While confession presupposes a doctrine of human sinfulness, it is important for our argument that the conception of sin must be individualistic. In this respect, Christian theology has clearly been ambiguous. In terms of strict monotheism, an omnipotent and omniscient God must be the author of the sin of mankind which He then punishes. The traditional problem of both Christian and Islamic theology is to reconcile God's goodness with God's power. Most solutions to the problem of theodicy have to minimise God's omnipotence in order to establish His goodness and they do this either through dualism where God is opposed by the Devil or by creating some space within which human freedom can operate, albeit on a limited basis. Again Weber sought to emphasise important differences between Catholicism and Protestantism. The oddity of Calvinism was that it combined a highly deterministic doctrine of election with a clear commitment to the importance of individualism in the doctrine of the priesthood of all believers. Each individual is personally responsible for their conduct since they can no longer depend on sacraments or priesthood. While Weber concentrated on these differences, his urban sociology suggested that Christianity as a whole was important for the development of western individualism. In *The City*, he argued that Christianity encouraged the growth of urban communities based on common religious norms rather than on tribal affiliation. Christianity thus provided the cultural context within which the individualist ethic of the urban artisan could flourish. While the problem of theodicy found no real philosophical solution in Christianity, the Christian notion of individual responsibility for sin greatly contributed to European individualistic moralities and in particular to the idea of a personal conscience. Regardless of the sociological importance of Christianity as a whole in the development of the modern notions of character and conscience, Weber clearly thought that it was Protestantism which developed a particularly radical version of moral individualism.

This problem – the historical development of cultural formulae for systematically connecting conscience with action – has been central to the sociology of Benjamin Nelson in his various studies of usury, science and religion.[1] Stated briefly, Nelson's argument is that, prior to the sixteenth century, the conscience of the individual was tested in terms of the formulae of the Forum of Penance and the Court of Conscience. Within this scheme, the priest occupied the position of moral judge who, in terms of casuistic theories of conjecturalism, fictionalism and probabilism, was in authority to make moral decisions. In Germany, the Lutheran critique of the tripartite moral system of casuistry, cure of souls and conscience produced an absolute split between the inner world of individual freedom, now dominated by the personal conscience, and the other world of political bondage. The notion that the state was a necessary institution to protect society from human evil was conjoined with an expansion of the role of conscience within the individual. Over time, this radical split between private conscience and public morality did not rule out attempts to revise and renovate the principle of spiritual direction, once freed from its Catholic setting. The external institutions of casuistry, priesthood and penance were scrapped in favour of new, private obligations under such terms as 'the Inner light', 'the voice of conscience' and the 'light of reason'. The conduct of men was to be evaluated by reference to private judgments and self-regulation. Where some external moral reference was required, this was no longer ecclesiastical prescription; the scriptures, the natural law and the common good became the ultimate external criterion of the inner working of private conscience. In its secularised form, this external reference was eventually provided by a utilitarian 'moral arithmetic' in the shape of the felicific calculus. While these changes were taking place in northern Europe, the Catholic Church south of the Alps did not remain unchanged. The traditional system of confession was retained in its essentials, but, under the reforms of Loyola and the Jesuits, the notion of 'liberty of conscience' was greatly expanded and new systems of casuistry were developed in response to the social needs of the Catholic burgher class. The Protestant Reformation was crucial, therefore, in 'the revolutions in rationale systems in the sphere of conscience'.[2] The Reformation converted morality into a form of internal discourse, but this position could only be maintained on the basis of state regulation of the external social order.

The question of the uniqueness of the western confessional morality is thus one aspect of a wider problem concerning the role of monotheism in the 'uniqueness of the West'. However, if we argue that the Christian conception of prophetic monotheism, individual sin and personal conscience generate a confessional culture, then we are immediately faced with the problem of Judaism and Islam. Since Christianity can be regarded as the product of Old Testament monotheism and Islam, as the summation of both Christian and Jewish prophetic religion, we would expect some form of confessional tradition in Jewish and Islamic cultures. This question is analytically parallel to the problem of the absence of capitalism in Judaism and Islam.[3] It is, in fact, possible to provide illustrations of confessional practices in both religions. One obvious example in Judaism is the festival of Yom Kippur when various rituals are performed to obtain forgiveness of sins and pardon for misdemeanours against neighbours. After the Minhah service, the penitent receives a symbolic flagellation, makes a confession and later dresses in the white robe of mourning as a sign of humility.[4] In Islam, there are similarly a variety of prescribed rituals and actions relating to penitence and purification of sins. The concept of sin in Islam is predominantly individualistic in the sense that humanity as such is not regarded as sinful in essence. It is not the species but the individual who is sinful. The principal sins according to koranic teaching are polytheism, homicide, magic, usury, false witness and maltreatment of orphans. While criminals are encouraged to confess their sins to Islamic *qadi* judges, there is no sacramental priesthood in Islam with ritual keys of absolution. Instead the penitents are prompted to offer alms to the poor or to undertake the pilgrimage to Mecca. Although Islam recognises the importance of forgiveness for sins, there is no institutionalised sacrament of penance by which sins can be absolved by the Church.

Judaism, Christianity and Islam share in common a monotheistic theology, a doctrine of human sinfulness and a variety of penitential practices for dealing with human failure. Of course, it would be possible to argue that Christianity's trinitarianism and the role of Sufi saints in Islam bring into question their monotheistic orthodoxy, but this is not immediately relevant to our argument. Despite this common commitment, there appear to be important differences in the role of confession in these religions. One difference is that in Judaism and Islam the idea of sin as bodily pollution is central to their penitential practices. The Yom Kippur festival and Islamic prayer and pilgrimage are accompanied by a variety of customs which are aimed at cleaning the body from sinful pollutions. In Islam washing the body is a necessary part of prayer, fasting and pilgrimage following the koranic verse 'God makes water descend from the sky so that He may make you clean by means of it.' According to Jewish religious laws, immersion in water is a necessary prerequisite to the repentance of sins. While in early Christianity sin corrupted the body and therefore repentance of sins was both a spiritual and physical cure, the materialism of human sin gradually disappeared with the development of the theory of Court of Conscience. Sin became more a pollution of the inner self which only the cure of souls could reach and less a pollution of the body which ritual immersion could wash clean. This question of pollution leads us into the crux of the question of the universality of confession versus its uniqueness to the West.

We may notice, for example, that the term 'confession' is frequently used by anthropologists to describe the penitential rituals, in relation to taboo and pollution, of traditional or pre-industrial societies. One of the most frequently cited case studies is Knud Rasmussen's ethnography of the shamanism of Polar Eskimos.[5] Mircea Eliade, Claude Lévi-

Strauss and Ioan Lewis discuss the shamanistic *seance* as a ritual which involves the confession of sins.[6] According to Rasmussen, Eskimo religious beliefs are focused on the importance of correct behaviour towards hunting and social rules, the breaking of which cause famine and starvation and thereby threaten the life of the group. Surrounded as they are by imminent dangers, the Eskimos depend on their shamans or magicians (*Angakut*) to control the dangerous forces of the Sea Spirit and the dead. The problem is that the sinful behaviour of one individual who disregards a tribal taboo – such as the correct control of menstrual blood – spoils the hunting activity of the whole group. Customs have to be obeyed[7]

> in order to hold each other up; we are afraid of the great evil, perdlugssuaq. Men are so helpless in the face of illness. The people here do penance because the dead are strong in their vital sap, and boundless in their might.

Sin is a tangible phenomenon which, like an infectious disease, threatens to contaminate the collectivity. These sins are confessed during *seances*, when, in the presence of the shaman and the group, offences are publicly acknowledged. Sins which are concealed become doubly dangerous. The offences of women are particularly potent and the penitent woman will often accuse others of similar offences. Once these various taboo violations have been admitted, the shaman recommends appropriate penances and confirms that the powerful forces which surround the group have been satisfied. Hunting will now be successful. The *seance* is thus both a court and a religious service in which individual misconduct is collectively punished through the medium of the shaman.

In terms of this example, it is important to note that the confession is public and collective, the shaman is a person in authority and the sin is regarded as a polluting agent which is physically dangerous. If we regard confession as a public recognition of taboo violation which pollutes the whole group, then confession in this sense does appear to be virtually universal in human society. To take a rather extreme case, pure Buddhism as a non-theistic doctrine had originally very little systematic conception of sin, guilt and redemption. The historical explanation for this absence of 'sin consciousness' is to be found in Guatama Buddha's opposition to Brahmanistic purification rituals which, from a Buddhist perspective, are worthless since they do not assist in the negation of human desire. In Buddhist teaching, sin cannot be conceived arithmetically as a list of transgressions which can then be absolved by mechanistic absolution. Furthermore, the Buddhist monks are not a priesthood invested with sacramental powers. However, as Buddhism spread through Asia, various forms of ritualised confession began to emerge along with a conception of sin as pollution. This was particularly the case in Japanese Buddhism which was influenced by traditional Shintoism. Similarly in Tibetan Buddhism[8]

> guilt is a concrete, measurable evil, not merely universal and basic evil, and it is, moreover, an evil of an ethical or cultic kind that destroys a distinct, negative cosmic-religious power, which must be restored by particular cultic and ethical deeds, such as lustrations, or confession before the community of monks, or by repetition of the prayer formula, 'Om mani padme hum'. Guilt is conceived precisely as pollution or filth – hence the many synonyms for guilt and pollution in the Tibetan language.

The universality of confession would thus appear to hinge on the universality of the concept of pollution as the infringement of sacred norms. These violations of taboo produce contagion which can only be removed by rites of purification, especially public confession, by which the individual is returned to society and the existence of the group preserved. The uniqueness of the western confessional now appears to lie in the fact that it divorced the notion of sin from that of disease.

It may appear that to state the issue in these terms is to return us to a debate which animated nineteenth-century anthropology. It has been argued that the theme of taboo and contagion was a Victorian discovery and, in particular, a Protestant discovery.[9] Victorian Britain was itself a society dominated by taboos – table-legs had to be suitably covered from public view and 'trousers' were 'unmentionables'. The discovery of Polynesian taboos held a particular fascination for the Victorian mind. The intellectual and religious problem was to show how the survival of primitive notions of pollution in the Old Testament had been transcended by Christianity in which 'holiness' no longer had any connection with physical 'cleanliness'. Thus, in William Robertson Smith's lectures on the religion of the Semites in 1889 the idea of spiritual evolution was combined with that of social evolution whereby Christianity had 'spiritualised' primitive avoidance customs. Similarly, James Frazer in *The Golden Bough* argued that, while civilised people make a clear distinction between sin and pollution, 'the savage makes no such moral distinction between them; the conceptions of holiness and pollution are not yet differentiated in his mind.'[10] Victorian anthropologists maintained the superiority of their culture by attempting to show that Christianity was based on ethical, not hygienic, norms. In Frazer's view, confession had a primarily magical significance in removing pollution rather than a religious function in atoning for offences against a deity.

While the value-judgments and evolutionism of Victorian anthropology have been widely criticised, especially in terms of their treatment of pollution,[11] Frazer's view that Christian confession is very different from confession in other religious cultures has found some support in the phenomenology of religion. Within the history of religions perspective, one of the most important scholars of confession was Raffaele Pettazzoni. Pettazzoni occupied professorial chairs in the History of Religions at the universities of Bologna and Rome.[12] His analysis of sin and confession is to be seen in the context of his concern to differentiate the problem of monotheism in Christianity from the notion of 'the high god' in primeval religions. In his major study of confession – the three volume *La Confessione dei Peccati* – he demonstrated that the practice of confession of sins was widely distributed throughout the world religions in all ages. These confessional practices did not emerge as the result of Christian missionary influence, but were entirely independent and autonomous. While recognising the ubiquity of confessional rituals, Pettazzoni wanted to draw a sharp distinction between Christian and non-Christian rites. This distinction rested on the question of individual rather than communal responsibility for sin and on the separation of sin from disease. Drawing on his wide ethnographic knowledge, Pettazzoni noted that in, to use his terminology, primitive societies confession is always accompanied by rituals of purification, namely fumigation, immersion, blood-letting, ablutions and so forth. In Kikuyu, the word *kotahikio* ('confessing') is derived from *tahika* which means to vomit; thus, as the penitent lists each separate sin, he spits on the ground. Pettazzoni argues that, in confessing his sins, the penitent evokes their power through the spoken word. The defilement of the original sin is reactivated in the confession and this act brings past pollution into the present. The purification rituals of washing, spitting and fumigating are addressed to the pollution which is present in the words of the confession. Primitive confession is thus connected with objective breaches of social norms which produce physical pollution:[13]

> it is not the subjective factor in sin, the will to sin, which counts, but the objective, the actuality of the thing done. It is this actuality which is an evil, and it is firmly held that misfortune, pain and suffering will come of it.

The conception of sin in the Christian confessional is, by contrast, internal and subjective. Pettazzoni's studies of confession in classical antiquity tend to confirm his view that primitive confession aims to protect the group against pollution. While confession of sin was generally absent from Roman and Greek culture, the institution of confession on the island of Samothrace is particularly germane to Pettazzoni's thesis. In Samothrace, homicide was regarded as a threat to the sanctity of the whole island and consequently a danger to the social group. A special priest was responsible, therefore, for the confessing of murderers who had endangered the community.

While Pettazzoni draws upon an impressive range of comparative data to support his argument that in Christianity the confession of sins is addressed to God rather than to the problem of communal pollution, there is an element of special pleading in his thesis. To some extent he takes the ideal form of confession as stated in the official Christian orthodoxy to be the form of confession as practised by the laity. As we have seen, the absence of ritualised confession in pure Buddhism is not characteristic of popular Buddhism. The same issue arises in Christianity. The confession of sins is in principle based on a separation of ethical and pollution concepts, but in practice confession has often been associated with physical healing, especially in medieval times. We can illustrate this combination of spiritual and physical healing in the confessional by looking at the impact of the Lateran Council (1215) on Britain once confession had been made obligatory on the laity. Franciscan friars as confessors, manuals on sin, literature on penance and the cult of Mary became particularly important in the British religious context for a century and a half following the Council's declarations on confessional practice. The new regulations relating to confession required doctors to call confessors to see their patients, especially where the patient was seriously sick or when the doctor's diagnosis was uncertain. Many treatises of the period drew an analogy between sinner-priest and doctor-patient relationships. Thus, Robert Grosseteste, chancellor of Oxford University and bishop of Lincoln, in his *Templum Domini*, wrote about the parallel between disease and vice, ethical conduct and therapy. The English version of the *Manuel des Péchés* drew attention to the importance of the shrift for mental hygiene, while the *Oculus sacerdotis* provided spiritual advice for pregnant women, drunkards and for the melancholic.[14] In addition to confession, pilgrimages to holy shrines were also regarded as significant in the lay system of therapy. In the thirteenth and fourteenth centuries, it would be difficult to argue, therefore, that there was a clear differentiation between hygiene and spirituality. The interrogation of the conscience in the confessional was thought to have therapeutic effects for the body.

It is particularly interesting to examine missionary situations where an indigenous system of confession has interacted with an imported Catholic tradition of penance. This mutual penetration of penitential practices has been especially prevalent in the colonial history of South America. In the majority of primitive American tribes, disease was regarded as the result of sinful actions, of a predominantly sexual character, and was a divine punishment for such transgressions. The treatment of disease involved various forms of repentance including fasting, abstinence and blood-letting, but the crucial therapy for disease was the confession of sins. Among the Aztec, Maya and Inca, the sick patient was first asked what sin had been committed which would explain the illness being suffered. The Christian analogy between the cure of souls and the care of the body was readily grafted onto these indigenous religious beliefs and therapeutic ritual. The confession of sexual deviation within the Catholic tradition was, therefore, a perfectly intelligible activity from the perspective of aboriginal custom. There were other important parallels in practice and belief. Pre-Columbian culture emphasised the importance of the female principle in the etiology of disease. It was entirely appropriate to build the shrine of the Virgin on the former temple of Teteoinam, the Aztec mother of gods. In addition, the Church provided a complete[15]

> hagiology of patron saints against disease. In much the same way as the religious sculpture and portraiture of catholic saints appeared in colonial Spanish America, so one of the distinctive characteristics of that period is the richness of medical hagiology.

The cross-fertilisation of ritual and belief between local practices and official Christianity suggests that the medical/religious analogy in writers like Grosseteste has always received ample support in folk culture where the analogy has been translated into a practical identity.

While we can hold to some reservations about the arguments of Smith, Frazer and Pettazzoni that Christianity as an ethical religion differentiated spiritual sin from physical sickness, it does appear to be the case that Christianity did not develop a conception of sin as a material substance which threatened the life of the social group. Although the doctrine of the Fall of Adam does imply a collective sin inherited from generation to generation, the responsibility for sin was generally regarded in an individualistic fashion. These individualistic trends in the traditional Christian doctrine of sin were further emphasised by changes in the concepts of subjective intention and personal conscience under the impact of urban, mercantile culture. While Calvinism developed the idea of individual responsibility into a central principle of faith, it can be argued that individualism pre-dates the Reformation.[16] With these reservations in mind, the argument for the cultural uniqeness of the private confessional in Christianity remains intact. We have to add the further note that most of our discussion refers to western, especially Roman, Christianity, where the legal obligation of the individual to confess officially defined sins was an essential characteristic. The Greek Orthodox tradition, by contrast, is less legalistic in the conception of sin and the importance of confession. The Orthodox guidelines on confession do not recommend recalling every sin in detail since this elaborate reconstruction might further provoke sinful thoughts. In addition, the conception of sin as a contaminating substance was not entirely absent in the Orthodox Church. In the *Philokalia* – the authoritative statement of Orthodox spirituality – it is recalled that a young man, living with a spiritual father, habitually stole a rusk of bread from the table at meal times. He felt condemned by his own conscience but was too ashamed to admit his wrongdoing. One day, listening to his spiritual father warning the brethren of the cunning ways the Devil tempts monks, he fell on the ground and confessed his sin. As his guilty secret was acknowledged 'the energy of the demon could be seen coming out of my breast like the flame of a lamp. It filled the room with a nasty smell, so that those present thought that a lamp of sulphur was burning.'[17] While the Orthodox Church denies in principle that sin has an objective reality, in one of the few passages where the *Philokalia* specifically comments on confession, sin is recognised as a material phenomenon. Furthermore, in the devotion of Christian saints, Islamic Sufis and Jewish Hasidim, physical contact with the saint or contact with his blood, tears and spital is a contact with religious grace, charisma and baraka. Both sin and grace are persistently regarded as part of the material world.

There is, however, an alternative to the notion of the *cultural* uniqueness of the confessional which is based on the assumption of the universality of a *psychological* need to confess. This argument was presented most clearly in Erik Berggren's *The Psychology of Confession*. Berggren's comparative study of confessional institutions is based on a basic psychological model of the psychological necessity to confess transgressions of social norms. The individual's knowledge of his own sins produces a sense of guilt which is experienced as burdensome and depressing. Confession of these hidden sins produces a sense of relief and confession has, therefore, important cathartic consequences. The Protestant preachers who recognised the value of spiritual guidance grasped the importance of the fact that[18]

> people have an innate need to escape from the sins they have committed; the soundness of this insight is proved by the fact that, repeatedly, a renaissance of individual 'cure of souls' has followed when the initiative has been taken to provide it.

Part of Berggren's evidence for this claim is derived from the revival of confessional practices among evangelical Protestant movements in Germany and Sweden, and the Oxford Movement in the Church of England. Although the confessional answers to an innate psychological need, the confessional takes a special form within the Christian tradition. He notes, for example, that confession must be to a person in authority. The authority of the priest is crucial if the confession is to 'have the intended effect, deliverance from sin.'[19] In Protestant circles, the minister does not usually claim a sacramental authority to absolve sins, but he is thought to have a special knowledge of souls which allows him to offer guidance and comfort. While there is, according to Berggren, a psychological need to confess, confession always takes place within and depends on a definite institutional setting. The ritualised setting of confession, within the church nave, for example, was particularly important in the Oxford Movement. The institutional features of confession – authority, priesthood and sacrament – are ultimately subordinate to religious intention. The Christian confession is to be distinguished from psychoanalysis, lay testimony and avowals of responsibility by the fact that sin is regarded as an offence against God. Like Pettazzoni, therefore, Berggren emphasises the ethical character of the Christian view of sin.

Although Berggren wants to argue that confession has important psychological functions in removing anxiety and depression, he also recognises that the cathartic effects of confession may be undermined by exaggerated scrupulosity on the part of the confessant. Because a valid confession has to be a complete statement of sin, there is always the possibility that a sin has been omitted, disguised or forgotten. Minor sins may be exaggerated by the scrupulous lay person so that 'confession has the effect of increasing their burden of guilt.'[20] This problem raises a serious theoretical difficulty for any argument about the innate need to confess since it can be reasonably argued that it is the institution of confession and the culture of guilt which produces the need to confess rather than the need producing the institution. If the need to confess were as strong as Berggren claims, then it would be difficult to understand why confession is an obligation on the faithful. Unfortunately, there is a strong normative element to both Pettazzoni's and Berggren's position, namely that confession is morally desirable.

While confession has desirable effects, the ultimate cause of confession – the innate need – is morally neutral, but one difficulty with these phenomenological studies is that they neglect the element of compulsion which is embedded in ecclesiastical institutions. In our view there is a permanent paradox in the relationship between the ideal of spontaneous confession and the practical obligation to confess. Although the distinctiveness of the Christian confession may reside in its ethical character, we must also recognise that the obligation to confess has been an important part of the Church's missionary campaign against heretical belief and practice. Confession may have cathartic relevance for the individual, but the institution itself cannot be divorced from the problem of social control in society.

The Fourth Lateran Council of 1215 which made confession an obligation on all the faithful has to be seen in the context of the Church's struggle against heresy, especially Albigensianism. This heresy, which is also referred to as Catharism or dualism, was well established in southern France by the middle of the twelfth century. The first Cathar diocese was established by 1172 at Albi and the Cathars of Languedoc were subsequently known as Albigensians. The Cathars believed that there were two equal, co-eternal gods who had created the material world of evil powers and the spiritual world. They believed in one sacrament, the *consolamentum*, which was baptism by the laying-on of hands. At death, the soul of the consoled Cathar would rise to heaven to be reunited with the spiritual body. The *consolamentum* was administered to those who had achieved religious purity after a long period of training. These were the *perfecti* who renounced their possessions and family ties, living a life of asceticism and devotion. Albigensianism was a threat to Roman Catholicism because it taught that the Roman Church had been founded by the evil god and because they opposed ecclesiastical tithes. A *perfectus* from Montaillou declared:[21]

> There are four great devils ruling over the world: the lord Pope, the major devil whom I call Satan; the lord King of France is the second devil; the Bishop of Pamiers the third; and the lord Inquisitor of Carcassonne, the fourth.

Despite these profound differences, there was an important parallel between Albigensian asceticism and the world-renouncing discipline of orthodox monasticism. The Albigensian heresy spread among the French rural peasantry, but it also found converts in the polite society of the court where it developed alongside a new culture of spiritualised romance, troubadour poetry and chivalry.

Peaceful means of converting the Cathars having failed, the Albigensian crusade under the leadership of Simon de Montfort attempted to remove the heresy by force. The Fourth Lateran Council assembled in the middle of the political and military crisis of the crusade against the Cathars. The regulations passed by the Council, including those relating to regular confession, were aimed to root out indifference to the Church and heresy against it. The heresy laws were codified by which bishops were to make inquisitions for heresy so that offenders could be turned over to the secular authorities. The property of heretics was to be confiscated and princes who failed to co-operate with the inquisition were to be excommunicated. The Friars Preacher, an Order founded to fight against heresy, were licensed to preach and hear confessions in every parish. During the inquisition, suspects were required to name other heretics as proof of the validity of their repentance. They were tried in private without knowledge of the offences for which they were charged. Suspects who made a full confession of heresy were given appropriate penances which included pilgrimage, service in the Holy Land, ostracism or imprisonment in one of the Dominican prisons. Those who did not repent were burnt at the stake. The use of the crusade as a weapon against dissident Catholic princes had the effect of undermining the moral authority of the papacy and was not particularly successful against the Cathars.[22] Albigensianism continued to exist in the remote areas of Languedoc and was subjected to further inquisitions in the early part of the fourteenth century under Jacques Fournier. Confession in the thirteenth and fourteenth centuries was part of the moral apparatus of a Church which was attempting to create a powerful, centralised organisation against internal heresy and the external threat of Islam. The Avignon popes of the fourteenth century[23]

> showed a strong tendency to organize the Church as a vast administrative machine and to think of the Christian life as a matter of juridical relationships rather than as a real and living relationship between God and man. They thought in terms of dogma, imposed by laws and decretals, controlled by an Inquisition which stamped out heresy mercilessly: breaches of the law brought penalties – those of the Inquisition for heresy, those of the papal Penitentiary for lesser sins.

When Pettazzoni and Berggren argue that the Christian confessional is distinctive, they are, of course, referring to speaking the truth about ourselves before a priest. This truth about our sins emerges as either the result of an institutional obligation or from an innate need. They have largely ignored the role of the confession in the detection of errors. It is this darker side, so to speak, of the confession which has preoccupied historians of heresy, inquisition and witchcraft trials. While in this collection of essays on confession, we have analysed confession as a ritual of inclusion to counterbalance the emphasis on ceremonies of degradation in deviance theory, we do not wish to deny that historically confession has also played an important role as a repressive social institution. The importance of confession as a linkage between private conscience and public order gives rise to the ambiguous association of freedom, spontaneity and truth, on the one side, and obligation, compulsion and error, on the other. This paradoxical feature of confession is particularly evident in the history of judicial torture, witchcraft and confession.

When the Dominican order launched its inquisition against the Albigensians of Languedoc and the Pyrenees, they found below the dualistic heresy an older and darker religion, namely a substratum of devil worship and witchcraft. The mountainous areas of Catholic Europe – the Alps and the Pyrenees – were locations where orthodox, institutional Christianity had a superficial presence. These remote areas were successively centres of Catharism, witchcraft and finally Calvinism.[24] The employment of inquisitorial procedure, judicial torture and confession were thus part of a missionary campaign against regions which were places of political and religious dissent. The use of judicial torture against the Albigensians in 1252 came into general employment against witchcraft in 1326 and produced a rich crop of witchcraft confessions. On the basis of circumstantial evidence, suspects were subjected to crushing, stretching or ducking in order to extract a confession. If no confession was obtained by these methods, then this was taken as incontrovertible evidence of witchcraft. These confessions[25]

> were seen as the few visible projections of a vast and complex organization, and so every new confession supplied fresh evidence for deductive minds. The same logic which had constructed the great work of the Angelic Doctor would construct a series of demonological manuals confirming and extending each other. The climax, because of its timing and distribution, would be the *Malleus*.

There is thus a correlation between the use of judicial torture, the extraction of confessions and the incidence of witchcraft. Where judicial torture was not employed, as in England, the witchcraft craze failed to get established. The missionary fervour of Dominicans in France, of Calvinists in Scotland or of Protestants in England appears to produce the heresy to which it is opposed. However, as Trevor-Roper points out, fantastic witchcraft confessions were often secured without the use of torture and furthermore the disappearance of torture appears to follow the collapse of the theory of demonology and not vice versa. The decline of the witch-craze was bound up with important intellectual changes by which the witchcraft confession lost credibility. It was not that critics of witchcraft trials denied the existence of witches but rather that they began to see witches as simply melancholic women whose raving was not to be trusted at face value. In this light, heresy and witchcraft were products of social conflict between central and peripheral areas. The struggle of the Dominicans against the Catharism and witchcraft of Languedoc was an aspect of the struggle of feudal, Catholic centres of power against remote areas where the power of the Church to impose faith and feudal tithes was in question. The use of judicial torture to obtain confessions was part of a social and political struggle to control remote, quasi-Christian regions.

This explanation which suggests that confession was an aspect of political repression leaves two questions unanswered, namely why was sexual deviance such an important part of the charges brought against witches and why were women accused more frequently than men? According to the *incubus* and *succubus* theme, the pact with the devil inevitably involved a sexual relationship. The witches' sabbath was believed to involve a sexual orgy. Although the devil could have sexual intercourse with both men and women, it was typically presumed that these sexual unions involved women rather than men. It is certainly the case that witchcraft accusations were very unevenly distributed between the sexes. Throughout Europe, approximately 80 per cent of those accused of witchcraft were female.[26] A variety of explanations has been offered to account for this distribution. According to Macfarlane and Thomas, women, particularly single or widowed females, were the most dependent section of the community and thought to harbour envy or revenge against their more secure neighbours.[27] The curses of old women against their tight-fisted neighbours were enough to spark off a chain reaction of accusation, interrogation and confession. In this perspective, accusation and confession is part of the dynamic of intracommunal conflict where the economic support for dependent members has been seriously threatened by social change. More generally, witchcraft accusations have ben regarded as a form of scapegoating in which the low social status of women makes them particularly vulnerable to social conflicts.[28] Alternatively, witchcraft accusations have been interpreted as an aspect of the struggle between men and women to control a monopoly over healing and medicine. The witchcraft craze represents the attempt by male doctors to destroy the traditional role of women as healers, herbalists and midwives. The 'wise women' of traditional village life were attacked as charlatans and witches by an alliance of the law, Church and medical profession.[29] Alternatively, the conflict between the Church and women healers has been seen as a struggle between the priest and the magician as 'part of the depaganization of the west'.[30]

What these theories have in common is a view of confession as an instrument of intracommunal conflict, but what they fail to specify precisely is the traditional importance of women in the reproduction of society and in the distribution of property. In feudalism and early capitalism, the controlled fertility of women was essential for the conservation of property, especially where strict primogeniture was followed. It was crucial, therefore, for men to supervise the moral fidelity and biological fertility of their wives. Failure of reproduction and uncertainty of parentage were seen as major dangers to the economic and political fabric of society. We do not offer this claim as an explanation of witchcraft as such, but we do see female witchcraft as simply one aspect of the problem of female deviance – at least from the point of view of the male guardians of property and order. This claim is further developed in Chapter 4, but at this stage it is important to note that, while confession in the Dominican inquisition played an important part in the political control of remote regions, confession is equally important as a permanent feature of sexual control within the family. The assumption that women are morally weaker than men, are prone to witchcraft and melancholy and therefore require male supervision was an essential part of seventeenth-century demonology. James VI of Scotland had a clear-cut explanation for the preponderance of female witches;[31]

> The reason is easie, for as that sexe is frailer than men is, so it is easier to be intrapped in these grosse snares of the devil, as was over will be proved to be true, by the Serpent's deceiving of Eve at the beginning, which makes him the homlier with that sexe sensine.

The confession of sexual sins of women is thus a feature of the moral authority of men as heads of households operating through the medium of clerical authority within the Church. These two forms of authority, domestic and ecclesiastical, did, however, frequently come into conflict. One of the most persistent criticisms of the confessional in French anti-clericalism was that the priest, not the husband, controlled the wife because he had privileged access to her conscience, if not her person.[32]

In this chapter, we have examined the evidence to suggest that confession of sins is a universal feature of human societies. Wherever there is a clear religious distinction between the sacred and the profane, which also defines social membership, we can expect to find a confessional mechanism. There is no shortage of anthropological data to support this viewpoint. However, the anthropological literature suggests that non-Christian confessions are typically collective, public rituals which seek to remove sins which are thought to be a threat to the community. In such communities, sin, crime and disease are not clearly differentiated. The uniqueness of confession in western society lies in its individualism, privacy, obligatory character and in its ethical conception of sin. This individualistic conception of conscience, sin and responsibility had far-reaching consequences for economic behaviour, legal practice and psychoanalytic therapy. The doctrine of individual responsibility was a 'persistent leitmotif' which[33]

> certainly developed the sense of sin in the western mentality and encouraged the notion of individual responsibility: it therefore contributed to the progress of European civilisation in the Renaissance period, and this contribution becomes more impressive when one realizes that individual morality was barely adverted to by the classical Greeks.

In the work of Pettazzoni, Berggren and Delumeau, this sense of the uniqueness of the western conception of conscience carries with it an implication of normative superiority over non-Western confessional practice. We have attempted to avoid this normative implication by showing that in western culture the individual conscience which controls the interior life of the individual is linked to the public world of constraint by legal obligation. Confession as an obligation to speak the truth emerged in the struggle to depaganise Europe and became part of a system of social control over women and dependants. The uniqueness of the confessional lies in the fact that the voluntary, spontaneous confession of ethical sins was formally institutionalised within a bureaucratic setting and put to political ends. However, we have to balance this view of confession as an instrument of social control against the equally important legal and ecclesiastical institutions of pardon, indulgence and sanctuary. In order to avoid the normative view of confession we have drawn attention to the obligatory requirement to confess and to its repressive political usage. We have also criticised the notion of an innate need to confess by emphasising the importance of institutionalised confession, but in criticising phenomenology and psychology, we do not want to treat confession as nothing other than moral repression. Our final reservation about the uniqueness of the western confessional centres on the alleged differentiation between sin and disease in Christianity. In our view, spiritual confession has traditionally and persistently been connected with physical and mental healing. If Protestantism divorced sin and hygiene by abolishing shrines and saints, the relationship between the body, the word and the unconscious has been partly reassembled by psychoanalysis. Although Freud, as we have seen, differentiated religious confession of conscious sins from psychoanalytic investigation of unconscious interior conflicts, it is particularly instructive that George Groddeck, who regarded himself as a disciple of Freud, described the meaning of certain kinds of physical illness as 'the wish to punish one-self, to do penance'.[34] The notion that illness is produced by guilt for transgressions of moral regulations and that confession will simultaneously restore health by restoring group membership appears to be a perennial component of western culture.

Chapter 4
Power, knowledge and confession: the work of Michel Foucault

In these studies of confession, we have been concerned with the sociological significance of confession at two levels. A confession may be defined as any statement, to a person in authority, which is regarded as a full account of motives, actions and events relating to behaviour which is regarded as untoward. In particular, what we say *against* ourselves is typically taken to be reasonable grounds for the truthfulness of a confession. In both the every-day world and in the formal setting of legal process, confession is strategically important in the confirmation of our presuppositions of identity and character. At another level, we have been concerned to explore the contradictory social effects of the institution of confession in society. We are aware that confessions may be sociologically interpreted as either a form of social repression by which those who are legitimate holders of office ('a person in authority') exercise social control over confessants or as a social mechanism which has the effect of reaffirming social values and which thereby contributes to the integration of social groups. The first interpretation connects together power and knowledge, while the second relates knowledge to consensus. Our approach to confession has, through the notion of rituals of inclusion and exclusion, attempted to interpret the institution of confession as both an apparatus of political control and as a social mechanism of integration. In short, our argument is that analytical distinctions between theories of control and consensus are, when applied to particular social institutions like confession, necessarily difficult to maintain. This particular perspective does, therefore, relate directly to the very strong conjunction of *pouvoir-savoir*, 'power/knowledge', in the recent work of Michel Foucault. In this exposition of his work, we are not primarily concerned with his general views on epistemology and discourse.[1] Instead we draw attention to the importance of the role of confession in Foucault's analysis of 'power/knowledge' in *Discipline and Punish, I, Pierre Rivière, Having Slaughtered My Mother, My Sister and My Brother*, and *The History of Sexuality*, vol. 1. We conclude by providing a critical appraisal of Foucault's study in the light of our perspective on confession as part of a system of social closure.

The work of Michel Foucault is notoriously difficult to summarise, let alone to evaluate and criticise. Apart from the obvious problems of Foucault's style, his work represents a direct criticism of the logic of conventional scholarship and the authoritative canons by which judgments are made on writing. Since the 'order of words' (good and bad, sane and mad, normal and pervert) is inextricably part of a system of power in society, to accept uncritically the conventional forms of western rationality is also to acquiesce unreflectively in the hierarchical distribution of power in society. As a critique of power, Foucault's form of analysis is necessarily a critique of the forms of discourse which exhibit and sustain power. In providing a summary of Foucault's philosophy as the basis for understanding his discussion of confession, we run the obvious risk of rendering his analysis in a systematic form which is antithetical to the nature of his text. Unfortunately, without some discussion of the general principles which inform his writing as 'a discourse on discourses', his interpretation of murder, sexuality and confession would remain opaque.[2] There is one further difficulty. In providing a brief account of Foucault's central ideas, one is tempted to elucidate them by showing that they are rather like those of George Canguilhem[3] but rather different from those of Louis Althusser. Such comparisons are immediately problematic since, for Foucault, classifications in terms of sameness and difference are fundamental to the exercise of power. To classify Foucault is to employ a set of procedures which are ruled out by the discourse to which they are directed. With these major reservations in mind, we attempt to provide a summary of Foucault's conception of the relationships between knowledge of things and power over them.

Every society or social group at a particular point in time is characterised by the presence of one or more perspectives or modes of talking about things. These 'epistemes' form the basis of discourse about reality. Foucault employs the term 'discursive formation' rather than 'ideology' or 'theory' to refer to such frameworks. The coherence of these discursive formations is constituted, not by the objects they define, by the form of connection between concepts or by the persistence of certain themes, but by 'rules of formation' which determine the dispersion of statements within a theoretical space.[4] However, to suggest that a discursive formation allows us to talk about 'things' – madness, disease or sexual deviation – implies that these objects of discourse are 'prediscursive', that is, existing prior to and independently of discourse. For Foucault, the objects of discourse are created by discursive practices and arise only in discourse. The rules of formation constitute objects of discourse by categorising objects, defining them and classifying their dispersal. Discursive formations enable us to speak about things because, through them, we can make fundamental classifications in terms of sameness and difference. At the same time, they define what are permissible, reasonable, or appropriate statements. In short, a discursive formation determines what can or cannot be said. These rules of speech are also 'rules of exclusion' since they specify, not only what can be properly stated, but also who is to speak, to whom and under what circumstances. The authority of statements is bound up with the social location of the speaker within the hierarchical order of social roles. For Foucault, the authority of the medical profession is of particular interest since medical pronouncements[5]

> cannot come from anybody; their value, efficacy, even their therapeutic powers, and, generally speaking, their existence as medical statements cannot be dissociated from the statutorily defined person who has the right to make them, and to proclaim for them the power to overcome suffering and death.

We might also add that the authority to hear statements is also crucial since, for example, the absolution of sins is the privilege of ecclesiastical office rather than of the personality of the priest.

Foucault's attempt to provide an analysis of power and ideology in society must be seen against the background of his earlier concern with the history of ideas. Given his interest in the issue of discontinuities between discursive formations, Foucault sought to replace the conventional history of ideas by an 'archaeology of knowledge'. He claims that the history of ideas attempts to reduce knowledge to something else – class relations, economic interests or to the consciousness of the human subject. The history of ideas attempts to penetrate below the immediate discourse to a real substratum which informs and determines the knowledge in question. By contrast, archaeology is distinguished from the history of ideas in terms of four basic principles. First, archaeology does not consider discourse as a document which stands as the sign for something else. It takes the specificity of discourse itself as the object of analysis. Second, archaeology does not approach the history of ideas in terms of a continuous transition or 'gentle slope' from common-sense and unformed opinion to a stable, articulate science. It is concerned with the specificity of each discourse and their irreducible rules of formation. Third, it does not take the *oeuvres* of knowledge as sovereign and authoritative, but seeks to comprehend the rules of discourse which dominate and control such *oeuvres*. Finally, archaeology is not concerned with problems of origin and genesis, and does not attempt to recapture those moments when the author and *oeuvre* are connected as the point of departure of discourse. In more direct terms, an archaeology does not attempt to evaluate a text in terms of its originality or precocity and, therefore, does not raise the question of whether one author 'anticipates' the development of knowledge in a later author. It 'tries only to establish the *regularity* of statements' and, rather than drawing up a roll-call of founding fathers of knowledge, it attempts to 'uncover the regularity of a discursive practice.'[6]

One of the central emphases of *The Archaeology of Knowledge* is, therefore, to identify regularities in discursive formations rather than to reduce discursive practices to economic or political practices. The text is autonomous and irreducible, but does this mean that discursive formations have no relationship with social structure and, if so, how can an archaeology provide the starting-point for a theory of power and ideology? While Foucault does not want to deny that economic changes in society were related to the rise of classical political economy or that demographic changes in human populations in the eighteenth and nineteenth centuries were related to the discourse on family, he asserts that the nature of these 'events' and their relationship to discourse are also discursively structured. We can neither oppose one realm (the discursive) to some other (the non-discursive) nor can we connect them together in terms of a general theory. All discourse has institutional sites and social supports, but their relationship is not determined by a general theory of social totality. A discourse is not an ideology in the sense of mystifying human subjects and concealing their 'real interests' from them. A discourse does not impose mystification; it rather establishes an authoritative 'regime of truth':[7]

> if certain knowledges of 'Man' are able to serve a technological function in the domination of people, this is not so much thanks to their capacity to establish a reign of ideological mystification as to their ability to define a certain field of empirical truth.

Discourse creates the space within which human types (the madman, the deviant, the sick) can be located and treated. The practices of incarceration (in *Discipline and Punish*) and exclusion (in *The History of Sexuality*) are ideological or discursive practices of labelling of the power/knowledge couple. Discourse, through its endless series of classifications in terms of difference and sameness, generates categories of inclusion and exclusion by which human types can be located. These classificatory practices articulate with the hierarchy of social groups within a system of power-relationships. This system of power does not, therefore, rest on subordination through mystification. It is rather that the rules of proper discourse systematically preclude alternative classificatory schema and thereby rule out alternative ways of seeing and saying.

Discourse, precisely because it gives rise to practices of exclusion by classification, also establishes fundamental concepts of normality. Following on Canguilhem's study of pathology and abnormality in biology and physiology, Foucault has been particularly concerned with forms of deviation which define the boundaries of normality, sanity, health and legality. Whereas his early work centred on the problem of insanity and the development of medical discourse in *Madness and Civilisation* and *The Birth of the Clinic*, his recent research has taken up the question of legal and sexual deviation. The question of murder has a special saliency for Foucault's analysis of knowledge and power, since murder is not only a potent form of illegality, but also under certain social conditions a major challenge to political authority. Foucault has so far been primarily concerned with two forms of murder, namely regicide in *Discipline and Punish* and parricide in *I, Pierre Rivière*, and with the forms of knowledge (criminology, penology, psychology and sociology) which speak authoritatively on illegality. Regicide is a threat to kingship and to the whole fabric of society; there is the obvious parallel of murder as an attack on the body and regicide as an assault on the body politic. Parricide is a form of domestic murder which assails political authority within the family. Murder represents several layers of illegality – an attack on the body, a threat to social order, a challenge to political authority, a sin against divinity.

Irony is an important part of Foucault's style. The conventional view is that contemporary society is largely free from repressive morality, from superstition and ignorance, and from the social circumstances that gave rise to witchcraft trials, torture and political violence. In Foucault's perspective the growth of systematic knowledge does not have these liberal and humanistic consequences. Those human sciences which claim to liberate us from ignorance merely give rise to new forms of domination through scientific discourse. In both *Discipline and Punish* and *The History of Sexuality*, Foucault wants to rewrite conventional ways in which we construct the history of penology and the history of psychoanalysis. The rise of treatment-oriented penology and the growth of sexual therapy involve an extension of political control over the body through the medium of a detailed, scientific and organised discourse.

In *Discipline and Punish*, Foucault follows the transition from a situation in which the legal penalty for crime was the punishment of the body to one in which penal institutions exist to discipline the soul. In the first situation, the object of penal repression is the body of the convicted criminal and the purpose of this repression was to impose an abundance of pain in a ritualised, public spectacle. The execution of the criminal, rather than his trial and sentencing, was the focal point of this public drama. In the second situation, public pain is replaced by private discipline which seeks to cure the criminal of his disposition towards deviant behaviour. The spectacle of public execution disappears with the growth of prisons, reform centres and therapeutic institutions. The pain imposed upon the body now becomes minimal and secretive as the penalty for crime becomes the deprivation of rights and privileges normally associated with full citizenship. With these changes in the nature of punishment, there developed new questions and perspectives about crime and criminals. While classical legal theory was concerned with the question of criminal responsibility for illegal acts and with the level of expiation relevant to particular crimes, the new science of penology was more concerned with the nature of the criminal himself and with the causality of crime. If the aim of penal institutions was to treat, cure and reclaim the criminal, it was necessary to understand his history, his psychology and his biology. In order to discipline, it was important to know the criminal as a special type. The growth of scientific criminology is part of an extended apparatus of control which aims to discipline the body by incarceration and restraint, and to classify and to subordinate his soul. Criminal anthropology and criminology[8]

> find one of their precise functions here: by solemnly inscribing offences in the field of objects susceptible to scientific knowledge, they provide the mechanisms of legal punishment with a justifiable hold not only on offences, but on individuals; not only on what they do, but also on what they are, will be, may be.

While penal reformers and liberal criminologists are motivated by humanitarian motives, their knowledge is ironically part of an extensive system of social control by which the deviant is transformed into the docile inmate of total institutions.

Although Foucault is concerned with these very general changes in penology and penal institutions, it is important to notice that his argument starts with the particular issue of regicide in French society in the eighteenth century and specifically with the torture and execution of the regicide Damiens on 2 March 1757. The macabre details of Damiens's painful death, in which he was torn by pinchers, drawn by horses, quartered and burnt to ashes, provide Foucault with an obvious contrast to the discipline of inmates under such schemes as Bentham's panopticon. This particular event also permits Foucault to interpret the symbolism of execution of regicides in relation to monarchy. His argument here is based on Kantorowitz's *The King's Two Bodies*. According to medieval juridical theology, the king had an earthly, perishable body which was finite, but at the same time the king was the embodiment of a social reality which was not subject to the process of decay. Regicide was thus an attack, not only on the king's secular presence, but also an attack on the sacred reality of society. The rituals surrounding death on the scaffold are the negative symbols corresponding to kingly investiture so that the tortured body of the regicide 'represents the symmetrical, inverted figure of the king.'[9] To hang, draw and quarter the body of the regicide in a public festival was to destroy the body and soul of the condemned man in order to purge his offence in response to his attack on the two bodies of the monarch.

The spectacle on the scaffold appears to be a powerful illustration of the 'ceremonies of degradation' which we have described in other chapters. However, Foucault recognises that these scaffold rituals were shot through with social ambiguity, much of which was determined by the peculiar relationship between the crowd and the condemned criminal. The day of execution was often turned into a public carnival 'in which rules were inverted, authority mocked and criminals transformed into heroes.'[10] Public executions often sparked off crowd riots, especially in cases where the conviction was felt to be unjust. They were also occasions for protests against excessive punishment of crimes which were regarded as relatively trivial. While the execution of criminals was a symbolic legitimation of kingly authority, in practice they frequently had the opposite effect. Where the condemned man did not submit to legal and religious pressures, the address from the scaffold could turn into a condemnation of the judges, an abuse against the king and a vilification of God. It is against this uncertainty surrounding the social effects of torture and execution that the importance of voluntary confession of guilt becomes obvious.

With the exception of England, the criminal procedure in most European societies was conducted in secrecy without the involvement of the accused who remained ignorant of the nature of the charge and the evidence brought against him. The magistrates conducted the preliminary investigation, collected evidence from witnesses and accusers, and formulated the sentence without the intervention of the accused. Since judges possessed a privileged access to legal truth, legal judgment was secured privately and secretly. Foucault argues that there were two reasons why this form of legal process tended to result in a confession on the part of the accused person. First, the confession removed almost any obligation on the prosecution to secure further evidence. Second, it removed all ambiguity from the legal charge and confirmed the written truth of the legal process with the living word of the accused. The secret, documentary proceeding was animated by the public speech of the confessant. In formal, legal terms, the confession was not necessary for conviction and was regarded as simply one proof of guilt alongside many others. However, because a confession was such a powerful avowal of the legal process and the authority of legal judgment, every effort was made to obtain it. The employment of coercion to obtain a confession had to be subject to rules if the validity of a voluntary confession was to be maintained: 'that is why it had to be "spontaneous", why it had to be formulated before the competent court, why it had to be made in full consciousness, why it should not concern impossible things, etc.'[11] A confession is the free utterance of an author, confirming the written discourses of law, which has the effect of excluding him from the realm of normality and legality. Nothing could more perfectly illustrate Foucault's implicit argument that ideology is typically self-imposed and not the mechanical effect of the 'ideological state apparatus'.

The transition to a regime of therapeutic cure within the prison, the collapse of the theory of the divine right of kings, the abolition of public execution and the development of scientific criminology also meant that the central importance of criminal confession and the address from the gallows was drastically curtailed. Although Foucault does not make the point explicit, it is reasonable to assume that he regards confession as part of the discourse of guilt, punishment and expiation. The confession as part of the legal setting of secrecy no longer functions in the discourse of treatment and utility. The new emphasis on discipline and training in a penal framework designed to render inmates docile no longer requires the ritual of the scaffold, the *amende honorable* and the public confession. An alternative interpretation, and one which is perfectly compatible with Foucault's general argument, is that the traditional confession, with its heavy religious symbolism and ritual, was dispersed inside a scientific discourse and police technology. In our view, confession may still retain its traditional importance in confirming evidence and legitimating authority; what have changed are, to use Foucault's terminology, the practices and technology which surround the production of confessions. In particular, there is the 'humiliation' of the procedures by which suspects are interrogated with the emergence of truth drugs, handwriting tests, interrogation procedures and the interrogation cell. In this respect, Foucault's intellectual passion for discontinuities masks an important continuity in the importance of confession in law.

The importance of confession in *Discipline and Punish* is that when the author of a confession speaks against himself, he speaks for the law. His personal condemnation becomes a public affirmation of legal truth. This fact raises the problem of whether an insane person can produce a valid confession. If being insane rules out being responsible for our actions, can a madman's confession, admitting responsibility for an act, be legally admissible? It is this paradox that is the central issue of *I, Pierre Rivière*, written by Foucault and his students at the Collège de France.

On 3 June 1835, Pierre Rivière, a 20-year-old peasant from the commune of Aunay at the village of La Faucterie, murdered his mother, who was pregnant, his brother and his sister. The weapon used was a sharpened bill with which Pierre Rivière had inflicted gruesome wounds to the heads, necks and shoulders of his kin. For the next month, Pierre Rivière wandered in nearby woods and lanes, supporting himself by begging and collecting wild saffron bulbs. He was eventually apprehended on 2 July 1835, by the gendarmerie at Langannerie. During the legal proceedings, he wrote a long memoir, over a period of two weeks, describing the conflicts between his parents, their domestic unhappiness, his design to kill his mother, his own character and the events of his life leading up to the arrest. During the trial, one of the crucial questions before the jury was the problem of Rivière's sanity. While much of the medical opinion was divided and contradictory – a conflict between discourses – and statements from witnesses were inconclusive, it was eventually decided that Pierre Rivière was insane. His 'singular monomania' involved a deep dread of women and female animals. As a consequence, the death penalty was commuted by the royal prerogative to life imprisonment. During incarceration, Rivière became convinced that he was already dead and requested that his head should be removed. He hanged himself in October 1840.

The particular interest of the memoir for Foucault is that Rivière was simultaneously the author of a confession and the author of a crime. The two forms of authorship cannot be separated. Yet, through the charge of insanity, Rivière was robbed of this authorship in both instances. The discourse of the memoir was obliterated by the king's pardon and an official discourse of insanity imposed on Rivière's discourse of murder. Thus, by commuting the death sentence, 'the State in the person of the king reasserted its authority while simultaneously masking it behind an act of grace.'[12] Rivière's detailed memoir was thus a challenge to the authority of legal discourse and to the person of the king. Published confessions to murder in the nineteenth century and earlier were normally ritualistic admissions of guilt, abject pleas for mercy and pathetic confirmations of the justness of the legal sentence. By contrast, the Rivière memoir is a long, detailed memoir which, in many respects, departs from the conventions of the published broadsheet confession. The existence of the memoir is unusual in the sense that Rivière was an uneducated person, but had managed to produce a literate and imaginative account of the crime and the events surrounding it. The reasons for the crime which emerge in the memoir, interrogation and subsequent reports are highly ambiguous. During the preliminary interrogation, he claimed that 'God appeared to me in the company of angels and gave me the order to justify his providence.'[13] He was not apparently troubled by the death penalty since he had received a divine command to kill. In the memoir itself, Rivière admits 'the design of playing the role' of a madman with a religious obligation to kill. At other times, he justified his crime in terms of the tribulations which his mother, over many years, had heaped upon his father. He killed his sister and brother for their tacit support of his mother in this situation of domestic conflict. The report of the presiding judge admitted that there was little evidence to show the presence of 'normal motives' for murder. The hearings 'disclosed nothing to raise any presumption that Rivière was animated by any feelings of hatred, revenge, jealousy or greed towards his mother, his brother or his sister.'[14] In the absence of an obvious criminal motive, expert opinion was drawn towards the conclusion that Rivière was mad.

Local witnesses confirmed the fact that, during childhood, the accused had been known as 'Rivière's idiot' or 'Rivière's madman'. Accounts were given of how Pierre had maliciously killed pet birds, threatened children, talked to himself, constructed bizarre 'weapons' and cut off the heads of cabbages in his father's garden. Legal opinion was initially divided. On the one hand, the existence of the memoir itself was proof of intelligence and ability. On the other hand, the coherence of the memoir stood in a paradoxical relationship to the horror of the crime. The memoir was itself an outrage against all conventions of decency. Eventually medical opinion, considering the history of madness which ran in the family, came down on the side of a judgment of insanity. Rivière had all the biological stigmata of the born criminal:[15]

> he habitually keeps his head, which is of average size, lowered; the forehead is low and narrow, the eyebrows knitted, the gaze ill-

> assured, timid, and furtive, his speech has something childish and unmanly about it; his answers are slow, he often smiles vacantly, his poise is awkward, his gait strange and jerky.

Madness was already present in his mother's family and his brother was also regarded as an idiot who could not attend the sacraments because he was incapable of comprehending the basic truths of Christianity. Rivière's social isolation as the village idiot had starved him of normal feelings of warmth towards his mother and fellow men. The moments of apparent lucidity of the crime and the coherence of the memoir were explained by the fact that, as forensic medicine confirms, the traumatic events of the murder momentarily produced a period of mental calm and stability. While Rivière thought of adopting the role of a madman as a method of avoiding the death penalty after the crime, the murder itself was an act of insanity. The written memoir did not, therefore, rule out the existence of insanity.

The Pierre Rivière case presents Foucault with a dramatic illustration of the conflict of discourse and the power to discourse. The legal and medical interpretations of the memoir were battles over the right to speak and the rights of authorship. It is for that reason that Foucault and his students are largely reticent as to the meaning and significance of the memoir. The dossier was published in order 'to draw a map' of the struggle between and within the various legal, medical and moral discourses. Any attempt to interpret the text would have involved imposing a scheme of scholarly discourse on Rivière's memoir thus duplicating the existing imposition of legal and medical discourses. To subject the text to psychiatric or psychoanalytical commentary would be an exercise of power against Rivière's authorship of the memoir. Towards the end of the dossier, Foucault does permit himself two general observations. The first is to note the unusual qualities of the memoir as a literary, detailed statement in contrast to the conventional published confession of the period. The second is to comment on the complex relationship between the crime and the written memoir. In his first project, a draft was to be prepared at the time of the murder and a finished manuscript sent to the authorities by which time Rivière would have committed suicide. According to a second project, the memoir was to precede the murder and, in a sense, produce the crime of which it was the narrative. In the actual event, the murder was followed by a period of wandering in the countryside when he issued several false statements. The true memoir was produced at the request of the examining judge. The final document was 'neither confession nor defense, but rather a factor in the crime'.[16]

The reticence which Foucault exhibits in relation to the Rivière memoir wholly disappears in Foucault's treatment of sexual confessions in *The History of Sexuality*. As with many of his earlier studies, at one level the study of sexuality is a critique of conventional views of the history of sexuality which assume an increasing liberalisation of social attitudes towards sexual relationships. In most conventional histories, there is the assumption that European societies have progressed from sexual repression to sexual permissiveness. The standard view is that, through the repressive institution of the Victorian family, the bourgeoisie turned sexuality into a social taboo, a silent and forbidden area of human relationships. By contrast, with the decline of parental authority, the Freudian revolution in psychoanalysis and changes in the social and legal status of women, sexuality has been liberated from repressive social norms. Against this conventional periodisation of sexuality, Foucault attempts to show that, over the last three centuries, there has been a 'discursive explosion' of the talk about sex. The paradox is that we have become increasingly verbose about the silence surrounding sexuality. The result is a compulsion to fill this silence with rigorous confession of our secret sexuality. These imperatives to confess had their origin in certain changes of the Christian confessional in the post-Reformation period.

In *The Protestant Ethic and Spirit of Capitalism*, Max Weber argued that the Reformation drove the ascetic discipline out of the monastery into the every-day world, making religious discipline the obligation of lay people. Foucault believes that this process was especially important in the creation of a discourse on sex. Confession of sexual behaviour had been a monastic obligation, but, with the enforcement of regular confession for the laity, in the period of the Counter-Reformation, it became a rule for all. According to the new imperative, 'Not only will you confess to acts contravening the law, but you will seek to transform your desire, your every desire, into discourse.'[17] The desire of the body was now to be processed through the 'endless mill of speech'. There is, according to Foucault, an important continuity between the Christian confessional manual with its codification of sex and its typologies of sin and later 'scandalous literature', especially that of de Sade and Frank Harris, which systematically set out to 'tell all'. The link between this sacred and profane literature is that the confession had become one of the central western institutions for the production of the truth of sex. Whereas in medieval times, the identity and moral value of a person accused of crime was vouchsafed by independent witnesses, the development of the confessional meant that our personal identity was determined by the truth we spoke about ourselves. There has been an externalisation of the inner speech about ourselves through the mechanism of confessional statements. The West has[18]

> become a singularly confessing society. The confession has spread its effects far and wide. It plays a part in justice, medicine, education, family relationships, and love relations, in the most ordinary affairs of every day life, and in the most solemn rituals; one confesses one's crimes, one's sins, one's thoughts and desires, one's illnesses and troubles; one goes about telling, with the greatest precision, whatever is most difficult to tell.

There is an important parallel here between the analysis of the confessional in the production of the truth of sex and the emergence of clinical medicine in *The Birth of the Clinic* in which, under the clinical gaze, the disease eventually declares its truth.

Given its constitutive role in the production of truth, confession is intimately interwoven with the exercise and presence of power. The official discourse of law requires that the confession must be free from constraint. Similarly, philosophy has traditionally regarded freedom as a requirement of the production of true statements. By contrast, Foucault argues that torture and confession have always gone hand-in-hand. The truth produced by confession is connected with, however silently and secretly, restraint, coercion, imposed obligation and compulsion. While a confession speaks of internal sins, it is addressed to an authority with the right to hear and interpret. The ritual of confession takes place within a relationship of power[19]

> for one does not confess without the presence (or virtual presence) of a partner who is not simply the interlocutor but the authority who requires the confession, prescribes and appreciates it, and intervenes in order to judge, punish, forgive, console, and reconcile.

The agency of control lies, not in the one who produces truth, but in the one who receives the confession.

From a historical perspective, the confession has now largely replaced that other mechanism for the production of knowledge of sex, namely the *ars erotica*. Through the practice and pleasure of sex, knowledge was produced which had to remain secretive since its value was diminished by being divulged. The knowledge produced by confession has, by definition, to be made public. In Foucault's view, the *ars erotica* have been displaced by this new mechanism of knowledge production and we now have, not the *ars erotica*, but the *scientia sexualis*. The initial discourse on sex resulting from the Christian confessional has been reconstituted in medical, legal and scientific discourses on sex. The traditional rituals of confession are now required to operate under norms of scientific regularity. The confession is now inscribed in the formal examination, questionnaire, interrogation and hypnosis. Through the scientific discourse of psychoanalysis, sexuality has become the primary causal model of all forms of normal and abnormal behaviour, from the everyday to the most unusual. Confession is no longer about what the subject consciously hides from himself, but what is hidden from him in the unconscious. The confession is no longer a test, but a sign of the hidden which can only be interpreted through the medium of scientific discourse. The language of sin was replaced by that of morbidity, pathology and deviation which required medical intervention. Through these procedures, the confession has been detached from the sacrament of penance and adapted to scientific discourse. The nineteenth-century bourgeoisie did not, therefore, hide sex in an envelope of silence; it erected a series of scientific discourses to explore, elaborate and codify sexuality not in the *ars erotica* but in *scientia sexualis*.

Sexuality, through these scientific discourses, became extended and all-pervasive. At the same time, there was the production of a new range of human types which marked the boundary between sexual normality and abnormality. The Victorian pattern of late marriage for educated, middle-class women produced the hysterical woman whose sexual disturbance required the interpretative skills of doctors and psychiatrists. The development of public schools, where children were not subject to parental scrutiny, created a new medical category, the masturbating child. Demographic changes, contraceptive techniques and a new social ethic of parenthood and prosperity produced the 'Malthusian couple'. Sexual perversity contaminated every section of society. The system of alliance (kinship, marriage and the distribution of possession) has now been overshadowed by the 'deployment of sexuality' (the system of pleasures for the production and consumption of the body). The role of the family in contemporary society is to provide the site for the deployment of sexuality. The family lost some of its economic functions as the unit of consumption and reproduction to become the focal point of affection, romance, love and pleasure. the discourse on sex is part of the dynamics of knowledge/power in that it provides categories of exclusion (the pervert) and informs the immanent power relationships of society through the vehicle of the family. Sexuality, and knowledge of it, thus becomes the basis for all-pervasive, hidden, immanent power-relations operating throughout society. Sexuality, knowledge of and power over it, becomes the principal means of access to the body, the family, the wider society and the basic processes of the life of the species.

These studies of murder and sexuality attempt to show that the intellectual disciplines which promise to liberate us from a dark past have the effect of extending and deepening the exercise of power through discourses which classify, quantify and code our lives. As we have indicated, this form of historical irony is not uncommon, at least in sociology. It was Max Weber who noted that rationality as embodied in modern science, secularity and bureaucracy had destroyed the enchanted garden of magic only to enslave modern man in 'the iron cage'.[20] This 'tragic vision' of the contradictory relationship between human purpose and social consequences has also become a powerful theme within the work of the Frankfurt School. For Horkheimer, Adorno and Marcuse, instrumental rationality serves the interests of the dominant class as positivist science is increasingly applied, not merely to capitalist economic production, but to political and intellectual control of society. The Enlightenment which opposed priestcraft and royal despotism has been gradually transformed into the handmaid of new and subtle forms of political authoritarianism. The difference between Foucault and the Frankfurt School is, however, that the latter have opposed the official discourse of positivist science with a substantive rationality, the ultimate aim of which is to spell out the contours of the good society. The point of their critique is to unmask the artificial restraints that control people in order to extend their freedom of action. To extend valid knowledge of society also entails an extension of political freedom. Foucault's 'discourse on discourses' (apologists to the contrary) appears to offer no such critique. His position offers no end to discourse by returning us to a mythical past without language and difference, since in the beginning was the word. There is no future without discourse. Furthermore, Foucault does not offer a 'discourse of liberation' to oppose the 'discourse on power'. His studies so far are characterised by neutrality or, more precisely, negative neutrality. Foucault does not offer an alternative to the discourses on the clinic and the prison. His studies are not[21]

> written in favour of one kind of medicine as against another kind of medicine, or against medicine and in favour of an absence of medicine. It is a structural study that sets out to disentangle the conditions of its history from the density of discourse, as do others of my works.

Foucault's apparent neutrality could be interpreted in one of two ways. As a positive perspective, it could be argued that his analysis of discourse provides an insight into the nature of power through the 'rules of exclusion' created by the knowledge/power couple. This study of the 'discourse of power' provides, as it were, a theoretical space in which the critique of power can be located. The problem is that Foucault has done very little by way of filling that theoretical space. Alternatively, we might be tempted to read Foucault's analysis of discourses in an entirely romantic way. Just as the scaffold often converted criminal into heroes, so Foucault's studies of the clinic, the prison and the confessional turn madmen, inmates and perverts into cultural heroes. There are obviously very strong objections to such an interpretation. There can, however, be no doubt that Pierre Rivière is the 'hero' of the memoir by virtue of his shameful authorship of it. Foucault's work carries with it the same implications which have been attached to Becker's *Outsiders*. By treating deviants as the victims of power through labelling, we implicitly neglect the victims of crime. Since the victims of crime have been the traditional concern of the law, the state and the police, radical sociology may feel the need to develop deviancy theory against the official victimology. The 'tragedy' of Rivière was his loss of authorship. How then are we to write about the loss of authorship on the part of his mother, sister and brother?

To state this argument less emotively, one problem with Foucault's analysis is that it concentrates overwhelmingly on the exclusionary effects of discourse and treats pardon and legal mercy as simply ideological devices. To know and to punish are examples of power; to know and to forgive are equally an exercise of the same power. Foucault will not, therefore, allow rituals of inclusion any theoretical autonomy since they are, in fact, subtle forms of exclusion. Foucault's solution to the possibility of ritual inclusion is to draw a distinction between the existence of an apparatus of power and its effectivity. Power is not omnipresent and omnipotent, since there is often a gap between the potential of power and its effects. Foucault's concepts of power 'serve to analyse not the perfect correspondence between the orders of discourse, practice and effects, but the manner in which they fail to correspond and the positive significance that can attach to such discrepancies.'[22] The problem with this interpretation is common to any defence of structuralism. Once it is admitted that the relationship between practice and effects, institutions and consequences may well be largely contingent, it is difficult to see what the necessary connections between structure and historical event are. If it is possible to provide historical evidence that the gap between power potentiality and effectivity was particularly great, that the range and authority of official discourse was especially limited and that, in any case, Foucault's periodisation of discourse is doubtful, can the theory be maintained on the grounds that non-correspondence between discourse, practices and effects is precisely what the theory seeks to explain? Since, like Foucault, we are concerned with the problem of changes in confession from medieval to modern times, we can start our historical criticism of Foucault with the problem of murder and pardon.

It is characteristic of Foucault's studies to take extreme and dramatic events or situations to illustrate the main thrust of his argument. Thus, he employs a sharp contrast between the brutal execution of the regicide Damiens and the detailed control of the body in the panoptican scheme of Bentham. The peculiarities of the Pierre Rivière case are the basis for an implicit statement of the operation of the French legal system. The reform of the confessional in the Counter-Reformation is taken as the basis for a study of how the confessional worked in practice. The selection of these extreme and unusual events is, to say the least, dubious. To take the case of murder, the scaffold scenes which have a central part to play in the early sections of *Discipline and Punish* present a particularly slanted image of the operation of the law prior to industrialisation. To make an obvious point, the ability to execute a murderer presupposes the existence of a system of arrest, detention and trial, but in most traditional European societies these simple operations were often difficult to perform. As we have consistently maintained in these studies of confession, it is highly misleading to think of legal institutions as uniformly effective and equally misleading to think of societal reaction to deviance as consistently hostile. Any theory of 'the discourse of law' must also develop a theory of the apparatus by which that discourse is produced and reproduced through the social structure. In our view, Foucault's theory of discourse is very weak in terms of explaining how discourse is produced and distributed. It is one thing to identify a discourse (in terms of regularities and continuities), but it is another thing to show how that discourse had effects. There appears to be a gap, therefore, between Foucault's analysis of discourse and the day-to-day consequences and operation of that discourse. To state this in a simplified form, it is often the failure and weakness of the institutions of social control and official discourse rather than its strength and effectiveness which are significant in the analysis of pre-modern societies. The operation of pardon, sanctuary and confession in medieval England provides a clear illustration of this situation.

In pre-industrial England, there were a variety of legal and social institutions by which a criminal could avoid arrest, conviction and punishment. The arrest process was often prolonged, offering felons an opportunity to seek sanctuary in a church. If they stayed within the church for forty days and nights, they secured the right to abjure the realm. Having obtained a confession of guilt and an oath to abjure the realm, the coroner specified a port for departure and a time-limit to get there. This exclusion of felons from their community was, of course, a particularly serious punishment, but many felons simply adopted a new identity in a neighbouring area or became outlaws. Those felons who did not abjure the realm did not necessarily go straight to gaol since bail or mainprize were very common. The conviction of felons could be further delayed by the right of the accused to challenge up to thirty-six of the jurors called to his trial. In addition, various categories of people were exempt from punishment. Under the privilege of benefit of clergy, a cleric found guilty of homicide would be sent for retrial in an ecclesiastical court where his punishment would be some form of penance. Children under 12 years of age, the insane, those who killed by accident or in self-defence and soldiers who had served in the king's army could expect a pardon. Female felons who were pregnant could not be hanged and, spending their incarceration in mixed prison conditions, many prolonged their lives by repeated pregnancies. The consequence of these institutions of privilege and pardon was that [23]

> society did not end up convicting many of the suspects. Less than a third of those tried for felonies were convicted. This meant that society had to live with a number of robbers, burglars, petty thieves, and murderers in their midst.... Medieval communities were willing to tolerate crime and criminals in their midst rather than convicting them and, although everyone from the king on down complained bitterly about the social cost, no one tried to rectify the situation because they had vested interests in maintaining the status quo.

A variety of social factors explain this tolerance of crime, especially homicide. While medieval communities were ready to hang strangers with alacrity, it was recognised that similar treatment of local villagers could set off a wave of revenge killing. Furthermore, in a society where most adult males carried weapons, disputes often resulted in woundings or death. Violent murders were the not uncommon consequences of interpersonal conflict. These attitudes also reflected the essentially private nature of medieval criminal law. It was expected that most disputes would be settled by those directly involved and, where the community felt collectively threatened by gangs of criminals, it was forced to rely on the hue-and-cry system to mobilise the public.[24]

While legal mercy and royal pardon may have had desirable ideological conseqences in legitimating the authorities, they must be seen against a background of social tolerance of certain crimes, ineffectual social control, inadequate procedures of arrest and detention, and widespread brigandage. To compare the punishment of the body in the special circumstances of regicide with the discipline of the soul through the incarceration of the body involves a very peculiar contrast. The most significant discontinuities between these two systems or situations are perhaps rather more mundane and less dramatic. With the arrival of a modern police force, the disappearance of 'badlands' and outlaws, the change in public opinion regarding the private nature of crime, the processes of arrest, conviction and detention are now more effective and efficient.

The principal assumption of Foucault's theory of discourse is that legal discourse operates to exclude certain social categories (murderer, deviant, madman) and thereby to articulate the hierarchical distribution of power in society. In particular, the discourse of law legitimates the exercise of power which is manifest in the practices of execution and incarceration. The theory neglects, therefore, to consider how this discourse has effects on the holders of social power. While it is clearly the case that legal discourse has effects on subordinate groups, legal discourse is also important for the practices of dominant groups. It is important to recognise that much of the violence and illegality of medieval times was attributable to the fact that the aristocracy was militarised. Professional men of war, returning from foreign wars or crusades, came to terrorise their own communities since they were often dependent on plunder for their means of existence. The development of codes of duty for knights was an attempt to regularise warfare and to limit the role of force in society. The growth of the Catholic confessional has to be understood in terms of its effects on the dominant, not the subordinate, group. Confessional theory and practice were formulated in response to the threat of militarised aristocracy to social stability and the threat of female deviance to the distribution of property in the dominant land-owning class.

The early penitential system was specifically concerned to elaborate a system of exact penalties relating to acts of violence against communal enemies on the part of the knightly class.[25] Cluniac spirituality provided a means by which the sins of violence perpetrated by knights in their secular calling could be vicariously expiated by members of monastic orders. The religious discourse of the period was aimed, not at the peasantry, but at the nobility in that the religious merit of monks cancelled out the violence of knights. The growth of a system of penance for knights was part of a wider attempt to 'spiritualise' knighthood in the period of the crusades. Religious conventions under the title of 'Truce and Peace of God' proscribed acts of violence on certain specified occasions and sought to protect women, clergy, children and peasants from the effects of war and domestic disturbance. Through the 'soldier's oath' and the ideology of religious chivalry, the Church attempted to limit internal conflict and to legitimate the use of force against the enemies of the community and religion. Although the confessional and other ecclesiastical institutions were designed to curb the behaviour of the dominant class, it would be wrong to exaggerate the effectiveness of these institutions. There are three factors which reduced the apparent harshness of the Church's teaching on sin in the early formulation of the sacrament of penance. The first is the partial eclipse of Thomistic theology and its replacement by the sacramental theology of Duns Scotus, which permitted a more lenient approach to the problem of human sinfulness. Second, the nobility were often in a position to select their own private confessors, who, in any case, had to be recruited from the upper strata of the ecclesiastical hierarchy. Third, and this is a point which Foucault wholly neglects, the system of penance was offset by a corresponding system of indulgence. As the severity of penance decreased, indulgences became widely available and highly commercialised. According to the theory of the Church as the Treasury of Merit, the Church possessed a monopoly of the store of grace which had been accumulated as a result of the blood of Christ and his martyrs. These indulgences served to cancel out the pains of social exclusion which attended the expiation of sins.

We have suggested, however briefly, that discourse may be directed, not so much at subordinate groups, but at the dominant class. A weaker version of this argument would simply be that dominant groups are often more exposed to official discourses than is the case for subordinates.[26] We are attempting to suggest the ironic argument that the effectivity of discourse may be limited to those who speak rather than those who hear. In the case of the confessional, Foucault largely admits this possibility. The new regulations of the seventeenth century made regular confession an obligation for all, but it would appear that 'it could scarcely have applied to any but a tiny elite; the great majority of the faithful who only went to confession on rare occasions in the course of the year escaped such complex prescriptions.'[27] Foucault recognises, therefore, that he is referring to an ideal of religious practice, not its actuality. This admission does raise a crucial problem for Foucault's analysis of discourse. If a dominant discourse expresses the social distribution of power by subordinating groups to the categories which are generated by that discourse, then it seems odd that subordinate groups are apparently less influenced by the discourse than the 'tiny elite'. As an alternative to Foucault, we have suggested that the confessional developed as a response to social violence, especially the violence resulting from the activities of noble knights. The discourse was addressed to violent knights rather than unruly peasants. The principal section of society, which was more or less permanently addressed by this discourse, was women, especially virgins and married women in the dominant class.

Where the accumulation of property crucially depends on a successful pattern of dynastic marriage, it is crucially important for heads of households under a system of inheritance by primogeniture to control the sexuality of their wives, daughters and first-born sons. Adultery was a sin, but also a major threat to legitimate descent and inheritance. It is for this reason that repudiation of barren wives and strict control of daughters was combined with an emphasis on sexual restraint for eldest sons.[28] The behaviour of junior males or 'youths' was of no particular interest. In the feudal period, therefore, the regular confession of noble women was an important aspect of the moral apparatus by which property owners controlled their women-folk through the intermediary of the priest. The sexual deviance of peasants has no such implication for the distribution of property. Although the law attempted to control peasant sexuality, it was not in terms of priestly control of moral consciousness.[29] Although capitalism had a major impact on the structure of the family, it did not automatically change the position of upper- and middle-class women in relation to the continuing importance of dynastic marriage. It can be argued that the sexual repression of women actually increased in the eighteenth and nineteenth centuries with new legal regulations governing 'strict settlement'.[30] It was not until there was an emphasis on credentialism over descent that the property functions of women began to change.[31] Changes in the law of divorce provide very clear evidence of this development.

There is an important continuity in the social status of women and their sexual control from feudal to capitalist times. The historical continuity provides further difficulties for Foucault's analysis of sexuality, especially for his interpretation of the hysterical woman. Foucault's argument is that the 'hysterization' of the body of the 'idle woman' was part of a new discourse of sex on the part of the nineteenth-century bourgeoisie. In the nineteenth century 'the hysterization of their bodies and their sex was carried out in the name of the responsibility they owed to the health of their children, the solidity of the family institution, and the safeguarding of society.'[32] There is, of course, ample evidence of a middle-class concern for the educated, idle spinster and of medical theories of female psychology in terms of the malfunctioning of reproductive systems. From Brudenell Carter's *On the Pathology and Treatment of Hysteria* (1853) to *Studies in Hysteria* (1893) by Freud and Breuer, it was commonly argued that women were more sexually charged than men and therefore required greater moral restraint. Their emotional outbursts were caused by problems of menstruation and reproduction. In the 1880s, female hysteria was treated by surgical removal of the clitoris or ovary. These well-known historical facts clearly support Foucault's interpretation of the new discourse of sex, but if we take a longer historical perspective entirely different interpretations are suggested. For one thing, the problem of the hysterical woman and the theory of the sexual basis of female melancholy was well established by the early seventeenth century.

Women have been traditionally regarded as subject to pernicious vapours and incapacitating melancholy. The cause of these maladies has been traditionally located in menstrual blood, giving rise to weeping, complaining and fretfulness. It was noted by Richard Burton in *The Anatomy of Melancholy* (1621) that gentlewomen who were economically idle or socially isolated were prone to such distempers, while common working women rarely suffered from melancholy. Burton's remedy was a mixture of work and religion. Women in the wealthy social classes of the seventeenth century appear to have been 'hysterised' long before the arrival of William Acton's *The Functions and Disorders of The Reproductive Organs* in 1865. Indeed much of the continuity of this view of women can be explained in terms of the persistence of the discourse on sex that goes back to Aristotle and Galen. In Aristotelianism, women were by nature and morality inferior to men and had to marry in order to be placed under the authority of a particular male. Aristotle's ethics and teleology were influential in the formation of Galen's humoral theory of disease and this combination of Aristotelian teleology of the body and Galenic disease theory came to dominate medical science for centuries.[33] In particular, Galen's theory of hysterical stupor in women became part of the basic discourse of Renaissance medicine which conceptualised male/female differences in terms of a series of dichotomies, namely hot/cold, reasonable/unreasonable, dominant/submissive.[34] Despite the revolution in medical understanding of reproductive functions brought about by writers like Gabriele Falloppio in *Observationes Anatomicae*

(1561), the equation of moral inferiority with female anatomy remained intact. Foucault's attempt to treat the hysterical woman as the specific product of a nineteenth-century discourse on sexuality cannot, therefore, be maintained.

We have criticised Foucault on three grounds. First, by concentrating on the rules of exclusion of discourse, he has failed to deal adequately with processes of social inclusion. Where he does deal with legal mercy, royal pardon and confession, he merely treats these institutions as a subtle ideological justification of exclusionary power. Social exclusion logically requires an independent analysis of social inclusion. Second, we have made both general and particular criticisms of Foucault's historical analysis of confession, criminal justice and the place of women in society. His analysis of regicide and parricide provides a one-sided view of legal institutions. Third, we have criticised Foucault for not developing an adequate theory of the apparatus of discourse. While he refers to the sites of discourse, he fails to discuss, in detail, the problem of audiences for discourse. We have suggested that he neglects the question of the effects of discourse on dominant groups. As an alternative to Foucault, we have argued that confession had important functions for the dominant social class in the transmission of property and in the control of noblemen at arms. Despite these criticisms, Foucault has provided a powerful and provocative analysis of the nature and significance of confession in society. In particular, Foucault has identified the critical issue of confession in relation to authorship, authority and responsibility.

Chapter 5
Confession in popular literature

One important aspect of confession we have yet to discuss is its contribution to the entertainment of the general public. From this perspective, a significant milestone in British penal history was the abolition of public executions in 1868. This came about largely as the result of a long campaign by intellectuals and reformers appalled by the unruly behaviour of the crowds of people who often travelled for miles to witness a hanging. Charles Dickens who was present at the execution of Courvoisier for the murder of Lord William Russell described his experience to readers of the *Daily News* in February 1846:[1]

> I did not see one token in all the immense crowd of any emotion suitable to the occasion. No sorrow, no salutary terror, no abhorrence, no seriousness, nothing but ribaldry, debauchery, levity, drunkenness and flaunting vice in fifty other shapes. I should have deemed it impossible that I could have ever felt any large assemblage of my fellow-creatures to be so odious.

Ten years later Dr William Palmer was hanged in front of Stafford gaol for poisoning John Parsons Cook at Rugeley. Public interest in the trial was so great that thousands of people poured into Stafford to witness the hanging. The town assumed, writes Robert Graves,[2]

> more the appearance of some anticipated festivity than of the fearful spectacle so soon to take place. The streets, despite torrents of rain which fell during nearly the whole of Friday, were thronged. The public houses did a roaring trade, and in many of them jocund songs and merry dances were kept up all night with untiring energy by holidaymakers who had travelled far to feast their eyes on Dr Palmer's death-struggles. One favourite resort was the house where the hangman had located himself, everyone being anxious to catch a glimpse of the man who was to be Dr Palmer's executioner.

The following morning Palmer walked with dignity to the scaffold, prayed briefly with the chaplain, shook hands with the hangman, and dropped suddenly to his death. This relatively dignified and speedy procedure did not find favour with the estimated crowd of 20,000 many of whom had gathered in expectation of a long and cowardly death agony as befitted a poisoner. 'Cheat', they roared, and 'Twister', for not having had their money's worth.[3] William Palmer was moreover a further source of disappointment: he had refused to confess.

The campaign to abolish public executions finally succeeded after years of debate and protracted inquiry because it became increasingly difficult for educated opinion to reconcile the theory of the exemplary nature of public hangings with the mood and behaviour of the majority of those for whom the spectacle had been arranged. The death cell comportment of William Burke, the notorious Edinburgh murderer, who in collaboration with Hare had provided bodies for Dr Knox to dissect, and his behaviour on the scaffold was in stark contrast to that of the large crowd gathered to witness his final public appearance in 1829. He made two full confessions and on the eve of his execution slept well. He now found, he said, waiting for death irksome and longed for his soul to fly to heaven. At 5.30 in the morning he asked for his fetters to be struck from his feet: 'So may all my earthly chains fall.' After spending half an hour alone with two priests he dressed in the 'dead clothes', took a glass of wine, and walked out of the prison to be greeted by pandemonium. This hostile reception temporarily shook his composure but he soon recovered and continued to pray with the priests who provided the only consolation left to him.[4] 'In all the vast multitude', wrote one reporter, 'there was not manifested one solitary expression of sympathy. No one said, "God bless him", but each vied with another in showing their exultation by shouting, clapping of hands, and waving of hats'.[5]

Scenes such as these, and the increasing publicity given to them in the press during the first half of the nineteenth century convinced the authorities that the lesson of the scaffold would only retain its solemnity if hangings took place in private behind prison walls. The traditional idea that justice must be seen to be done would be upheld by professional dignitaries who would witness the execution on behalf of the public who would in turn be assured that the law had taken its proper course. Thus the ritual function of execution and the remedial properties of confession would be retained while the unseemly holiday atmosphere would be abolished and a proper moral tone restored. The public would now have to depend on the printed word for descriptions of the convict, his final comportment, and the mechanics of judicial murder. By 1879 the admission of representatives of the press to executions in British prisons had been rigidly curtailed, a change in policy which James Berry the executioner heartily approved:[6]

> I know that there is a large section of the public that thinks the exclusion of the reporters must mean that there is something going on which there is a desire to hush up. I am a servant of the public, as also are the sheriffs, the governor, and the other officials connected with an execution, and the public, through its representatives on the press, ought to have some assurance that the details of each execution are carried out decently and in order. . . . If the Governor of the gaol or the Sheriff were to give three admissions for each execution, with the understanding that any representative suspected of not being bona fide would be refused admission even if he presented his ticket, I think that every real objection would be met.

As Berry also pointed out, the sentence of the law was announced to those members of the public gathered outside the prison gate by a notice suitably couched in brief officialese and endorsed by the surgeon of the prison. Everything, in short, was being done to ensure the dignity and respectability of the death penalty.

There was still one place, however, where something of the old atmosphere of public executions could be recreated for public consumption and that was Madame Tussaud's. There, in the celebrated Chamber of Horrors, effigies of murderers who had been executed were exhibited, where possible, in the clothes they had worn on the gallows. The ostensible aim of Madame Tussaud's was, as with the scaffold, to improve the morals of the nation, and long before the abolition of executions in public their catalogues had adopted a high moral tone. One, on sale in 1860, typically reassured the public 'that so far from the exhibition of the likenesses of criminals creating a desire to imitate them, experience teaches them that it has a direct tendency to the contrary.'[7] In pursuit of this respectable goal the exhibitors were able to capitalise on two other outstanding characteristics of murder, both judicial and domestic, the capacity to shock and inspire the kind of moral outrage to which Burke and William Palmer were exposed. Carefully blended, these three elements – morality, revulsion, didacticism – combine into a heady mixture with high entertainment value. The Chamber of Horrors was to the Victorians, more than to generations of the present day, indeed 'a horrible place':[8]

> There is Horror in the dull cold light descending from above upon those figures in the Old Bailey dock, all with the same expression on their faces, upturned, inquisitive, bewildered. There is Horror in the unpicturesqueness of this aspect of crime – crime in coats and trousers being more horrible (because nearer to us) than crime in

> doublets and trunk hose. There is Horror in the inflated smiling heads, cast after death by hanging.

Once it was no longer possible to catch even a distant view of a murderer's end crowds in London flocked to Madame Tussaud's where they could get closer not to the reality of murder but its replication in wax. In effect the distancing of the public from the reality of crime and punishment accentuated the dramatisation of evil. In 1912, for example, Guy Thorne summed up the effect of Tussaud's creations on the popular imagination:[9]

> Row upon row of faces which differ in every way from one another and yet are dreadfully alike. For these great sinister dolls, so unreal and so real, have all a likeness. The smirk of cruelty and cunning seems to lie upon their waxen masks. Colder than life, far colder than death, they give forth emanations which strike the very heart with woe and desolation.

In his treatise on the principles and mechanics of capital punishment in late Victorian Britain, James Berry paid particular attention to the problem of penitence. He was, like most of the latter-day hangmen, a religious man and therefore concerned to justify the death penalty as congruent with religion and acceptable unto God. There were, he said, two classes of penitent. In the first place there was 'true repentance': a state of mind evident in those who genuinely recoiled in horror from the deed they had done. Such murderers had usually committed their crime 'without intent or premeditation. . . . In a fit of frenzy or under peculiar circumstances.' But, second, there were those pseudo-penitents who expressed no remorse or whose expressions of regret were a sham designed only to procure sympathy and hopefully a commutation of sentence. Pseudo-penitents were drawn in the main from the ranks of professional criminals:[10]

> These are usually men whose crimes have shown a refinement of cruelty and callousness that is positively revolting. . . . They are the miserable men whose lives have been spent in defying and blaspheming God, but who, when they see death before them, whine and howl, and beg for the intercession of the chaplain or any other godly person they may meet with, not because they repent of their sins, but because they are frightened almost to death by the thought of a fiery hell, which has been painted before their imaginations in glowing colours.

There was also a third class of condemned prisoners: those who were not penitent at all. These too are professional criminals. Men who regard the law as fair game and life as a battle of wits where the prizes go to the most agile and cunning. The lives of these offenders came to an end, said Berry, not on the gallows but in the courtroom when sentence is pronounced. The game is up and the only regret they feel is 'personal and purely selfish'. All three classes of murderer deserved to pay the supreme penalty but the truly repentant had the consolation of knowing their punishment would cease in this world and their misery would soon come to a perpetual end.[11]

Berry's treatise is typically Victorian in that it exemplifies the uneasy and ambivalent combination of religion, law and criminology which characterised the official approach to the problem of crime. Prior to the nineteenth century crime was not by and large seen as the product of depressing social conditions, special circumstances, or 'the criminal mind' to which only experts had access. On the contrary, it was seen as an integral feature of the plight of everyman. Crime was the predictable result of an understandable failure to resist temptation to sin to which all men were prone. The role of confession in the popular literature of murder and its punishment was to confirm the common frailties of mankind fallen from Grace:[12]

> My death each hour I do attend
> I have deserved long since to die.
> When on the ladder you shall me view
> Thinke I am nearer heaven than you.

These lines, attributed to Luke Hutton, a highwayman hanged at York in 1598, express a sentiment still close to the hearts of the Victorians exposed, as they were, to a much more extensive and sophisticated murder literature than previous generations.

As the latter years of the nineteenth century unfolded, a population sheltered in the main from the realities of punishment began to depend more and more on the printed word for information about the nature and extent of criminal activity. Detected murder is a comparatively rare feature of the criminal calendar and the attention it attracts, as befits 'the ultimate deviancy',[13] out of all proportion to its recorded incidence. Because the majority of individuals never *knowingly* encounter a murderer face to face, it is left to the popular media to provide descriptions and interpretations of murder for public consumption. This popular literature of murder pays lip-service to the *status quo*: to borrow Grenander's phrase, it 'strokes the norms of a mass audience.'[14] It does not set out to challenge the assumptions and values of society but accepts the standard of the day from which it seeks to profit. The view reinforced in literature of 'real life' murder, then, is the time-honoured notion that the murderer is at best a weak-willed sinner upon whom (admittedly) fortune may have borne very hardly or at worst (and most exciting of all for the reading public), a monster of iniquity whose existence on God's earth should not be tolerated for a moment longer than is necessary.

Two examples separated by almost forty years will serve to illustrate this point. First, from the introduction to the very popular *Fifty Most Amazing Crimes of The Last Hundred Years* where it is written:[15]

> If one reviews all the condemned criminals in this collection, taking into account all possible motives, situations, and states of mind, nowhere does one find a sympathetic character.
> The murderers towards whom the public mind finds least antipathy are those who have killed, either on the spur of the moment, under great provocation, or as the result of what are held to be long-suffered injustices, as in the case of Crippen and Constance Kent. Portraits of criminals all show marks of depravity: meanness, mercilessness, vanity, snobbishness. An evil-looking lot.

Second, the following observation taken from Edgar Lustgarten's compendium of 1975:[16]

> I never aimed at a gallery of friends and freaks; rather at one in which the human subjects – by method, motive, or other circumstances – are representative of their generation. Each, maybe, intrinsically evil, but shaped by contemporary environment and ethos. Each the instrument of forces universal and eternal, but also the token of a phase of history.

Thus the popular view of murder is that circumstances do alter cases but we must never lose sight of the doctrine of individual responsibility. The very enormity of the crime – and its rarity – sets homicide apart even though the motives are usually commonplace. The confession of the murderer, in itself often a relatively unremarkable statement of guilt, sets the seal on a religio-legal process which in its essentials has changed little over the centuries. In very few cases do undetected murderers make voluntary confessions. The ideal confessant is a rare species as we have noted. In the majority of cases confessions are the product of the process of criminal prosecution and the determination of guilt. It is not surprising, therefore, that it is in popular literature that we find the least ambiguous testimony to the remedial properties of confession.

By the 1860s the sales of the simple and highly stylised broadsheets and street ballads through which news of murder and its punishment had been traditionally disseminated were declining under competition from newspapers, cheap journals and books which the invention of new printing methods had made possible. Trial reports became lengthier and with the abolition of public executions the main focus of interest shifted from the gallows to the dock where the comportment of the accused could be observed by those who could get into the courtroom. Popular interest was increasingly taken up with details of the life and character of the accused and the victim as elaborated through courtroom interrogation by counsel for the prosecution and the defence. As we have previously noted, relatively few murders are cleared up as a result of a spontaneous confession though many innocent people feel compelled to confess to crimes they have not committed. The solution of a murder is thus the outcome of a number of interrelated activities of which the eliciting of a confession is only one. Many confessions take the form of simple admissions of responsibility to be filed alongside the rest of the documents of the case.

When, in 1865, Constance Kent astonished the world by confessing to the unsolved murder of her half-brother five years earlier, her confession consisted of a brief statement providing no insight into motive or circumstance:[17]

> I, Constance Emilie Kent, alone and unaided, on the night of 29th June 1860 murdered at Road Hill House, Wiltshire, one Francis Savile Kent. Before the deed was done no one knew of my intention, nor afterwards of my guilt. No one assisted me in the crime, nor in the evasion of discovery.

The resulting trial was a perfunctory affair lasting only a few minutes. The judge accepted her responsibility but 'spoke in a voice choked with tears as he passed sentence; it was reported that the "greater part of the assembly as well as the jury were in tears".'[18]

Even more abbreviated was the confession of Franz Müller who committed the first British railway murder in 1864. Boarding a train at Fenchurch Street station one evening he found himself travelling with a much more prosperous passenger who he bludgeoned to death, stole his watch and chain, and threw out of the window. The motive was commonplace enough but the setting, one of the great triumphs of the Industrial Revolution, added new terrors to public transport. Having been found guilty Müller protested his innocence almost till the end, his only confession a few words of admission confided in German to the Lutheran minister standing by him on the public scaffold. Officialdom heaved a sigh of relief: Müller had fulfilled one of the great requirements of law by what could be interpreted as a penitent death. Whether James Berry would have described him as a 'true penitent' is a moot point but the street press had no difficulty in accommodating him:[19]

Oh! I must die a malefactor,
In front of Newgate's dismal door,
In the midst of health and vigour,
Aged only twenty-four.
I never thought the law would take me,
When I sailed o'er the raging main,
All my courage did forsake me –
A murderer in the railway train.
Swift the moments are approaching,
On the gallows I must die,
The cruel hangman stands before me,
On the wretched tree so high,
I am full of grief and anguish,
Full of sorrow, care, and pain –
A warning take by poor Franz Müller,
The murderer in the railway train.

Of necessity last minute confessions on the scaffold were hurried and to the point – an admission of guilt was all that time allowed or, at that late stage, all the authorities required. The law had taken its full course. Since the middle of the eighteenth century when an act requiring the condemned to be hanged two days after sentence was revoked, the law had provided an extended interval to enable the offender to show penitence and make his peace with God. When Berry was writing his memoirs the period between sentence and execution had been extended to three weeks which he considered excessive.[20] After the sentence of the court the prisoner was transferred to the condemned cell where he was under the constant surveillance of two warders. Each day he would be visited by the prison governor, doctor and chaplain. In practice this period was used by his lawyers to appeal against sentence or petition for mercy.[21]

> Also during this time the government official who was responsible for the case papers would be studying the case and collecting all relevant information, including an opinion on the man's sanity if this had not been an issue in the court hearing, and would then make a final report to the Home Secretary. It was this minister who had the final decision on whether the sentence should be confirmed or commuted to life imprisonment.

If at the end of this time the death sentence was unchanged, improved arrangements for speedy and humane executions which Berry did much to pioneer, allowed a time lapse of less than twenty seconds between the moment the chief officer entered the cell and the body of the condemned hung between the doors of the trap[22] The time for an extended confession had passed for ever as Samuel Dougal discovered when standing on the scaffold at Springfield gaol, Chelmsford, in 1903 after being found guilty of shooting a wealthy spinster:[23]

> Dougal denied the murder until his last moments. . . . Then, as the executioner went to pull the lever, the prison chaplain called out 'Guilty or Not Guilty Dougal?' From behind the white hood came Dougal's last word before dying – 'Guilty'.

In his book, *Criminals Confess,* Belton Cobb points out that the foremost feature of 'any crime story, whether it be truth or fiction, is invariably, "Who did it?".'[24] He shows how certain confessions, published during the eighteenth and early nineteenth centuries, shed light on the motives and methods of those concerned which would otherwise be shrouded in mystery. The confessions to which he refers are, however, rather unusual examples of extended accounts written by the malefactors themselves being put to death. As such they are substitutes for the detailed trial reports which only became available to the general reader during the latter half of the nineteenth century when the murder industry began the process of rapid expansion which has continued to the present day. In addition to the proliferation of trial reports and other studies of 'true crime', the growing respectability of reading about such an unsavoury topic as murder was clearly evident in the emergence of detective fiction, given an added impetus in the 1880s with the publication of Sir Arthur Conan Doyle's first Sherlock Holmes story, *A Study in Scarlet*.

In detective fiction the power of conscience as a major force behind the discovery of iniquity and the location of responsibility was subordinated to the scientific skills of the (usually private) investigator who, having identified the malefactor, would (possibly) hand him over to the authorities for punishment. The situation was neatly summed up during the 'golden age of the detective story' by H. Douglas Thomson who wrote in 1931:[25]

> Few murderers in the detective story are sentenced at the Old Bailey, and in only one story that I have read has there been a description of the execution. . . . The truth of the matter is that we expect the villain to make a 'good end'. He has been responsible for some share in our entertainment. Let him choose the means of his

> death, and 'die like a gentleman'.... Where is heard the 'jingle of the bracelets', there must there also be the 'fetid breath of almonds'.

Whatever the fate of the detected murderer, the hallmark of the classic detective story is the infallibility of the detective who does not allow a crime to remain long concealed. Detective fiction differs sharply from picaresque novels where the criminal is a romantic and amusing rogue who commands the reader's sympathy and even admiration. In the former our sympathy is on the side of law and order epitomised by the detective who is differentiated from the conventional police force by the possession of superior powers. It is, writes A. E. Murch, 'an important point that the Detective Story, in direct contrast to the Crime Story, recognises the activities of the criminal as reprehensible and not to be tolerated, much less regarded with amusement or admiration.'[26] To the middle classes who comprised a large proportion of the detective-story reading public it was respectable to read about crime because the offender always met his just deserts. The moral, as the organisers of Madame Tussaud's and newspaper proprietors claimed, was plain. No one could be accused of glorifying crime. There was, as the journalist William Bolitho stoutly affirmed in his collection of essays on the murders of Burke and Hare, George Joseph Smith, and others who had taken several lives, 'no such thing as a nice murder'.[27]

There was therefore no scope in the profitable detective story formula, closely tailored as it was to the demands of an extensive readership, for spontaneous confession. Murderers, like many in real life, made strenuous efforts to conceal their crimes and only confessed when overwhelming evidence of their guilt was made public. Classic detective stories faithfully reflected reality in so far as any confession was incidental to an investigation and served the ultimate function of legitimating religion and law. Since the aim of such stories, like the aim of the popular press, was to entertain, publishers could ill afford to waste time and money by taxing the brains of readers with detailed socio-economic or psychological analyses of murder and its motives which were, in any case, often curtly dismissed by judges in the courts. As Lord Haldane observed:[28]

> Overwork means undue congestion of certain lobes of the brain. In order to draw the blood from these lobes, other contiguous lobes must be stimulated. A week in the country merely means that you brood on your work. Detective novels act like iodine on a gum and serve as a counter-irritant.

Detective fiction was justified as an escape from reality but it was an escape which drew on certain aspects of the reality of the detection and prosecution of murder, confirming the popular view of murder as a sin and a crime for which the offender should pay with his life; commanding sympathy at the last only through signs of 'true repentance'.

Not all fictional representations of murder fall, of course, into this category. Indeed, in what is generally regarded as 'the grandfather of the detective story' – William Godwin's *Caleb Williams*, first published in 1794 – Caleb Williams gains little pleasure from the pursuit and final unmasking of the villain Falkland who has ruined his life and sent two innocent men to the gallows for a murder he committed. The closing pages of the novel are given over to Falkland's confession. He is dying and admits his guilt:[29]

> 'Williams,' said he, 'you have conquered! I see too late the greatness and elevation of your mind. I confess that it is to my fault and not yours, that it is to the excess of jealousy that was ever burning in my bosom, that I owe my ruin. I could have resisted any plan of malicious accusation you might have brought against me. But I see that the artless and manly story you have told has carried conviction to every hearer. All my prospects are concluded. All that I most ardently desired is for ever frustrated. I have spent a life of the basest cruelty, to cover one act of momentary vice, and to protect myself against the prejudices of my species. I stand now completely detected. My name will be consecrated to infamy, while your heroism, your patience, and your virtues will be for ever admired. You have inflicted on me the most fatal of all mischiefs; but I bless the hand that wounds me. And now' – turning to the magistrate – 'and now, do with me as you please. I am prepared to suffer all the vengeance of the law. You cannot inflict on me more than I deserve. You cannot hate me, more than I hate myself. I am the most execrable of all villains. I have for many years (I know not how long) dragged on a miserable existence in unsupportable pain. I am at last, in recompense for all my labours and my crimes, dismissed from it with the disappointment of my only remaining hope, the destruction of that for the sake of which alone I consented to exist. It was worthy of such a life, that it should continue just long enough to witness this final overthrow. If however you wish to punish me, you must be speedy in your justice; for, as reputation was the blood that warmed my heart, so I feel that death and infamy must seize me altogether.'

The language is close to the 'sorrowful lamentations' of contemporary broadsheets and street ballads but the analysis of the relations between good and evil is, as Ian Ousby has argued, much more complex. Detection in this novel[30]

> begins as an activity apparently designed to establish moral and intellectual clarity. The detective, voluntarily or involuntarily, assumes the role of an agent of justice, seeking to distinguish good from evil and to identify the source of evil. Caleb's relationship with Falkland, however, progressively suggests that good and evil do not admit of so simple a polarisation. Inextricably linked, the detective and the criminal are similar in their characters and in their fates. Rather than emerging as antithetical or antagonistic in their relations, they grow into symbiotic twins.

Unlike the many detective stories which diverted the Victorians and subsequent generations, *Caleb Williams* does not have a happy ending. The moral issues are, as is often the case in real life, unresolved: the confession of the offender does not close the case. In terms of the definition, therefore, Godwin's novel is much more than a detective story in the classic mould. As Julian Symons has pointed out, one major characteristic of detective fiction is the stereotyping of good and evil.[31] The detective embodies righteousness and the offender has long been estranged from his fellows by his secret dread. The fact that his identity remains unknown until the final dénouement only serves to remind us that his normality is a masquerade. He only confesses (sometimes revelling in his iniquity) because he is given no other choice. Like the sex killer Thomas Allaway, hanged in 1922, the villain of the piece admits he has been found out when he decides there is not much point in keeping silent. Allaway protested his innocence until the last moment, hoping during the period between sentence and execution for a reprieve.[32]

Containing a closed circle of suspects and determined by rigid rules the detective story of the 'golden age' is a fairy tale. What crime literature offered to its readers for half a century from 1890 onwards 'was a reassuring world in which those who tried to disturb the established order were always discovered and punished.'[33] But out of this literature emerged, on the fictional side, a new type of crime story during the 1930s; defined by Symons as the 'crime novel'. The detective story, he argues, has now changed into the crime novel and the two are as different as chalk and cheese. The crime novel is a study of character and situation; there is often no detective, no clues, little interest in the murderer's method and sometimes the 'puzzle value' is low. Frequently the lives of the characters are shown continuing after the crime which is seen to be the result of particular pressures in their lives; an added feature, rarely found in the detective story, may well be a sceptical approach to specific aspects of law and order or the workings of society.[34] In terms of these characteristics the whole novel takes over the function of the traditional confession to murder and does it more effectively. Describing the last days of the mass murderer William Burke in his condemned cell in Edinburgh, William Bolitho observed:[35]

> His remarks and occupations in the condemned cell have been preserved. They have little to tell us but what we knew before: that a man who has confessed to sixteen murders in the space of nine months, is still a human being

The crime novel is more effective in the role of confession because, like other detailed psychological and sociological analyses of particular murders,[36] it offers an extended account of the interaction between character, situation, and social structure from which these unusual events arise. This form of extended confession no longer claims the common humanity of offender and offended in the grounds of the sinful heritage of all mankind but on the potential of all people to act in a murderous fashion when under similar pressures. The crime novel offers imaginative insight while criminological analyses of real crimes reconstruct events and actions leading up to the taking of a life and at their best these reconstructions incorporate subjective (from the offender's point of view) and objective (socio-economic, cultural and situational) perspectives. In short, we are offered a contemporary and secular variation of the old adage: 'there but for the Grace of God go I.'

There are many examples of this secular approach to murder which has, like the criminal law, retained aspects of traditional Christianity or what J.G. Cawelti has described in his analysis of popular fiction as a 'residual moralism'.[37] To conclude this essay on confession as an integral feature of some of the most popular forms of mass entertainment we shall consider two examples both written during the inter-war years when the British crime novel was just beginning to disentangle itself from classical detective fiction. They are in chronological order: C.S. Forester's *Payment Deferred*, first published in 1926;[38] and Ernest Raymond's *We, The Accused*, originally published in 1935 and recently the subject of a successful television adaptation.[39] Both novels have run into several editions.

Payment Deferred fulfils one of Symons's main criteria for a crime novel in so far as the murderer, Mr Marble, is known to us from the outset. This is necessarily the case because Forester has created a study of the corrosive effects of guilt. The story opens, therefore, with a murder. Mr Marble, a lower middle-class family man with a respectable job in a bank, is in debt and does not know where to turn to pay off his creditors:[40]

> His mind was numb. The grim feeling of blank despair was swamped by complete lassitude of soul. He realised vaguely that his oft-repeated threat of sending the children to bed without any supper would soon be carried into effect despite himself. He would be sacked from the bank, and he would never get another job. He knew that well enough.

Overtaken by the accumulation of small bills, Mr Marble finds a solution to his problems in the shape of his nephew from Australia who pays an unexpected visit to the poverty-stricken suburban home. Mr Marble's nephew is well-dressed and has with him plenty of money – sufficient to resolve his uncle's difficulties. Mesmerised by the contrast between his straitened circumstances and his nephew's affluence, Marble, unknown to his wife, poisons him with potassium cyanide from the photographic cabinet and buries the body in his muddy backyard. The money in his victim's wallet relieves the immediate pressures on the Marble family but does not bring them happiness. Marble becomes obsessed with evading discovery and, as one anxiety is heaped upon another, his marriage disintegrates and his wife kills herself after discovering his infidelity. To complete the irony, Marble is hanged for her murder. He is by the time of his wife's suicide so preoccupied with the fear of detection he fails to exhibit appropriate grief and the presence of cyanide in the house, Marble's collection of books on crime and medical jurisprudence, and the letter from the other woman combine to convince the authorities of his guilt.

Mr Marble is not a pleasant character but the circumstances leading up to his crime – the depressing effects of respectable poverty – are immediately recognisable as in the second of Forester's crime novels, *Plain Murder,* published in 1930.[41] So is his state of mind: a condition of constant anxiety produced in the first instance by seedy respectability and latterly the consequence of his opportunistic offence. The lesson, familiar to readers of classical detective fiction, is that a criminal, especially a murderer, may prosper materially but morally and in terms of human relationships, crime does not pay. In this story, however, the age-old theme is developed with skill and insight. Marble's crime is not detected; he is the victim of the very values he kills to maintain: a man strong enough to take another life when the opportunity arises yet conventional enough to dread the consequences even when he is successfully avoiding discovery. In other words his inner life is of the kind the theory of confession leads us to expect. A person who in the end is tormented by secret guilt and cannot live comfortably with his deed:[42]

> And he was paying heavily enough for those few Treasury notes. That heart of his which had thumped so heavily on that stormy evening thumped just as heavily at other times now. He could not keep his mind from working out possible occurrences in the future, and some new morbid thought of the arrival of the police, instigated by the officials of Medland's (the victim's) hotel, or of some unexpected inquiry by the Bank as to whence had come the money which had so suddenly come into his possession, would set his heart pounding away until he could only lean back in his chair and gasp. He would wake sweating in the night too, with the fevered blood running hot under his skin, as some fantastic possibility developed in his sleeping mind. Then he would writhe and toss in his bed, muttering faintly to himself, tortured with fears of the known and the unknown. And sometimes, when he had been sleeping very badly, one or two horrible memories returned to him: memories of a pair of staring eyes, and of a boyish face, the mouth smeared with foam. That was the worst of all.

Our second fictitious murderer who shares the common humanity for which the theory and practice of confession searches also comes from a lower middle-class background but the circumstances of his crime – reminiscent of the Crippen case – are much different. He is Paul Arthur Presset, 50 years old, and a schoolmaster in a small private college. Married to an overbearing and oppressive woman whose social pretensions are a constant irritant and a reminder of his failure in her eyes, he meets another and younger woman and they fall in love. The author skilfully and convincingly traces the train of thought which leads Presset, a kind and gentle man, to dispose of his wife in the hope of a deeper and more authentic relationship with his lover. As in the Crippen case 'the other woman' is innocent and ultimately acquitted of complicity after the couple, who run away together, have been tracked down by the police. In effect the novel is an extended confession: our sympathy for the murderer is engaged from the outset; we are not asked to condone his offence but we do not find it difficult to understand how such a person, caught up in such a set of relationships, might be tempted to act.

Thus we follow Presset into the condemned cell and from there on his brief journey to the gallows. His lover now knows he killed his wife but he stands redeemed in her eyes by virtue of his dignity, responsibility, and acceptance of the truth of Christianity. He is, as James Berry would have said, truly repentant. On the morning of the execution Presset is not surprisingly very much in the prison governor's thoughts:[43]

> How on earth could that decent little fellow, considerate for all, have done so shocking a deed? Last night when he went to say goodbye to him, Presset, considerate to the last, had said: 'I can never thank you enough, sir, for all your kindness. And these gentlemen, too, and the others; I'm sure they've all been kindness itself. I don't want anyone to be upset about me. I dare say I deserve it, and anyhow, I'm not sorry to go. So please don't let anybody worry.' Whereon the Governor had been moved to say with swelling eyes, 'Goodbye, and God bless you.'

Chapter 6
Confessing to murder: critical notes on the sociology of motivation

> In all criminal cases . . . there existed areas of darkness between judge and delinquent, impenetrable to both: there were unplumbed depths in the human conscience to which light could never penetrate save through the guilty party's confession.[1]

Two recent developments in the sociology of deviance, the study of motivational accounts and the labelling process, are closely related to each other empirically and theoretically.[2] It has been argued that formal agents of social control, and in a wider context although less predictably, members of other social networks, impute typical 'motives' to deviant individuals which represent official explanations of 'bad character' and which it is assumed play an important part in the development of deviant identity.[3] The public imputation of criminal intent characteristically subsumed under labelling theory is thus considered one specific aspect of a general process of becoming deviant. Although studies of accounts and labels have contributed to sociological understanding of the processes by which people (a) react to deviance and (b) become deviant there are considerable gaps in our appreciation of the criminal career.[4]

The crux of the matter is that certain difficulties bar the way not only to an adequate external conceptualisation of criminal motivation, but also to a rounded understanding of the complexities of societal reaction to news of criminal behaviour on the part of a particular individual. It is our contention therefore that an exploration of confessions, particularly confessions to murder, will shed some light on those critical 'areas of darkness' apparently separating the judges from the judged. Accordingly we wish to consider two important features of the traditional confession/interrogation relationship: the historical development and secularisation of confessional ideology and consequent tensions between the theory and practice of confessing with reference to English murder cases. We shall draw on these to fashion a sociological critique of certain aspects of contemporary views of confessions as admissible evidence. In short, we wish to make a further contribution to the study of the conviction process;[5] to attempt to enlarge our understanding of one possible stage in the criminal career, namely confessing to murder.

Our point of departure is the conventional English interpretation of the meaning of 'confession' as the *acknowledgment of fault* or offence to others through the *formal declaration of injury*.[6] In our language the word itself carries essentially pragmatic overtones which overshadow the subtler meanings found in some other parts of the world.[7] Although it implies the underlying active principles of conscience, knowledge, and consciousness, in practice it foreshortens their complexity by relating much more closely to administrative considerations. The English legal response to the problem of an external understanding of self-knowledge, consciousness of motivation etc., on the part of the offender, is to discover credibility almost exclusively within the notion of self-blame (conscience) and to define confession as simply any statement wholly or partly adverse to an accused person.[8] Within the 'law and order context' to which this shift of emphasis has conventionally responded the fuller and subtler phenomenology of a confessional statement (revealing the inner workings of the self) is reduced to the mechanistic revelation of pre-existing collections of fact to which the legal labels 'admissible/inadmissible' may be appropriately attached by agents of social control predominantly concerned with 'clearing up' responsibility for an offence. Clearly such an administrative approach to the problem of guilt favours the legitimate social order. Moreover, from a wider sociological viewpoint, it has tended to focus analytical attention almost exclusively on societal reaction to a criminal offence. A glance at the history of English criminal law provides a useful illustration. Radzinowicz has shown that the familiar custom of exhorting a convicted offender to confess before execution in public was an ancient practice informed by attitudes 'seldom articulated but. . . always there'.[9] These were the view that execution was an act of expiation and sacrifice and perhaps more conveniently, given the imperfections of forensic science and criminal investigation of murder generally,[10] the notion that a confession happily relieved judges and executioners of the burden of responsibility and guilt. Execution as expiation and sacrifice, writes Radzinowicz, would only 'acquire a deeper meaning' if the condemned man 'himself consented to it'.[11] The foremost ingredient here was, and still remains, acquiescence to higher authority mediated through an apparent experience of consensus over the everyday meanings and motivations of murder, bridging the gap between the accused and his accusors.[12] It is the function of 'interrogation tactics' to reconcile the two apparently conflicting parties and to bring about a peaceful solution to the problem.[13]

Confessions of the kind to which Radzinowicz refers, of course, were nearly always the product of legal proceedings against the confessant. One example, the alleged confession of George Sparkes published commercially as a broadsheet at the time of his execution, illustrates the legitimating idiom:[14]

> My dear Mother, I am now in the condemned cell, and must die for the murder of a good neighbour, and kind friend Mr Blackmore, I coveted his money, I did not intend to kill him, but you know I was going to get married and wanted to exalt myself above my station, but now wretch that I am, what disgrace my pride has brought me to, what anguish do I now feel, what disgrace upon my family, what sorrow to you my aged widowed mother, God help you, you taught me what was right, but I didn't hearken to it, for I took to gambling and drink, which ruined me, I murdered Mr Blackmore, I am told I am to die next Friday, I hope the Lord will have mercy on my soul, I had none on Mr Blackmore, give my love to all my friends and brother who I hope will forgive me, I am your wretched son. (George Sparkes, The Condemned Cell, 25 March 1853)

Despite the sense of outrage provoked by Sparkes's crime this 'confession' has a recognisable quality: the murder is totally individualised. It has its origins within a flaw in the personality of the offender, but a flaw which may be supernaturally redeemed even if it cannot be tolerated and rectified in this world.

As far as confession to the English murder is concerned, the concept of conscience (public awareness of fault and consequent self-blame leading to some attempt to make amends) has mirrored prevailing motivational constructions of deviance.[15] Death by 'unnatural causes' (i.e. death by relatively obvious physical violence, excluding legitimate conflict) has been seen as the outcome of some flaw in the personality of the offender. To the Elizabethans, for instance, murder was a mortal, albeit recurring sin for which offenders would fry in hell; correspondingly men and women would only traverse that particular spiritual barrier if compelled by what were conceived to be overbearing passions.[16] The presence of irresistible motive forces of this order could be subsequently confessed when and if a murder was detected. Closer to our own time George Orwell reflected on this persistent cultural theme when he outlined the characteristics of the perfect English murderer as[17]

> A little man of the *professional class*. . . living an *intensely respect-*

> *able* life somewhere in the suburbs, and preferably in a semi-detached house, *which will allow the neighbours to hear suspicious sounds through the wall.* He should be either chairman of the local Conservative Party branch, or a leading Nonconformist and strong Temperance advocate. He should go astray through cherishing *a guilty passion* for his secretary or the wife of a social professional man, and should only bring himself *to the point of murder after long and terrible wrestles with his conscience.*

What is striking about published confessions to murder through the ages (whether 'abnormal' or 'normal' murder, to use the current Home Office classification) is that the whole gamut of underlying social processes achieves expression in terms of a simple formula.[18] It is hardly surprising then that our murders have traditionally been represented as puzzles amenable to solution through empirical investigation. As Raymond Williams has written in another context, complex relations between groups of people are seen as 'decipherable by an abstract mode of detection rather than by full and connected analysis of any more general undertaking'.[19] Such an abstract mode of detection, aimed primarily at unmasking the character responsible for the deed through the accumulation of clues and point-scoring in the interrogation situation, has been facilitated by the strategic utilisation of institutions of privacy: privacy is nowadays considered vital for the successful operationalisation of interrogation tactics.[20]

Some years before the abolition of public executions in 1868, representatives of 'the establishment' had come to agree that in spite of its traditional advantages the practice of exhorting confessions following conviction could have a negative return. It could, they suggested, possibly shake the faith of the public in the integrity and skill of the law as an agent of truth and perhaps even provide the prisoner with an opportunity to manipulate the situation hopefully in his favour.[21] From 1845 only authorised personnel were allowed to visit a condemned prisoner and criminal confessions began to assume the private form we recognise today, the existence of which is occasionally revealed to a wider public in the press and other documents. The validity of these confessions was increasingly adjusted according to their value as corroborative evidence, though the traditional religious element of atonement did not cease to be important. Professional and administrative considerations were looming large and today we have reached the position where confessions derive their significance, as the Eleventh Report of the Criminal Law Revision Committee has attested, primarily from their perceived value in catching criminals: that is, maintaining law and order.[22]

An ideal case

While the Criminal Law Revision Committee confined their interest in confessions to pragmatic considerations impinging on the nationwide war against crime, they were also compelled to acknowledge that ideologically confessions have been accredited as a special type of motivational account offering peculiar insight, otherwise unobtainable, into the hidden depths of the confessant's personality, thereby illuminating previously puzzling aspects of his known behaviour. Faced with the practical everyday difficulties of clearing up reported crime, the police and the courts typically strive to reconcile ever present tensions between the theory and practice of confessions. Not surprisingly in this troublesome context, the ideal type of confession becomes the voluntary statement provided by an authentic lawbreaker who has 'given himself up'.

In July 1971 a middle-aged man walked into a Manchester newspaper office and calmly told a reporter that nineteen years previously he had killed a prostitute in Liverpool.[23] The murder itself was not particularly unusual. The victim was battered to death on a piece of waste land after she and the murderer had been drinking. There was insufficient evidence for the police to trace the man responsible. The victim herself was a notorious figure in the neighbourhood, notorious as a 'roller' – a prostitute who robbed her clients. Unlike many domestic murders, the situation was such that the range of suspects was considerable. Just the sort of situation where a confession might provide the vital corroborative detail necessary to make an adequate connection between cause and effect.

Describing the offence, the confessant revealed sufficient information to convince the authorities he was responsible for the death. Moreover he provided a causative link between his past offence and his present conduct, characterised as a concatenation of strange behavioural incidents and psychological experiences, seen as the product of the recurring image of the battered face of the victim. Once he had confessed, the offender experienced considerable relief from a series of psychological symptoms, including nightmares and sleeplessness; not to mention behaviour disorders such as petty violence, rows with his wife, jealousy and petty criminality. Having given himself up, he made it possible for the judge to pass a lenient sentence of twelve months, described as a kind of atonement adequate to redress the balance of wrong to the community. It is clear from the judge's comments that he felt retribution had been adequately visited upon the offender in the form of years of unhappiness, validated by his voluntary confession.[24]

Although the reported confession describing this criminal act is brief, the social meanings extend well beyond the boundaries of the immediate motives for the deed (in this case, apparently, drunken anger over attempted theft by the prostitute). We learn retrospectively from the confessant's account that the enormity of his offence, which he successfully covered up after the event, assumed such proportions in his mind that it could only be diminished by major remedial action. In other words, the offender's voluntary statement to the police that he was responsible for the murder of a prostitute was not only seen to be the authentic product of twenty guilt-ridden years of private non-shareable torment, but also represented a visible public process of status passage with wider social implications. Mental stress is very often clinically and popularly associated with anti-social behaviour and this is particularly the case in many studies of the psychology of murder, but when we come to confession we sometimes find the pattern of association reversed. The Liverpool case provides an ideal illustration of the way in which mental stress can be interpreted as producing social benefit. We can see that the confession has two crucial dimensions: it is part of a process of self-authentication whereby an individual, through his mental suffering, lays claim to fundamental personal worth, despite having committed a deviant act; from the point of view of the wider legitimate society, confession reaffirms its central beliefs.

When the confession was finally made, it fulfilled ideally the two social requirements previously outlined. Besides providing the police with unique evidence indicating responsibility for the offence, it was clearly seen to be the result of the kind of personal suffering typically associated with the 'compulsion to confess'. Second, this public avowal of private, guilty secrets had the effect of sustaining the useful legal concept of 'the man of conscience'. We *know* the confessant had a guilty conscience because he confessed it and his actions both before and after the confession offer further proof of the validity of his account. Serving his token prison sentence enabled him to feel he had atoned and was regenerated: he felt at peace.

Returning to the wider perspective: confessions in a police station or court of law must be validated against external evidence to achieve a successful prosecution and to reverse, or at least mitigate, the degradation process. We can see then that legal proceedings (detection, interrogation, trial, sentencing) are not necessarily degradation ceremonies effectively isolating a proved offender from society; in certain circumstances these proceedings may well restore an individual's sense of personal worth besides restoring his social acceptability, although these two aspects need not be co-terminous.[25] Also we may note that the development of what we call a guilty conscience may appear independently of any direct physical experience of external rejection or stigmatisation.[26]

Why, from a sociological point of view, should the Liverpool case be regarded as an ideal, typical instance of a confession to murder? First, it represents a situation where ambiguity is totally minimised: the empirical features of the case neatly accommodated the conventional wisdom regarding all true confessions as voluntary moral actions. Second, as a published social document, the case reaffirms the ideological distinction between the essentially 'good' and 'bad' people among us. All these factors are in turn responsive to an underlying individualistic ideology attributing guilt to flaws in individual personality. However, at the same time this ideology assumes that normal people will be moved by guilt, should they find themselves committing illegal acts (particularly that most heinous act, murder). Anyone failing to respond to these 'natural forces' may be labelled as hardened, unregenerate or simply inhuman.

In spite of changes in penal practice since the nineteenth century, confession continues to enable the offender to demonstrate his unity with society; to lay claim to a particular social significance or status. It follows that what he reveals must make sense to those around him, otherwise he will be categorised as dangerous or mentally ill. The compulsion to confess must be conceptualised as a shared phenomenon common to all decent people providing proof of non-alienation from the conventional social order.

Another way of looking at the problem is to compare historically the wide range of murders and confessions with the ideal type described above. These overall factors can be summarised as follows: there are situations where one or more suspects have been detained, but where a confession is necessary to make a formal charge; situations where the evidence is strong enough in itself to make a formal charge; situations where a confession would not add to the existing evidence but might be deemed appropriate. Added to these complexities are cases of multiple confessions,[27] extorted confessions,[28] crank confessions,[29] and confessions after the fact.[30] When any of these factors intrude, the process of guilt, confession, and reconciliation cannot be smoothly integrated and the behaviour of participants reflects these contingencies, as occurred in the United States when Albert De Salvo confessed initially to being the Boston Strangler.[31] Consequently, agents of social control may feel that the moral image of the law is under threat, with the effect that a confession can assume added symbolic significance even when obtained under considerable pressure and when forensic evidence as to responsibility for the offence is unambiguous. Historically a position has been achieved where the symbolic significance of the confession as a legitimation of law and order has been retained, whilst at the same time there is greater willingness to concede that confessions are the result of systematic interrogation procedures designed to break down the resistance of suspects by inducing such mental strain that they make 'voluntary' confessions.

The ideology of confession

Historians of the legal tradition have commented on the fact that there is a noticeable continuity, however implicit, between religion and law.[32] Since the religious dimension is particularly evident in the legal view of criminal confession (with its emphasis on guilt, punishment and reconciliation), our appreciation of the nature of confession as a stage in the conviction process may be aided by a brief examination of the religious tradition. There are a number of interesting parallels which become evident in comparing religious and legal interpretations of confession. In both legal theory and the theology of penance, the concept of confession is riddled with ambiguity and contradiction. This ideology of confession is only indirectly and uncertainly connected with the actual day-to-day practice of confessing, whether in the confessional or in the police station. At a more general level, there has been an important connection between the redeeming work of the Church and that of the politico-legal order. From Tudor times onwards, the confession as part of the address from the scaffold followed a set pattern in which offenders recognised the legality of their execution, acknowledged their misdemeanours and ended by asking the audience to pray that 'God and king would mercifully forgive them their trespasses, and then, in a closing burst of loyalty, they expressed the hope that their gracious sovereign might long and happily reign over the kingdom in peace and tranquility'.[33] Why should men going to a painful death, often on trumped-up charges of treason, make no complaint about their treatment or condemn their persecutors? Part of the explanation seems to be that they hoped by confessing to remove the more gruesome aspects of the execution procedure and to protect the families they left behind. Many of them also accepted that the royal personage was surrounded by an aura of divinity and that, since they were guilty, they must be sinful men in need of social redemption. Historically, a confession prior to execution has proved a valuable means of demonstrating the benefits of loyalty to sovereign powers.

Although the meaning of 'confession' has a social history, there does seem to be an enduring core meaning and significance which characterises its application in particular instances. The root meaning is a religious one – confession being the central feature of the sacrament of penance which dates back to the origins of Christianity. The skeletal definition of confession involves the notion of the autonomous individual, driven by the burden of guilt, voluntarily and disinterestedly acknowledging personal guilt and responsibility for sin before an authoritative person. Contemporary English law retains these essential elements by holding to the view that admissible evidence flows from a true confession, produced by guilt and freely offered to a person in authority. The contemporary attitude of legal theorists is still based largely on the Warickshall case which states that 'free and voluntary confession is deserving of the highest credit, because it is presumed to flow from the strongest sense of guilt, and therefore it is admitted as proof of the crime to which it refers.'[34] The legal position resembles the characteristic Catholic definition which points out that confession 'consists in accusing ourselves of our sins to a priest who has received authority to give absolution'.[35] Although both the legal and religious view of confession places heavy emphasis on the individual nature of guilt, the root meaning also entails a social perspective in the sense that, having made a confession, the sinner is restored to the community by cancellation of wrongdoing. Confession is closely associated with a number of key theological terms, including forgiveness, reconciliation and justification. E. J. Bicknell, for example, argues that confession involves a reconciliation between the sinner and God's family when the confessant comes to an awareness that he has sinned 'against the peace and unity of the whole household'.[36] Similarly, the confessed murderer becomes acceptable to his interrogators because he has shown himself capable of such normal, social emotions as remorse, regret and shame. James Berry, the nineteenth-century executioner, made a distinction between murderers who exhibited sentiments of remorse and those who died unreconciled. The victims who caused him 'most trouble' morally were the few cases in which they have been devoutly penitent, and almost seem to welcome death as a release from a burden too heavy to be borne and an expiation for the sin which they deplored.[37] Religious and legal personnel have, therefore, typically regarded confession as a remedial activity which is capable of restoring the social bond and reasserting the boundaries of the moral community. By acknowledging the 'normal' emotions of remorse in an act of self-condemnation, the confessant confirms the official view of human personality.

Although Christian definitions of penance seem to be unambiguous, detailed inspection of the main terms of 'confession' show them to be full of difficulties. Legal and religious ideologies claim that the true confession must be voluntary, but in practice the churches and the legal system rely on various institutional mechanisms for producing a regular flow of confessions. In Protestant revivalism, a general confession of sin went hand in hand with emotional conversionism: both events were often produced by manipulating feelings of guilt and fear of damnation.[38] The Catholic Church has also occasionally resorted to inducement and terror to stimulate the confession of sins. Perhaps one of the most interesting examples of what might be called 'confessional apparatus' was the French *confessional à surprise* in which a panel painting of Christ was, by touching a concealed button, transformed into a picture of the devil complete with terrifying eyes and tusks, and accompanied by loud noises from whistles and pipes. Without this gimmickry, the Church has regularised confession through tradition and through eccleciastical law which requires adult members to make confession of their sins at least once a year. Ideologically, confession is voluntary and spontaneous (the result of inner psychological mechanisms of guilt), but in reality it is induced by dogma, custom and institution. The same hiatus between the ideological stress on voluntary confession backed up by the institutional practice of inducing and constructing appropriate confessions exists in the legal system. Both in England and the United States, there is a consistent claim that admissible evidence can only derive from voluntary admission of guilt, but the police at the same time have relatively sophisticated techniques and psychological theories for obtaining confessions from suspects.[39] Even where the law has taken cognizance of developments in police methods (as in the *Miranda* decision),[40] the implementation of these legal pronouncements has often been inadequate. In any case, modern police methods of interrogation, at least in the United States, are so subtle and indirect that it would be virtually impossible to draw up operational criteria which would distinguish clearly between oppressive techniques of questioning and text-book methods of interrogation routinely employed.

The problem of voluntary confession can also be connected with the criterion of disinterest on the part of the confessant. The Church has generally held that confessions must be disinterested if they are to be valid, but simultaneously it is thought that there are definite spiritual benefits to be obtained from penance. There does appear to be an element of bargain in all confessions in which sins are exchanged for what theologians have called 'satisfactions'. Similarly, while the law holds that any confession induced by 'the flattery of hope' must be invalid, there is ample evidence of widespread existence of various forms of bargain justice in which a confession of criminal guilt could be expected to produce leniency on the part of policemen and legal officials. These bargaining factors, which seem to be a regular part of coping with difficulties in the administration of justice,[41] are completely ignored by, for example, the Criminal Law Revision Committee. The Committee's statement that 'mere exhortation on religious or moral grounds' does not render a confession inadmissible and that there 'must be a fear of prejudice, or hope of advantage'[42] is inadequate as a guideline in a situation where police methods of interrogation are now technically advanced and where some form of bargain is a common aspect of deciding upon a charge.

The third major ambiguity in the religio-legal ideology of confession can be seen as a tension between confession as a spontaneous outpouring of the humble soul and the recognition that both priest and penitent (interrogator and suspect) must acquire some elementary knowledge of how, when and where to confess. While the confession is assumed to be unpractised and spontaneous, the Church has issued numerous manuals (most of which are in Latin) on confession and there is an oral tradition which passes on confessional lore to seminarists. One objective of these manuals is to provide the priest with an understanding of the strategies which a penitent may use to cover up a genuine confession. Although officially the priest and confessant are expected to trust each other, these manuals imply that the penitent will use evasive action to mask his real sins and deliberately mislead the priest. The confessor has to break through this moral disguise in order to expose the man. Frank Lake, commenting on confessions in modern clinical theology, observed that confession can often be an inverted form of 'self-righteousness and perfectionism' and that the neurotic confessant can be expected to bring to the confessional 'ancient peccadilloes such as masturbation at the age of 9, free love at the age of 10, or travelling without a railway ticket at the age of 11'.[43] Similarly, the penitent must himself develop some conception of what is relevant as confessional material. Hence, the confession can be seen as an attempt to arrive at some mutually acceptable point mid-way between moral enormity which may scandalise the priest and a peccadillo which the priest may discount. The same type of tension between the spontaneous confession of legal theory and the constructed confession of interrogation practice occurs in police work. While the law requires the free, spontaneous confession, the police must attempt to break through what they regard as irrelevance or subterfuge (by employing the 'Mutt and Jeff' routine, for example, as recommended in police manuals).[44] The interrogator must bring the suspect towards constructing a confession which will be suitable as a piece of legal evidence rather than as simply a part of the suspect's personal biography.

Our argument is that the Christian tradition has developed an ideology of confession which has provided a suitable vocabulary of motives by which penitents can give accounts of untoward behaviour. This ideology, which in turn made a substantial contribution to the underlying assumptions of criminal confessions, was never without ambiguity; these ambiguities had to be resolved by practitioners in the confessional itself. These approved motives were set within the wider social context of the Church and obviously this institutional setting has changed considerably over time. There was, for example, a massive process of secularisation of religious beliefs and institutions in the nineteenth century which rendered much of the traditional confessional vocabulary obsolete. In nineteenth-century France, as secularisation weakened the cultural hegemony of the Catholic Church, a bitter conflict of interpretation developed over the confessional. Both Protestants and secular anticlericals came to regard confession as a vicious form of priestcraft and religious control. Probably the best-known criticism of the confession as a form of clerical domination was presented by J. Michelet in 1845.[45] Michelet complained that confession undermined the authority of the husband and threatened family morality by allowing the priest to come between man and wife. The priests contaminated women by putting 'terrible ideas into innocent minds'. Anti-clericals were also divided between those who took the view that confessors were too lax so that unconditional absolution permitted continuous sinning and those who thought that confessors were too strict, making the penitent's life a misery. Within the Church, Jesuits attempted to liberalise the sacrament of penance, while Jansenists revived the doctrine of man's total depravity. It was under these conditions that the coherence of traditional vocabularies of motive was brought into question.

While the conflict over confession may have sharpened in France after the Revolution, in more general terms the traditional confessional had long been under attack from Protestantism. It is interesting to note that Theodore Reik has argued that, although Catholicism had channelled the psychological 'compulsion to confess' into the objective obligation of the institutional confessional, Protestantism had turned men in on themselves by removing the institutionalised form so that the external confession had once more become internal. By achieving this situation, Protestantism had unwittingly contributed to the secularisation of confession by 'preparing for the future development that will go beyond confession and perhaps replace religion by other social institutions'.[46] In Reik's view, Protestantism had in part contributed to the emergence of secular psychoanalysis of the 'compulsion to confess' by contributing to the over-all secularisation of Christianity. We must, however, be careful not to overstate Reik's claim that Protestant denominations did not produce external, institutional forms of social control which had parallels with the Catholic confessional. For example, Methodism created a form of institutional confession control in its class and band meetings in which laymen would publicly confess their sins and shortcomings, submitting themselves to the inspection and interrogation of their class leader. What transformed the class meeting was not so much doctrinal emphasis on the inner, subjective consciousness, but growing social respectability as Methodism became a predominantly middle-class denomination. For nineteenth-century Methodists, respectable people have nothing to confess; hence, the interrogation of the class meeting was a moral affront. A Methodist magazine in 1867 put the view that, since class leaders were often poor and illiterate, it was 'unseemly for a person of respectability and education to be taught by a humble artisan'.[47] Lay people had come to feel that the idea of the 'burden of guilt' was incompatible with their social status. This social development resulted in a thorough transformation of the traditional language of hell and spiritual terror which had been important ingredients of conversion and confession.

In contemporary society, the former drama of the scaffold address and the Christian confessional has been partly replaced by routinised police interrogation and the pastoral talk. It is evident, however, that secularisation, at least in this country, does not simply mean the disappearance of religion. Some writers have thought that there can be a beneficial exchange between religion and consulting psychology, for example, so that psychologists could 'include more widely a revised form of confessional catharsis in their procedures'.[48] Traditional religious concepts are taken over by new institutions, but in certain cases religious themes can remain intact as archaic social forms. In particular, religious concepts seem to retain a hold over such institutions as the family, the monarchy and the law. It is interesting that the Criminal Law Revision Committee should believe that there is a strong argument 'entitled to the highest respect' for preserving the professional privilege of ministers of religion. The Committee no doubt detected a parallel between the work of the law and that of the Church since wrongdoers should be encouraged to confess to their minister of religion; the minister may be 'able to persuade him to lead a better life'.[49] Such a state of affairs, in its view, is in the best 'interests of religion, morality and society'.[50] That the clergy and legal personnel share a common ideology, which specifies the ways in which evil men can be redeemed, should come as no surprise; higher echelons of the Church and legal profession are, after all, recruited from the same social classes and trained in the same public schools. Bishops and judges, according to Alasdair MacIntyre, 'still live within a moral framework and use a moral vocabulary' which has been undermined elsewhere in society and they do not find it intellectually difficult to assert that the 'Courts have a responsibility for maintaining moral standards' and that there are unambiguous solutions to the most complex of contemporary moral issues.[51]

The sociology of motivation

Our concern with confessing to murder reflects a traditional criminological interest in especially unusual or untoward acts. Richard D. Altick has noted in his study of murders and manners in the age of Victoria that murder has exercised a hold over men's primitive emotions and imagination which has been 'renewed from society to society and age to age'.[52] He traces a 'crimson thread' running through 'the fabric of Victorian social history'. Even more importantly from our point of view, he documents the way in which the early Victorian period saw the institutionalisation of homicide as 'a popular entertainment, a spectator sport'. One of our main arguments is that the process of secularisation, which we referred to earlier as conditioning the nature of confession and enhancing men's awareness not only of a newly discovered personality structure but a different order or relationship to God through men, was accompanied by the emergence of murder as mass entertainment. The growth of a mass audience fostered by trends in urbanisation and the deliberate creation of interest in murder by the popular press was not diminished by the abolition of public executions in 1868. From the point of view of confessions, the abolition of capital punishment in public did mean a change in the form and content of published confessions which, for all but the privileged few, are the only source of information of a convicted murderer's state of mind. Although these confessions lay traditional emphasis on repentance, making one's peace with God, and so justifying punishment, it is possible to detect the faint signs of new elements both in the confession and by implication in the motivation of murder: increasing preoccupation with criminal psychology[53] (particularly the notion of mental pathology), a corresponding shift in the kinds of explanations acceptable to the general public,[54] the growth of modern forensic criminology geared to scientific detection, and much later the development of scientific interrogation drawing upon the insights of experimental psychology, behaviouristic psychiatry, and technological innovation.

Because the public reaction to murder in this country has been informed for several decades by fascinated horror, confession to murder has continued to be a particularly sensitive index of the way in which the meanings of motivational statements are filtered; filtered, that is, in a way which reflects dominant ideas of how a confession should be done and presented 'properly', rather than suggesting what possible modes of consciousness underlie the actual act. This filtering process can be conceptualised as follows: (1) the murder; (2) suspect; (3) private interrogation; (4) formal charge; (5) public trial; (6) conviction.

Clearly, a published confession to murder must always be the product of these processes. Moreover, in this context the only kind of spontaneous confession possible is one emerging from a privately experienced sense of guilt. All other confessions involve the confessant in some form of confrontation with representatives of public institutions. Along with the development of murder as public entertainment, the growth of criminal psychology, scientific detection and scientific interrogation have modified the cultural ambience of the basic legal framework and thereby altered the implications of confession in modern society. While therefore legal *ideology* retains its anachronistic appeal to the fear of God (moral guilt), penal practice is now much more pragmatic and recognised as such by the public. As we have stated, it is now generally accepted that confessions are the outcomes of skilful interrogation processes which are detailed in police manuals, particularly in the United States.[55] It is in these processes that we perceive most clearly the relationship between experimental psychology, technical innovation and political ideology: interrogation processes are now clearly geared towards purging individuals of secrets dangerous to the State.

As we have suggested earlier, English murders have had over the last century and a half a strong domestic quality; comparatively speaking, we have seen few political murders and it is a criminological fact that statistically one has a greater chance of being murdered by one's relatives or intimate friends than by strangers on the streets or by other criminals.[56] Because England has been relatively settled politically since the late seventeenth century, domestic murder has assumed a particular significance in this country, all the more compelling in the relative absence of political assassination and violent political conflict.[57] In addition, 'it does seem likely that the Victorian mass's sustained enthusiasm for murder was in part a product of their intellectually empty and emotionally stunted lives, so tightly confined by economic and social circumstances.'[58] In short, a happy conjunction between the forces of social control and popular entertainment; whatever the class of murder occupying public attention, the events of the crime have always been described in such a way as to sustain social stability through a reaffirmation of conventional notions of criminals and non-criminal man. Murder has been understandable not in terms of its origins within a conflictual society, riddled by social inequality, but as the individual product of flawed personalities who may be able to redeem themselves by confessing the error of their ways. These inescapable and under-researched historical features raise problems for the interpretation, both in sociology and in life, of confessional statements describing motives of murder.

The sociology of motives attempts broadly to understand motives as aspects of social interaction where actors request explanations of activity. In this respect a motive is seen primarily as a statement or response (including non-verbal) which will satisfy such questions as 'Did you do X?' and 'Why did you do X?'. From a pragmatic point of view, interrogation situations represent ideal manifestations of what is seen to be a general social phenomenon susceptible to sociological analysis. Erving Goffman, for example, has devoted a paper to analysing problems of communication in situations where, 'when a respectable motive is given for action' (in our case, murder), we 'suspect an ulterior one'. An important ingredient for these situations for Goffman is 'the resources or capacities' the interactants bring into the situation.[59] What experimental research has shown, and this includes studies of methods of eliciting confessions under drugs and psychological pressures, is that truthful responses tend to correspond to the expectations of the interrogators rather than possessing some absolute value.[60]

Recently, Scott and Lyman attempted to summarise contemporary sociological analysis of motives in a typology of accounts. Our critical comments on current notions of motivation in sociological theory can be usefully directed against their typology.[61] An account is a 'linguistic device employed whenever an action is subjected to valuative inquiry', that is, an account is a set of sentences produced in conversation when a social actor is called upon to explain unusual, unexpected, untoward behaviour or beliefs. There are two basic types of accounts: excuses involving recognition of the untoward nature of an act, but denying responsibility and justifications involving acceptance of responsibility, but denying the pejorative nature of the act. According to Scott and Lyman, accounts are accepted (honoured) because they are appropriate in certain situations where they match common 'background expectancies'. These expectancies refer to sets of 'taken-for-granted ideas that permit the interactants to interpret remarks as accounts in the first place'.[62] Consequently, accounting situations can be regarded as contexts in which people bargain over behaviour by attempting to get different sorts of motivational descriptions to fit their untoward behaviour and that of others. It follows that one major task of the sociology of motivation must be to understand the nature of interrogations and confessions which are salient features of conversations where imputations are being made about 'bad character'.

In presenting observations on recent treatments of motives, it may be appropriate to start with general criticisms before turning to more specific issues about imputing motives for murder. First, the notion of 'background expectancies' in Scott and Lyman is largely unanalysed and far too primitive theoretically to do the work asked of it. Since the 'honouring of an account' and 'background expectancies' are equivalent, the explanation of why any particular account is accepted tends to be circular. The only real clue which suggests the existence of common expectancies is the fact that an account has been accepted. Thus, the notion of 'to honour an account' is too simple and we need to start by making some elementary distinctions between different ways of accepting an account. An account may be accepted by an interrogator because it is thought to be real, sincere and appropriate; this seems to be the situation discussed by Scott and Lyman. Alternatively, an account may be pragmatically accepted (rather than 'honoured') because (1) it does not really matter to an interrogator whether the account is altogether reliable; (2) the cost of challenging an account is not worth the possible embarrassment or social upset which might follow; or (3) a person may have no choice in presenting an account. Where an account is forced from a person by processes of brainwashing, by the use of drugs or by some other forceful method, 'background expectancies' and 'taken-for-granted ideas' may be at a minimum.[63] The various ways in which a vocabulary of motives may be shared by social actors is certainly far more problematic than is sometimes suggested in sociological discussion of accounts and motives.[64]

Second, most typologies of accounts, including Scott and Lyman's, are incomplete since they often ignore an account-type which is crucial to the whole process of criminal convictions, namely confessions. Unlike excuses and justifications, a confession involves, at least in principle, a social actor accepting full responsibility for untoward behaviour *and* accepting the pejorative implications associated with it. It may be that sociologists have largely ignored confessions because they have been more concerned with the strategies by which people neutralise responsibility than with the ways in which suspects are brought to an acceptance of it.[65]

More importantly, much recent analysis of motives as features of social interaction implies that an account must be some form of direct communication, whether verbal or non-verbal; unfortunately, the significance of silence (refusal to provide an account) in contexts where an actor is requested to give an explanation of himself has been generally neglected. The decision which faces a suspect whether to make a general confession or appeal to legal rights of silence is an important one. As K.H. Basso points out any 'adequate ethnography of communication' (and by extension of any adequate sociology of motives) must take into account the fact that for an outsider entering 'an alien society, a knowledge of when *not* to speak may be as basic to the production of culturally acceptable behaviour as a knowledge of what to say'.[66] Of course, since murder is typically domestic, involving offenders with no previous history of major crime, the accused is a person entering the alien, culturally distant world of the police station.

The issue of the choice between silence or confession illustrates a range of difficulties in the legal process which it is worth considering in more detail. The legal tradition has been highly ambiguous (if not contradictory) in its interpretation of silence so that an accused may not have any clear rules of procedure for specifying the conditions of appropriate silence. The traditional position in English law has been that an innocent man has nothing to tell and, therefore, silence is compatible with innocence. The Criminal Law Revision Committee, however, has argued for the opposite interpretation – an innocent man has nothing to hide and will proclaim his innocence to the public. Silence would consequently be evidence of guilt. In the Committee's view, the present 'right of silence' is 'contrary to common sense' and 'gives an unnecessary advantage to the guilty' without helping the innocent.[67] The problem of this appeal to 'common sense' (apart from the fact that there may well be different types of common-sense knowledge) is that, although we have a *legal* right to silence, we all feel a *social* duty to speak. One of the basic rules of conversational practice is that silence will be typically interpreted as a form of rudeness. The conflict between these legal rights and norms of conversation was illustrated recently in a study of draft protestors in the United States by John Griffiths and Richard Ayres, who noted three different reasons why draft protestors felt bound to make some statement to FBI agents despite their partial awareness that they were not legally required to answer questions.[68] First, since the protestors did not have a comprehensive knowledge of their legal position, they were not able to make a rational, informed choice between remaining silent or making a statement. Because of this ignorance of the law, suspects tended to redefine the legal confrontation as a moral situation: they felt obliged to show FBI agents that their protest was morally valid. Second, although these suspects were of equal or higher social status than their interrogators, they were nervous in the interview situation when faced by a person in authority. Engaging in a moral justification of their protest probably helped to ease what was for them a tense situation. Finally, in every-day conversation when we are spoken to, we are expected to reply; these every-day expectations were carried over by suspects into the context of formal interrogation. For suspects, the interview by FBI agents was a *social*, not a *legal* encounter. Thus the protestors were not able to isolate in social interaction the legal right of silence from the social expectation to hold a conversation and the agents did nothing to indicate that anything other than an every-day encounter was taking place.

Conclusion

Although contemporary theories of accounts and motives are clearly important for future criminological theory and research, the notion of 'accounts' needs considerable refinement and elaboration. In particular, the view that accounts are accepted because two social actors (suspect and interrogator) share common, assumed expectancies is over-simplified. Confessions and other admissions of guilt to the police or other legal personnel may be accepted without any sharing of important assumptions. The interview context, the status of police and the methods of questioning, backed by the paraphernalia of modern psychiatry, conspire to induce an account in such a way that it will match the dominant theories of the legal *status quo*. The same account, however, may be interpreted in entirely different ways (as every-day conversation or as a legal statement) by suspect and interrogator despite the fact that the account is, at least in some respects, mutually acceptable. There are many reasons why we give accounts, many types of accounts and many conditions on which they are accepted. While these problems can only be approached by careful sociological interpretation of the actual process of conversations within specific social contexts, we have also argued that any vocabulary of motives (in our case, motives for murder) must also be located within their wider historical and social setting; they must also be understood as ideologies, full of ambiguity and contradiction, which have complex social histories.

To understand the motives which may be allocated to a murder in the course of constructing a confession, we must examine the history of murder as a social phenomenon, the history of confessions and the development of ideologies whose main terms involve notions of guilt and redemption. The peculiar problem which we have attempted to isolate is the fact that quasi-religious ideologies of personal guilt persist in the legal tradition while the actual practice of confessing is much more closely tied to the secular sciences of forensic medicine, psychiatry and experimental psychology.

Chapter 7
Confession, guilt and responsibility

Confessing to murder

It is generally recognised in Britain that murder has three characteristics. First, it is comparatively rare; second, there is a high detection rate; and finally, and most important, the motives of the majority of murderers – vanity, lust, jealousy, greed, hatred, revenge and fear – are sharper versions of recognisable every-day experiences and as such not too difficult to understand. Enthusiastic followers of murder trials often assert that most killings 'have domestic qualities which form the basis of popular interest' since ordinary people 'can identify with the circumstances which lead to the possibility of murder'.[1] This common assumption has for centuries been linked with the horror and outrage we also associate with 'the ultimate deviancy of murder'. The appeal of true crime stories, according to Wilson, lies in the fact that[2]

> you and I can read them with a certain horror that springs from identification with the murderer. . . as we read of William Corder going to such desperate lengths to untangle himself from Maria Marten we experience the same horrified fascination, glad not to be in his shoes.

Even when a 'repetitive' murderer oversteps the boundaries of enormity and is apparently responsible for several untimely deaths the motive itself may not be considered especially outlandish. Thus in the case of Mary Ann Cotton, who was suspected of at least 14 or 15 untimely deaths and was hanged at Durham Prison in March 1873, for the murder of her stepson, the broadsheet which celebrates her 'Trial, Sentence, and Condemnation' typically allots only a couple of lines to the alleged immediate motive (the 'money the burial clubs paid'):[3]

> The West Auckland Poisoner at last has been tried
> That she is guilty cannot be denied,
> Her crimes have struck terror all over the land,
> And deep indignation on every hand.
> No feelings of pity was in her hard heart,

> She never has acted a good woman's part;
> With dark deeds of murder she perill'd her soul,
> And her children destroyed for possession of gold.

Domestic murder, by which we mean violence which has no explicit political motive, is therefore at once unspeakable and banal. Like other forms of civilian violence with which it is often closely allied,[4] murder is not infrequently the outcome of tensions and temptations which are built into the fabric of every-day life. In industrial societies generally it is a well-documented fact that[5]

> Nearly half of all known murders. . . are committed by friends and close relatives of the victim. The culprit is there on the spot, often the only and self-confessed suspect. He may indeed ring the police himself, or act as his own executioner.

In England and Wales the studies, sponsored by the Home Office, of deaths recorded by the police as murder have concluded that the pattern has remained relatively unchanged during the past two decades when the majority of victims 'were closely associated with the suspects and were killed for personal or emotional reasons, especially rage, quarrels and jealousy', and the same is true for Scotland.[6] In addition, the long-standing debate about the merits of capital punishment also confirms that the causes of murder are constitutive of ordinary domestic relations. In the wake of these facts and other studies of interpersonal violence[7] our use of the term 'domesticity' is not restricted simply to intimate relations between family members but embraces the wider notion of private citizenship and 'civil society'. We are referring to those areas of private life covered by the family, school, church and so on: areas which are in varying degrees separated from 'public' life but which are not completely independent or obvious of the existing social and political set-up. It is in this context that confession becomes an important bridge between the generalised hostile reaction which news of a murder is expected to provoke and the particular willingness to accept that even outside the protection of the rules of war the taking of human life may well be 'understandable' and consequently forgiveable.

Confession is normally considered to be a private act of contrition for wrong-doing during the course of which an individual accepts responsibility for his offence and reveals that he has, like other men, a conscience and shares with them an essentially moral status. One of England's most famous hangmen, James Berry, who retired prematurely in 1892, recorded his practice of approaching 'in a kindly manner' those few prisoners who had not confessed to urge them 'to confess the justice of the sentence in order that I may feel sure that I am not hanging an innocent person'.[8] In common with the masters he served his motives were undoubtedly mixed but his method of persuasion was entirely religious. After measuring a condemned man, we are told, he would hand him a piece of paper containing the following lines:[9]

My brother – sit and think,
While yet on earth some hours are left to thee;
Kneel to thy God, who does not from thee shrink,
And lay thy sins on Christ, who died for thee.

He rests His wounded hand
With loving-kindness on thy sin-stained brow
And says, 'Here at thy side I ready stand
To make thy scarlet sins as white as snow.

I did not shed My blood
For sinless angels good and pure and true;
For hopeless sinners flowed that crimson blood,
My heart's blood ran for you, My son, for you.

Though thou has grieved me sore,
My arms of mercy still are open wide,
I still hold open Heaven's shining door.
Come, then, take refuge in My wounded side.

Men shun thee – but not I.
Come close to Me, I love My erring sheep.
My blood can cleanse thy sins of blackest dye.
I understand, if thou can'st only weep.'

Words fail thee – never mind.
The Saviour can read e'en a sigh, a tear;
I came, sin-stricken hearts to heal and bind
And died to save thee; to My heart thou'rt dear,

Come now: the time is short.
Longing to pardon and to bless I wait.
Look up to Me, My sheep so dearly bought,
And say, 'Forgive me ere it is too late'.

Thus Berry who described himself as the last link in the 'chain of legal retribution' considered that confession was an important stage in the process of restoring the essential humanity of the malefactor for whom he believed Christ had died. 'I am at liberty to state', he proudly wrote, 'That of all the people I have executed, only two or three have died without fully and freely confessing their guilt.'[10] In his eyes the confession transformed the guilty criminal into the penitent human soul and acceptable fellow member of the human race.

In the Christian tradition 'conscience' has a pervasive juridical connotation as in 'the Court of Conscience' where the guilty self is exposed to an interior prosecution.[11] A confession came to mean speaking fully (*confateri*) about the trial of the self via the interrogation of conscience. A basic definition of religious confession refers to 'accusing ourselves of our sins to a priest who has received authority to give absolution'.[12] This religious view of confession is close to both professional psychological analysis of confession and the every-day usage. Psychologists have treated confession as a typical response to any transgression of group rules where an internalised sense of guilt drives the individual to self-criticism. While as we have seen some aspect of this religious view of confession finds its way into the legal tradition, confession within the court has a more specific meaning. As Radzinowicz has pointed out, a criminal's confession helps to legitimate both the judicial system (i.e. the rule of law) and the penal system; and in the case of the death penalty, to absolve authority from guilt.[13] Other writers have argued that confessions have an important part to play in a murder trial because it is an awesome ritual of sacrifice and not a search for justice. 'Authorities use such trials to make us believe that social disorder does not lie in faults in our relationship as superiors and inferiors, but in the evil machinations of some dark villain who threatens us all.'[14] It is, however, also possible to argue that the formula of confession both in law and religion serves certain important functions for the individual and is not simply in all cases the outcome of crude external pressures. It seems clear that confession is a socially constructed means of celebrating the value for the individual and society of sincerity and honesty. In other words, the symbolic and functional necessity of values which are in opposition to lying and deceit.

It is because of this that the English law has for several centuries insisted upon voluntariness, disinterest and spontaneity as hallmarks of a valid confession. As it stands this law is enshrined in R. v. Warickshall (168 E. R. 234) which clearly stated the reliability principle:

> A free and voluntary confession is deserving of the highest credit, because it is presumed to flow from the strongest sense of guilt and therefore it is admitted as proof of the crime to which it refers; but a confession forced from the mind by the flattery of hope, or by the torture of fear comes in so questionable a shape when it is to be considered as the evidence of guilt, that no credit ought to be given to it; and therefore it is rejected.

In a historical context where for centuries the law has distinguished between justifiable and non-justifiable homicide confession is an important guide to the presence of criminal intent or 'the strongest sense of guilt' and it acknowledges the right of the individual to make admission or statements which are apparently against his or her own interests. But it must be added that the notion 'against one's own interests' is a legal abstraction which fails to take into account the particular nature of murder and its detection and the situation of the accused both when he or she comes to trial and after sentence. From a sociological point of view insufficient attention has been paid to the social processes through which suspect and interrogator come to perform the social activity of confessing. Confessions must be viewed not as pre-existing collections of facts but as accounts of criminal responsibility produced by participants in the interrogation process. Confessions are constructed not discovered. Our argument is therefore that although the process of making a confession takes place when the confessant is undeniably under some form of pressure and the confession so obtained validates legal authority, it also reflects an ethical system that is not reducible to the immediate interests of the participants. The legal system can thus be said to possess a relative autonomy from the particular interests of the parties involved; an autonomy which owes much to the influence of religion.

For the early Church, confession was infrequent, public and voluntary. The existence of sins among the faithful was obviously problematic and the Church only grudgingly accepted the development of the confessional since it conflicted with the belief in the efficacy of baptism and with the belief in Christ as Redeemer. The history of religious confessions shifts from infrequent, voluntary public acts of contrition and absolution through to confession as regular, obligatory, secret and private. John McNeil, in his study of the cure of souls, wrote that while 'in the early period the offender was hesitantly admitted to one, possibly a second, act of penance, every Christian was now under obligation to come to penance not less than once a year.'[15] A priestly monopoly over the hearing of confessions was established as early as 1216 when the Lateran Canon made confession a compulsory obligation and gave priests the sole right to hear confessions of their flock. To assist parish priests in this work, numerous penitential manuals were written for their guidance and new rulings had to be worked out to deal with anomalous situations. The period 1300 to 1600 became the great age of summa for confessors in which a clerical elite formulated an encyclopedic version of moral conformity to ecclesiastical discipline. The canon of 1216 meant that a true confession had to be to someone in authority. The personal status of the priest was no longer regarded as important since it was his role within the Church which guaranteed the power of his absolution. The priest 'may even be immoral. But if he holds the keys of power he may forgive sins.'[16]

In the face of this institutional authority, an attitude of humility and contrition was expected of the confessant. The confession had to be 'bitter, speedy, complete and frequent.'[17] As the Church came to emphasise the importance of subjective guilt and the private motivation to contrition morality was no longer regarded simply as a set of external, objective laws and it was the internal conscience of the private individual which provided the psychological linkage with the requirements of external social order. Public adherence to orthodoxy was achieved by internalised, private guilt and by the methodological searching of conscience under the scrutiny of the priest. The mechanism for the maintenance of external social order was the internal 'court of conscience' and the institution for excommunication and social shame became subsidiary to 'a culture of guilt'.[18]

Confession and the fiduciary issue of indulgences therefore were social processes whereby the spiritually deviant could be symbolically restored to the community. Confession has, and retains, a ritual of inclusion which forms the counterpart to the rituals of exclusion, that is, anathematisation and excommunication. Thus, for example, in the medieval Celtic system, a murderer was punished by pilgrimage, by service in a Crusade or by service in a monastery which had the effect of removing the individual from the normal routines of family and social life in anticipation of his final restoration. During his pilgrimage the penitential murderer should like Cain be: 'a wanderer and fugitive upon the earth'. Furthermore indulgences were created to mitigate the harsh demands of penance.

The religious apparatus of sacraments, confession and pilgrimage provided the Church with a mechanism for dealing with the serious crime of murder in routine, manageable procedures which were uncomplicated by any particular concern with the motives of murder. The historian J. Bellamy pointed out that the only interest in motivation was shown by preachers who asserted that man's misdeeds sprang from spiritual frailty and native sin – pride, vanity, greed, lust, idleness and trickery – rather than the pressure of external events. For the clergy 'crime was a natural consequence of man's original fall from grace'. In this cultural climate it was possible for people to commit serious criminal offences when the opportunity arose and then to revert back to conventional life.[19] Provision for return or social inclusion which is embedded in the sacrament of penance has its counterpart in the common law of early England. Once a murder had been committed relatives and friends might take immediate revengeful action but there were many circumstances when this was not considered appropriate. Institutions of outlawry, sanctuary and later the King's pardon insured that many murderers remained alive. There were, as Joel Samaha illustrated for Elizabethan Essex, several reasons why offenders could escape the gallows. Those who were accused might go free if a pardon had been bought, if they were pregnant, lunatic or subject to benefit of clergy. In addition, even in an age increasingly concerned with law and order, many victims did not resort to the system of criminal justice to redress a wrong; those who reported crimes and named offenders often came under enormous pressure from neighbours and when a prosecution actually ensued it was possible to engage in plea-bargaining which could reduce a charge and did not exclude crimes of violence and murder. During Elizabeth's reign 640 people, many of whom were not hanged, were sentenced to death and the number of suspects winding up at the end of a rope averaged 14 for each year. The majority of these had not been found guilty of murder.[20]

The traditional view, expressed in a pamphlet on the death of Sir Thomas Overbury in 1613, that: 'murder is wide-mouthed' and 'will not let God rest till he grant revenge'[21] can be seen as a general condemnation of domestic murder and a reflection of the view that murderers were not a special order of humanity motivated by unusual desires. The process of confession has, throughout the history of this crime, enabled detected murderers to reveal they were subject to the human errors and weaknesses which beset all men:[22]

> My dear mother,
> I am now in the condemned cell, and must die for the murder of a good neighbour, and kind friend Mr Blackmore, I coveted his money, I did not intend to kill him, but you know I was going to get married and wanted to exalt myself above my station, but now

> wretch that I am, what disgrace my pride has brought me to, what anguish do I now feel, what disgrace upon my family, what sorrow to you my aged widowed mother, God help you, you taught me what was right, but I didn't hearken to it, for I took to gambling and drink, which ruined me, I murdered Mr Blackmore, I am told I am to die next Friday, I hope the Lord will have mercy on my soul, I had none on Mr Blackmore, give my love to all my friends and brother who I hope will forgive me, I am your wretched son George Sparkes, The Condemned Cell, 25 March 1853.

There is no evidence in this confession, which is formulated according to the traditional conventions of street literature, to support the view that George Sparkes was regarded as anything but an ordinary man who recognised he had gone astray and was consequently anxious to make amends. His last public appearance was in the 'normal' role of repentant sinner. Had he persistently *refused* to confess the story might well have been somewhat different since it was unwillingness to confess and not the actual trial or execution of the offender which represented the final stage in his degradation and social exclusion.

Confessions were not of great interest to the authorities and to the wider public by which they were avidly consumed because they illuminated the dark corners of an alien criminal mind but precisely because they were acts of communication which confirmed the existence of a shared ethical view and a common human nature. Before the development of forensic psychiatry and psychoanalysis confessions were not expected to provide a detailed guide to a convoluted and disturbed inner life but to celebrate the sanctity of an ordered domestic life and to warn others against possible sources of disruption. An examination of confessions in cheap books, broadsheets, and newspapers and other published accounts of murder trials shows that, at least until the later years of the last century, they follow a basic descriptive formula which (a) provides often lurid details of the offence, (b) makes appropriate expressions of horror and revulsion and (c) invites the reader to dwell on the unhappy plight of the convict who is overtaken by remorse. Thus in 1879 artistic representations of 'The Dream of Kate Webster' on 'The Night Before The Execution' show her lying in tormented sleep, her hands clasped, jaw tensed, as the ghastly images of the murder she committed pass before her tightly closed eyes. Beside her bed is the figure of a nun who prays over an open Bible and a crucifix in anticipation of ultimate 'Mercy' and redemption.[23]

To be acceptable a confession had to be couched in conventional terms of remorse which included the admission of guilt, the acceptance of punishment and the 'Hope of Heaven'. All the available evidence indicates that the formula which governed the lucrative creation and publication of dying confessions was itself a reflection of the actual practice of eliciting these final words during or at the close of a successful prosecution. The fact that a minority of those who were hanged went submissively to the gallows with a consistent denial on their lips and that some stoutly resisted or threw down abuse from the scaffold on their captors and the Christian faith only confirms the general rule. The abolition of public executions in 1868 and the final abolition of capital punishment in 1969 are, of course, milestones in our penal history and as such complicate the picture but neither of these major events has disposed once and for all of the personal need to confess or of the identity change a confession can produce. To recognise also that confessions are often made by interested parties to skilled and powerful agents of control is not to negate the dependence of law on minimal consensual values which certain crimes violate. In his recent study of the activities of the Ordinary of Newgate, Linebaugh has shown how successive incumbents in the eighteenth century used their position to extract confessions from those who were eventually hanged. Amidst the wretched and debilitating conditions of Newgate their duties were to: 'read prayers, preach and instruct the prisoners' and in particular to prepare those who were condemned to death for the life beyond the grave. The popular demand for dying confessions often stimulated the Christian zeal of the Ordinary who sold the words he had extracted to the publishers. Linebaugh writes:

> The Ordinary was probably expert at the manipulations made possible by this situation – denying the sacrament to some, interrupting the feverish rest of others, or messing about with what they wanted the world to remember them by in their 'last words'.

In most cases, he seems to have found something to report though there were some men and women who refused to make even a private confession.[24]

Until the abolition of public executions in 1868, the offender not only died dramatically and often slowly before a large audience whose motives for attendance were mixed,[25] but often made a public confession which was presented according to a time-honoured formula which at least gave him an opportunity to acknowledge technical responsibility and sense of guilt. Offenders who refused to participate in this process were often seen as thoroughly degraded beings, and as such totally divorced from the rest of the community. A typical response occurs in the following account of the trial and execution of George Chennel and his servant for the murder of Chennel's father and the housekeeper in 1817.

> The execution of these atrocious murderers took place, according to their sentence. . . and it was thought due to public justice and public feeling, that the neighbourhood which had been alarmed and horror-struck at the atrocity of their crime, should likewise witness their punishment, and hear their confession, if disposed to make any.

The Newgate Calendar recalls that the two prisoners were at first unwilling to make a confession and were:

> determined to persist in their denial of guilt, and resolved rather to take the chance of pardon for unconfessed crimes in another world, of which they had no habitual or vivid impressions, than to brave the horrors of their fellow men in this by admitting the monstrous atrocity of their crimes.

Both Chennel and Chalcraft were earnestly exhorted by the Ordinary of Guildford gaol and the Ordinary of Horsemonger Lane gaol to make a full disclosure of the crimes they had committed against society yet although attentive to prayers and Scripture, the men consistently refused to confess. The whole of Chennel's behaviour was described as that of a man: 'completely besotted in his intellect or hardened in his crimes, dead to any feelings of remorse, incapable of any spiritual reflection, and insensible to any thing but visible objects.' Their bodies were hanged for an hour at Godalming and were then cut down and given to two surgeons for dissection, and later exposure to the gaze of thousands who 'throughout the day eagerly rushed in to see them'.[26]

This trial illustrates the general principle that only those murderers who refused to confess were ultimately regarded as the most hardened criminals. The absence of signs of repentance or regret were read as a final indication of a hard-hearted irresponsibility. No matter how short, a confession served to demonstrate that the condemned person was now fully sensible to the burden of guilt which could be lifted from his shoulders by appropriate expressions of remorse. By means of the time-honoured formula the offender confirmed the popular view of murder – that the motives of a person who kills another in civilian life were understandable and forgiveable provided they were accompanied by evidence of the burden of guilt which must at some time be shared.

Before the last century the view was, therefore, that confession was a piece of voluntary evidence which also demonstrated the normality of the offender. This view has persisted until the present day although throughout the nineteenth century certain elaborations followed on a number of important changes. First, the growth of prisons and asylums which meant that a private world was created in which offenders could be executed and excluded from the public gaze. Second, the growth of scientific criminology and in particular psychology and psychiatry which created a group of secular experts with a professional interest in scrutinising confessions for signs of abnormality ('moral insanity'). Thus, for example, the McNaghten Rules of 1843 established an intellectual test for insanity which further institutionalised and routinised the scrutiny of confessions and other statements by prisoners for signs of impaired mental health.[27] The growth of this expertise represents a secularisation of previous explanations of abnormality. Third, the development of an organised police force and the gradual emergence of scientific detection. Fourth, the growth of more sophisticated techniques of interrogation. Fifth, legal reforms which made it possible for the accused to take an even more active role in the trial. Prior to the Criminal Evidence Act 1898 the accused was not allowed to act as a witness in his own defence. Sixth, the cultivation of the protection of privacy on a wider scale than ever before. The private life emerged as a highly valued cultural prize and it was necessary to develop some means of communication which bridged the new distances separating various sections of the population. In this context court proceedings and the role of the accused and other participants were made accessible by the press to the thousands who could not attend the actual proceedings. Whilst providing the basis for an extremely lucrative form of mass entertainment, lengthy descriptions of murder trials – especially those which were accompanied by a great furore – made it possible to explore the recorded evidence in the light of new theories of crime. While a murder could still be regarded as the dastardly result of greed, vanity, or unbridled passion, such motives were increasingly situated against a background of complex social and psychological pressures.[28]

These changes assisted the transition to a much more elaborate exploration of the social and psychological factors underlying criminal behaviour. With modernisation came the tendency for religion and law to drift apart in institutional and ideological terms. Nevertheless, religious personnel have continued to play a major role in the legal system and despite the massive changes outlined above confessions still continue to draw on a religious vocabulary as Rod Watson's analysis of contemporary confessional practice shows.[29]

In summary, institutionalised confessional practices serve three important functions: (a) confession is part of the apparatus of state control; responsibility for detected murders can be located and exemplary punishment handed out; (b) symbolically it is part of our cultural heritage which enables society to repair certain deviant acts; (c) it also offers the individual offender an opportunity for moral regeneration in the sense that having violated one of society's most sacred norms, he is provided with a means of reconciliation. That confession is part of society's ideological apparatus does not exclude the fact that it may be an authentic experience for the individual. Following Lemert's analysis of paranoia and social exclusion,[30] we suggest the process of confessing may involve interaction which provides necessary affirmation of a person's being in the world, defined as his ultimate acceptability as a moral agent. Confessions are socially constructed and institutionalised but they are also a process of self-confirmation; thus in what has often been described as a brutal legal process (i.e. condemnation and execution) the law paradoxically provides for the ultimate inclusion of the labelled deviant in the wider community.

Confession is therefore inherently contradictory. Although the Eleventh Report of the Criminal Law Revision Committee on general evidence[31] has provoked considerable criticism inside and outside the legal profession, there has been very little discussion of paragraphs 53-69: 'Confessions'. These paragraphs summarise the contemporary legal status of criminal confessions, defined as any statement wholly or partly adverse to an accused person. Traditionally, a confession to be valid, i.e. interpreted in a court of law as evidence of responsibility for a crime, must be made to 'a person in authority'.[32] Commensurate with the general aim of the Committee to modify 'rules which have ceased to be appropriate to modern conditions' where it was felt that the emergent sophistication of modern criminal classes rendered the police task of winning the war against crime increasingly arduous, the Committee focused on the criteria defining confessions as reliable evidence. The problem is to get confessions efficiently, while preserving traditional legal safeguards. By concentrating on these pragmatic tasks, the Committee failed to examine the crucial interdependence between the status of the confession as evidence and the actual process by which that confession is produced.

From a sociological, as distinct from a legal perspective, confessions must be viewed not as pre-existing collections of facts to which the legal labels 'admissible' or 'inadmissible' can be unambiguously attached once they are brought to light during an interrogation.[33] They are accounts of criminal responsibility produced by participants in the interrogation process to be offered as evidence for the prosecution.[34]

Thus, any meaning a confession may have rests upon its communicative significance as the outcome of specific interactions between the suspect and his interrogators and this communication work must be produced to fit into existing legal frameworks.

Upholding the traditional view that valid confessions are essentially voluntary (otherwise they are suspiciously regarded as the outcome of 'the flattery of hope', 'the fortune of fear' or, since 1964, 'oppression') the Committee explored the relationship between the reliability principle (truth) of a confession and the procedures by which that confession is obtained (disciplinary principle). Accordingly, in the Draft Bill to 'amend and, in part, restate the law of evidence in relation to criminal proceedings', the Committee recommended that in future a confession by the accused may constitute admissible evidence unless ambiguously obtained 'in consequence of any threat or inducement of a sort likely, *in the circumstances existing at the time*, to render unreliable any confession which might be made by the accused in consequence thereof' (emphasis added). In short, while the Committee occasionally asserted that the new recommendations would not disfavour the accused, there can be little doubt that these proposals are more responsive to their explicit concern with modifying the rules of evidence in favour of the prosecution. The over-all effect is to extend the range of communications which would be legally recognised as confessions and to augment the flow of confessions into the courts.

Fundamentally, as far as the accused is concerned, a dangerous ambiguity prejudical to the concept of the confession as truth ('what a person says against himself is likely to be true') remains:

> The majority consider that the right course is for the rules as to inadmissibility of a confession on account of a threat or inducement to be limited to threats and inducements of a kind *to produce an unreliable confession*, but for inadmissibility on account of oppression to remain [emphasis added].

Conveniently, oppression is a concept embracing any sort of procedure perceived as undermining the free will of the accused.

Underpinning the Committee's pragmatic brief is an uncritical acceptance of a commonsense view of confessions, which is founded ultimately upon the Christian tradition.[35] The Committee, as a body of lawyers, examined the question of confession in a narrow legal framework, without paying sufficient attention to the social contexts and processes by which the confessant (suspect) and the confessor (police interrogator) come to perform a social activity, namely confessing. The connection between legal and religious concepts is well known and applies no less to the confession. In Christian theology, the true confession occurs when an individual without compulsion or inducement disinterestedly confesses all his sins before 'a person in authority' (a priest). This ideal type stresses the spontaneity of the unpractised confession, but manuals on confessions and the training of priests recognise that the believer must be taught how to confess, what to confess and when. The Church induces confessions by its beliefs, rituals and institutions. The aim of the confession seeks to break the sinner.[36] Confessing, therefore, is a skill acquired by the mature, practised Christian, brought to an awareness of his need to confess by exposure to suggestions of guilt. In its view of confession, the law shares with religion a number of assumptions, laying emphasis on the untrained confession (arising out of a burden of guilt) and the view that confessions are true in so far as they are voluntary and independent of 'oppression' or bargain.

In attempting to locate criminal responsibility and criminal intent, the Committee fell back on the confession as emerging necessarily from what has been called 'the strongest sense of guilt'. At the same time, tribute was paid to the importance of creating appropriate conditions through, for example, modifying the rules of evidence by which confessions may be produced in court. Noticeably, the Committee felt that the definition of the 'person in authority' should not be extended to incorporate a wider audience, thereby recommending the abandonment of the current legal restriction. Thus, there was a recognition that the factors which lead people to confess are numerous: the confession involves a search for motives which will be accepted as appropriate by judge and jury. Part of this quest is embodied in the interrogation process which is a produce of learned skills, forming an essential feature of police training.

Confessions assume their strategic importance in the war against crime because factual evidence linking a suspect to an offence is frequently inadequate. It is hardly surprising, therefore, that the law cannot content itself with allowing the 'strongest sense of guilt' to produce unaided its desired effect. A more realistic note was struck by the murderer Charles Avinain who, from the steps of the guillotine, advised: 'Never confess'.

Lofland has recently suggested that the elaborate and long drawn out process of execution allowed the condemned to reassert their identity as normal men and women by the demonstration of courage and style. Precisely because their dying confessions and addresses from the scaffold followed the prescribed formulae which we have described earlier, they were able to reject labels of absolute deviance and identity, and to show that in most respects they were subject to the same temptations and possessed the same ultimate virtues as other men.

Accounts and labelling

If we turn to the sociology of accounts we find that none of the researchers in this field (Austin, Wright Mills, Scott and Lymann, Rotenberg) has explored the implications of confession as a special kind of account. An 'account' with regard to deviant action has two properties: (1) it is an explanation or justification of an untoward action in the past which is subsequently questioned; (2) as in the work of Matza and Sykes, it can be a technique for neutralising the capacity of certain rules to induce guilt when broken and thus to make possible present and future actions of deviance. Both these features are conventionally seen as ways of alleviating the burden of guilt and placing part or whole of the responsibility on others or on the force of circumstances. Thus in psychotherapy, psychiatry and sociology the chain of causation of a particular crime is elaborated, thereby mitigating the responsibility of the individual. In the laws relating to murder, it is also true, via distinctions between intentional and unintentional murder, that responsibility for an act can under certain circumstances be taken from the shoulders of the person who is technically responsible – thus by implication alleviating the subjective burden of guilt. Certain sociologists, however, have shown an appreciation of the subtle implications of these interactive processes between representatives of powerful social institutions of social control and individuals suspected of major crimes. Goffman, for example, has elaborated on the significance of apology for deviance and control in micro-interaction and its significance for wider institutions. In the cruder version of stigmatisation theory, following an infraction of the law, the individual is detected, brought to trial, punished and thus excluded, but the complete cycle may not stop at this point. The complete cycle of crime must include 'apprehension, trial and punishment, and return to society'.[37]

It is possible, as we stated at the beginning, to see confession as a special kind of self-stigmatisation during the course of which the confessant distances himself from his own actions, sits in judgment upon them, and in effect finds himself guilty. As Lewis has pointed out, conscience carries with it the notion of self-judgment.[38] Under what may be a painful self-examination the subject may feel tormented by guilt and consequently impelled to confess his deviance and seek forgiveness. Even when confession may not be disinterested, voluntary or spontaneous and in fact elicited, as Watson has shown, not through violence but through subtle conversational ploys, confessions illustrate that deviants are not necessarily locked for all time within the incomplete cycle of detection and punishment, and therefore within the deviant role. Rehabilitation may be a painful process and to regain acceptance it is usually necessary to apologise for the disruption which the deviant act has caused, and even more important, disown the deviant self. Confessions are thus a neglected form of apology which involves the individual separating himself into two parts: the part that is technically guilty of the offence and the part that disowns itself from guilt and swears allegiance to the norms which have been violated. Before the abolition of capital punishment and certainly before the abolition of public executions in 1868, confession had the power to restore the dignity of the offender even as he stood on that symbol of utter degradation – the gallows. If we look at the ideology of confessions in which the concepts of expiation, forgiveness and redemption play a central part, it is possible to accept the idea that many of those who were responsible for the implementation of this particular aspect of British penal policy rarely advocated the total and irreversible exclusion of the ordinary criminal. Even in the case of treason when the punishment was especially designed to horrify and thus deter, Bellamy has shown that considerable efforts were made to shift the condemned man from the role of traitor to that of penitent who was thus entitled to many of the rights of non-offenders (for example, the restoration of property and public sympathy). Confession, which has for centuries been a central feature in the prosecution of murder, thus indicates a religious and secular interest in restoring the offender's status as a fellow member of the human race. Confession therefore is a special mode of human communication specifically designed to bridge the gap between the convict and the community. Even when the crime is particularly horrifying the formal phraseology of the confession usually reflects these concerns.

Conclusion

In our view this can be taken to indicate that, as a special form of personal statement made in a particular institutional context, confession highlights the contradictory aspects of law as simultaneously a system of social inclusion and social exclusion. Further evidence for this claim can be taken from the differential reaction of the crowd at an execution, the reaction of the press and the willingness of the authorities to bring the full rigours of the law against only the minority of offenders who ultimately confess to evil intent. On the basis of highly selective evidence – as for instance drawn from the study of particular minority groups such as homosexuals – certain sociologists have concluded that a general theory of stigmatisation has relevance to all the social consequences of law enforcement. In other words, the process of stigmatisation or the successful imputation of a deviant identity is an integral feature of the legal process. What seems to be clear when historical data are taken into account is that the law is not always a 'degradation ceremony' which results in the permanent exclusion of the offender, and second, even those who are punished are not necessarily given deviant identities acceptable to all sections of the community. Vulgar labelling theory assumes the existence of a uniform public opinion which can somehow be formally manipulated by agents of social control and by the mass media. It is important to recognise that public reaction to the same crime, even a very serious crime, is mixed and changeable. Indeed the law may take steps to protect the offender from the negative effects of local opinion and public hostility, as in the celebrated case of William Palmer and 'trial by newspaper'.

Labelling theory has a very uncertain value as a predictive science of the consequences of public reaction to criminal and deviant behaviour. What is required is a more complicated approach which takes into account the significance of processes of self-labelling and the consequent intermeshing of subjective and cultural conceptions of innocence and guilt attached to particular crimes, such as murder. What is also needed is an approach which takes into account our relative ignorance of community reactions to law-breaking and of the extent to which the general public has a realistic understanding of the motives of crime which have been elaborated by criminologists since the middle of the nineteenth century.

If it is true that murder is relatively rare and that the detection rate is a fair measure of the amount of murder taking place in society, then it seems reasonable to argue that there is a relatively small number of people free in society nurturing guilty secrets of a homicidal nature. A recent example is obviously the so-called Yorkshire Ripper. If it is also the case that the majority of murderers cannot be classified as psychotic (seriously mentally disturbed) or, as what Camps calls 'repetitive murderers' who transcend the boundaries of enormity, then it does seem likely that this pattern of murder does reflect an ideology of guilt which has become established over the centuries. Guilt, of course, as Duster has argued, can take the form of guilt over the commission of an act regarded as reprehensible or immoral; guilt as a subjective feeling which may exist regardless of any actual act of wrongdoing or human error; and guilt as a formal pronouncement of culpability which is independent of the commission of an act or feelings of shame.[39] In this context where guilt has a number of different interpretations and the confession as evidence must usually be considered alongside other forms of evidence, confession reaffirms the complementarity of these processes by providing, at whatever point in the prosecution and disposal of the offender, a confirmatory indication of the validity of the set of social relations within which the offender is enmeshed. Thus the acknowledgment of a subjective sense of guilt is not simply functional or subordinate to the mighty workings of the legal system, but an important means of indicating the shared humanity upon which the justification of a whole way of life is based.

Conclusion
Oppression and confession

In the liberal history of ideas, truth is associated with political and social freedom, while error is connected with oppression and violence. In the history of Western society, therefore, the emerging individual conscience has to be protected from, on the one hand, the forces of irrationality and superstition, and, on the other, from various forms of political coercion which would silence that freedom of opinion which is the institutional framework of individuality. In the nineteenth century, these liberal assumptions were characteristic of political analysis, connecting writers like J.S. Mill and W.E.H. Lecky. For utilitarians, it was the dead weight of uneducated public opinion and conservative tradition which threatened to stifle the creative individuality of thought and the development of personal creativity. The extension of the political franchise promised to bring into the political process of parliamentary democracy the untutored voice of the political masses which would result inevitably in a deadening uniformity inimical to the free expression of the cultivated conscience. Mill's fears for liberty were greatly reinforced by the publication of de Tocqueville's *Democracy in America* in 1835 in which the dangers of democratic, mass uniformity were strongly articulated. Mill was subsequently prompted to make a comparison between the role of custom and tradition in Oriental Despotism and the political dangers of mass rule in Western society. The 'Chinese stationariness' which had squashed the growth of individualism in the Orient was now endangering the Occident through the institutionalisation of mass democracy. The only immediate solution was the recognition that good government could only be the province of 'the wisest, and these must always be the few'.[1]

The ambiguity of Mill's liberalism was that the growth of the individual conscience required the protection of wise, but firm, government and this requirement could not be maintained on the basis of universal equality. This liberal anxiety about the mob was connected with a series of other anxieties which Mill inherited from the classical utilitarianism of his father and Jeremy Bentham. While utilitarianism was founded on the principle of 'the greatest happiness of the greatest number', the main driving force of early liberalism was the fear of pain. Because privation was a constant threat, men in society required the protecting umbrella of sound laws and good government. In economic terms, utilitarian man was not so much motivated by the desire for profit, but by the fear of economic loss and financial catastrophe.[2] Furthermore, since these beneficial principles of utility were periodically brought into question by the criminal classes, the protection of individual liberties necessitated the existence of powerful custodial institutions. The point of Benthamite penology was to harness public opinion against the corrosive effects of criminality. Liberal fears thus found their architectural expression in Bentham's panopticon in which surveillance and discipline would guarantee moral improvement. Liberal fears produced a variety of illiberal mechanisms in politics and penology in the public sphere to safeguard the individual, liberal conscience in the private domain, but liberal thought remained blind to these contradictions. The threat to liberalism was external, not internal, and that threat was primarily one of irrationality as manifested in the mob, the criminal and the uneducated working class. This alliance between rationality and conscience was perhaps nowhere better illustrated than in the overtly confident argument of Lecky's *The Rise and Influence of Rationalism in Europe*, which appeared in 1865, the year which coincided with Mill's election to Westminster.

The rise of rationalism, for Lecky, was seen in terms of 'the struggle between the reason and the affections which leads to truth' and 'between the will and the desires which leads to virtue'.[3] The space separating reason and will from truth and virtue was haunted by the spectre of irrationality in the form of theological dogma, 'religious terrorism', miracles and witchcraft. The rise of rationalism involved the slow diminution of these dark forces before the triumphal passage of intellectual scepticism and tolerance. The progress of reason was marked by the decline of fear as the principal motive for duty, the disappearance of dogmatic education and the 'supremacy of conscience'. In particular, this rational development was indicated by the disappearance of persecution, especially religious persecution, so that the history of witchcraft provided 'an index of the course of civilisation'.[4] Witchcraft held a particular fascination for Lecky. The presence of witchcraft in European society rested upon strongly held beliefs in supernatural agencies intervening in the life of men and upon a system of coercive institutions to produce witchcraft confessions. In short, witchcraft required dogma and terrorism. The witchcraft trial had a special repugnance for the liberal view of history and Lecky provided ample, graphic descriptions of the role of violence in the production of confession. The punishment inflicted on these ancient, feeble women by the civil and religious authorities was 'worthy of an oriental imagination'.[5] The repugnance of the inquisition in Lecky's moral framework is that it was designed to force the individual to speak the truth. In the liberal scheme, truth emerged, in principle, from the free struggle between reason and affections, from the unfettered play between mind and body. Of course, the knowledge produced by the forced confession was not recognisable knowledge at all, but merely superstition and illusion. Persecution did, however, result in the confirmation of existing prejudices and illusions by producing self-confessed evidence of diabolical possession and of supernatural intervention. The march of rationalism was only possible with the disappearance of dogmatic super-naturalism and of those repressive practices which constantly reaffirmed illusionary beliefs.

The sociological and historical analysis of confession in the twentieth century no longer shares the optimistic evolutionism of liberal history in which the development of reason is inevitable and continuous. For some writers, the persecutions, oppression and interrogations of the modern period now make the mentality of the inquisitor all too familiar. Thus, Trevor-Roper in *The European Witch-Craze of the 16th and 17th Centuries* observes that with[6]

> the recrudescence, even in civilized societies, of barbarous fantasies in no way less bizarre and far more murderous than the witch-craze, we have been forced to think again, and thinking, to devalue the power of mere thought.

The pogroms against the Jews of Eastern Europe confirmed the view that apparently secular societies were no longer free from millenarian thought and irrational social movements.[7] While these events dramatically demonstrated the presence of powerful mythologies, mass society theory pointed to the more subtle pressures of the 'techniques of persuasion' which became available with improvements in the technology of communication.[8] However, what these modern critics of society shared in common with nineteenth-century liberalism was the view that reason was itself somehow divorced from the history of oppression. The witch-craze of the seventeenth century and the pogroms of the twentieth were illustrations of human irrationality; the liberal equations of reason and truth, will and virtue were left unquestioned. Not only is the history of rationalism distinct from the history of myth and superstition, but scientific thought is separated from the routine application of coercive measures and repressive practices in society. An alternative view of the history of rational calculation and political control can be located in Max Weber's studies of reason and religion.

In the conventional interpretation of Weber's remarks on the relationship between Protestant asceticism and rational science, Protestant culture is seen as a temporary prop for the genesis of Western science.

Protestantism legitimated the initial burst of scientific inquiry by allowing rational man to discover a divine order within the natural world. However, once the process of scientific institutionalisation was established, science, like capitalism itself, no longer required such religious legitimation. The classic expression of this interpretation of the temporary alliance between science and religion was presented by Robert Merton in 1970.[9] To perceive Protestantism in this light is to forget, however, that Weber saw Protestant asceticism as grounded, not in supreme confidence in the orderliness of natural phenomena, but in an acute salvational anxiety in relation to an unknown and distant God. It was an irrational anxiety, not rational certainty, which constituted their world view. Both rational capitalism and systematic science have their origins in an irrational quest. As Tenbruck so ably argues,[10]

> The rational discipline of life from which capitalism sprang was not just helped along by religious sanctions, it was rather created by them. Its rationalism was not merely supported by irrational elements, it was rather created by them. Its rationalism was not merely supported by irrational elements, it was irrational in itself because incessant work, discipline and dedication with no regard to tangible gratifications cannot be logically derived from any ends which naturally come to man.

Just as disciplined labour in excess of immediate needs of sufficiency is not 'natural' to man, so the quest for abstract, scientific knowledge lies outside a concern for every-day utility. As Weber also made plain in 'science as a vocation', science itself can generate no principles or values by which scientific practices can be unambiguously legitimated. Science and capitalism give rise to a disenchanted world, while the spirit of rational calculation, basic to both capitalist enterprises and scientific endeavour, becomes the guiding principles of society as an 'iron cage'. All areas of life become subject to the endless process of rationalisation. The increasing bureaucratisation of public relationships was simply one obvious illustration of the penetration of formally rational norms of procedure which infected science, law, religion, politics and personal life. For Weber, it is the 'fate' of our times for men to be reduced to mere 'cogs in a machine' under the subordination of capitalist production requirements and rational calculability of tasks. For Weber, the rise of rationalism does not correspond to growing freedom and individualism, but, on the contrary, with increasing social control, uniformity and coercion.

Max Weber's characterisation of capitalist society is to some extent shared by the Frankfurt School and Critical Theory, but they reject what they take to be Weber's implicit equation of rationality as the technical calculation of efficient means to known ends with reason *per se*. The nub of their rejection of Weberian rationality is that, while technical rationality may be harnessed to the practical needs of an industrial civilisation, there is an alternative mode of rationality which is substantive, reflexive and necessarily critical of the repressive structures of capitalism. This perspective on the critical and self-reflective nature of reasoning has been most fully articulated in Jürgen Habermas's theory of communication and cognitive interests. Habermas identifies three knowledge-constitutive interests: the technical, practical and emancipatory.[11] The empirical-analytical sciences embrace a technical cognitive interest, the historical-hermeneutic disciplines incorporate a practical interest and the critical social sciences involve an emancipatory cognitive interest. These three interests correspond to the three fundamental dimensions of social life: work, interaction and power. The main thrust of this aspect of Habermas's argument is that the cognitive interest of the empirical-analytical sciences is not the exclusive criterion of rationally valid knowledge and that these three interests are distinct and autonomous. In the context of this conclusion, Habermas's discussion of the emancipatory interest and the conditions for realising critical dialogue is the more significant feature of his theory.

Habermas has criticised both Marx and Freud for illegitimately conflating empirical-analytical knowledge with the emancipatory critique. The problem for Habermas has been to tease out the critical theory which is embedded in the positivist conception of the mode of production in Marx's political economy and in the unconscious in Freud's psychoanalysis. By rejecting Hegel's idealism, Marx gave a one-sided emphasis to instrumental actions and to instrumental rationality. The result was that the cognitive interests relating to labour were given priority over those relating to language and symbolic communications. The critical aspects of Marx's philosophy were subordinated to the quest for an empirical-analytical science of modes of production. Similarly, with his training in conventional medicine and neuropsychology, Freud based his analysis of the 'talking cure' in psychoanalysis on neurology. However, a mechanical 'distribution model only creates the semblance that psychoanalytical statements are about measurable transformations of energy.'[12] Clinical results from psychoanalytical sessions are not comparable to observations in the controlled experiments of the natural sciences since the distinctive feature of therapy is not exact control but the intersubjectivity between analyst and patient. In order to recognise the emancipatory critique which is submerged in historical materialism and psychoanalysis, Habermas has argued that critical theory is a type of analysis of language which exhibits the restraints and distortions which are present in human communication.[13] For Habermas, the production of valid, critical knowledge can only take place in situations of open dialogue and free communication. The participants must be free to engage in unrestricted and, in principle, unlimited debate, because it is only in these circumstances that self-reflective and self-critical awareness can emerge. The emancipatory interest seeks to expose the social and political constraints which distort such communication and render knowledge invalid. The forced confession is thus, *par excellence*, an example of distorted communication. Any analysis of human knowledge must necessarily involve an analysis of the conditions under which knowledge is produced. Habermas thus rejects the conventional positivist distinctions between description and evaluation, fact and value, since any examination of knowledge must entail a critical evaluation of the constraints on knowledge. Valid knowledge presupposes the good society.

While Habermas has been able to provide instances of distorted communication in industrial, capitalist society, his examples of free dialogue are rare and unsatisfactory. It is clearly important for Habermas's argument to provide convincing cases of unrestrained, reflexive dialogue otherwise the realisation of critical knowledge remains utopian. One crucial instance which Habermas does provide is that of psychoanalytic communication in Freudian therapy. For Habermas, the analyst, through open dialogue, provides the conditions by which the patient can arrive at self-knowledge through reflection. There are a number of objections to this position. It can be argued that psychoanalytical therapy is effective, not for the reasons provided by Habermas, but as the result of 'a complex pattern of negative and positive reinforcement'.[14] If we could understand the conditioning process, we would obtain the results of therapy without recourse to open dialogue. A more powerful objection is that Freudian analysis provides, in practice, a particularly good illustration of distorted rather than open communication. There are major inequalities between analyst and analysand at the level of basic skills, education, knowledge, control and status. While the analyst assumes a relationship of friendship and trust, he must distrust the patient's initial communication which disguises the conflicts within the unconscious. The patient's resistance to painful self-disclosure must be broken. The patient has to provide a fee as a mark of respect and as an indication of willingness to achieve a cure. The fee points to an impersonality within the relationship which lies behind the overtly personal nature of the dialogue between professional analyst and amateur patient. The patterns and conditions of interaction between psychoanalyst and patient may thus fall far short of Habermas's criteria of open discourse. Furthermore, Freudianism may itself be part of a general ideology of sexually oppressive relationships in advanced capitalism.

There is, therefore, a curious parallel between the liberal view of the relationship between knowledge and freedom and that presented by Habermas in critical theory. Both liberals and critical theorists agree that the growth of rational understanding requires maximum freedom from social and political restraints. The existence of oppression and persecution in society is inimicable to the achievement of full, critical self-knowledge and to rational thought. Being forced to talk under conditions of oppression and torture is thus the exact reverse of the open dialogue of the free society. There are obvious differences between the two positions since Habermas does not believe that the triumphal march of empirical-analytical knowledge is to be equated with reason *in toto*. Habermas has been far more pessimistic than most liberals about the realisation of free dialogue, but, despite all their differences over questions of epistemology and philosophy, there remains a parallel between Popper's view of the Open Society and Habermas's notion of a community based on rational consensus. Popper's principal interest was the openness of the scientific community within which hypotheses could be refuted in a critical dialogue, but the scientific community was also a model for how an Open Society could be organised. In a similar fashion, the psychoanalytical dialogue provides Habermas with the clue to the discursive processes of the rational, critical society.

One general difficulty for any theory which wants to make a strong connection between freedom and knowledge is that it must assume that, as the result of voluntary, open discourse, some sort of rational consensus will emerge which is sufficiently broad to incorporate the great majority of the population. At one level, this is simply the problem of coping with systematic disagreements which may persist between parties to a critical dialogue. More fundamentally, there is the question of dealing with social groups, either inside or outside a given discursive community, who reject, or appear to reject, the institutionalisation of the conditions upon which discourse is founded. Do the conditions of free dialogue also embrace those social categories – madmen, criminals and terrorists – whose actions appear to question the basis of open discussion? The liberal dilemma is the selection of coercive measures to restrain the actions of those who threaten freedom. We have already discussed the response of utilitarian liberalism to those groups – criminals and the working class – which were thought to challenge liberty and individual creativity. In contemporary society, should the natural and social sciences be employed to constrain the behaviour of those deviant groups which in practice undermine the liberty of the majority? If, hypothetically, eugenics, sociobiology and criminology could be used to minimise the threat to free dialogue from certain classes, then open communication would actually require certain forms of constraint. This is not an idle question since this is precisely the justification for the state, the law and the police by which the existence of a repressive apparatus is necessary to protect the freedom of the majority against minorities. The issue is how to define 'minorities' and how to distinguish between lawful restraint and illegal oppression. Given the importance of obtaining confessions of guilt for serious crimes which threaten civil liberties, the problem of defining oppressive interrogation becomes central to the relationship between social order and individual freedom.

The writer who has most perceptively recognised the significance of the madman and the criminal as a question mark standing over the liberal history of reason is Michel Foucault. Against the liberal perspective, Foucault argues that the modern history of Western society is constituted by the 'will to knowledge' and this quest to know necessarily involves injustice and unhappiness. Power and knowledge can never be separated:[15]

> we should abandon the whole tradition that allows us to imagine that knowledge can exist only where the power relations are suspended and that knowledge can develop only outside its injunctions, its demands and its interests. . . . We should admit rather . . . that power and knowledge directly imply one another; that there is no power relation without the correlative constitution of a field of knowledge, nor any knowledge that does not presuppose and constitute at the same time power relations.

Repression in society is not solely a question of centralised, monolithic power; it has to be conceived in terms of a complexity of mechanisms which produce repression through the establishment of discourse, power and knowledge. Advances in knowledge are intimately bound up with the establishment of localised centres of power – the asylum, the prison, the clinic, the psychoanalytical couch, the school – through which the discourses of madness, penology, medicine, sexuality and pedagogy operate. The growth of rational, calculating knowledge is not separated from the growth of local, institutionalised power and the rise of rationalism is not to be seen as a long struggle against witchcraft and superstition, since 'modern rationalism and science have the same ignorable origins as the lunatic asylum.'[16]

Foucault rejects all teleological views of knowledge and its history, but treats each discourse as constituting its object of analysis at the point of its inception. In *Madness and Civilization*, for example, he argues that madness was not waiting to be discovered by psychiatry, since there was no uniform, unchanging phenomenon called 'madness' prior to psychiatric discourse. Madness is constituted by the arrival of scientific discourse and by a set of power relations which materialised in the asylum. Similarly, we cannot conceive of our society as liberated from repression and persecution, since repression is exercised through a variety of rational discourses which codify, categorise and order individuals. The liberal view which contrasts Victorian sexual repression with modern permissiveness is one illustration of this teleology which Foucault persistently questions. Our compulsion to confess our sexual life provides a useful illustration of this theme:[17]

> The obligation to confess is now relayed through so many different points, is so deeply ingrained in us, that we no longer perceive it as the effect of a power that constrains us; on the contrary, it seems to us that truth, lodged in our most secret nature, 'demands' only to surface; that if it fails to do so, this is because a constraint holds it in place, the violence of power weighs it down, and it can finally be articulated only at the price of a kind of liberation.

Since freely speaking is connected conventionally with truly speaking, we have grown blind to the subtle power of the discourses of sexuality which force us to endless self-disclosures.

While Foucault draws attention to the subtle, immanent power relations which are expressed through the 'need' to confess, liberal anxieties about confession have focused either on the use of physical brutality to obtain admissions of guilt or on the use of scientific techniques to induce confessions and changes of belief. Public reaction against the use of physical force by the police to obtain confessions from suspects has typically been unambiguously forceful; the reaction to the allegations of brutality against IRA suspects at Castlereagh would be one obvious illustration of this point.[18] There has also been consistent anxiety about the use of scientific techniques by foreign powers in the conditioning of alleged criminals or prisoners of war. In the literature on brainwashing, frequent attention has been drawn to the use of confinement and isolation to induce confessions from American soldiers in the Korean war.[19] A more difficult problem, at least from the point of view of liberal assumptions, is to draw a line between 'normal' police practices of questioning suspects and oppressive interrogation. In America, while street interrogations and arrests have been occasions for conflicts between the police and citizens, especially in ghetto areas,[20] the regular employment of interrogation tactics in the police station has been a more sensitive area of concern.[21]

In addition to the obvious suspicion that, with skilful interrogation, the innocent may be induced to make incriminating statements, it is difficult to determine at what stage 'oppressive questioning' undermines the criterion of voluntariness as the basis of legally admissible evidence. One illustration of this dilemma is the routine use of Inbau and Reid's classic manual on interrogation by the American police force.[22] This manual provides an account of the various psychological and interactional technics which create the optimum conditions by which confessions can be obtained. These technics include the management of the interactional setting, the manipulation of the suspect's sense of guilt and self-respect, and the control of the suspect's subjective view of the crime and the benefits of confession. These manipulations of the interrogation context are designed to create the feeling in the suspect that confession is personally and socially desirable. Under these social and psychological pressures, making an untrue confession may appear to the suspect as a solution to the interrogation process. As Irving and Hilgendorf argue,[23]

> social pressures can be brought to bear on him (the suspect) so that in extreme cases the immediate desire for social approval and self esteem may outweigh the longer term consequences of a false confession, and induce the suspect to construct an untrue statement.

However, while these 'abnormal' outcomes might cast some doubt on the use of these interrogational tactics in specific cases, there does, in principle, appear to be a contradiction between practice and the court's requirement that confessions have to be made voluntarily. On the basis of their empirical research and theoretical analysis, Irving and Hilgendorf conclude that there is no set of reliable criteria, either in theory or in practice, which will unambiguously give meaning to the notions of 'oppression' and 'voluntariness'. Nevertheless, these two principles are recognised as having some 'force as moral imperatives governing the limits of what is acceptable practice'.[24]

As we have argued throughout these studies on confession, the central question is not why people confess, but how they remain silent. Although there is a formal right for suspects to remain silent, there are good grounds for believing that, by the very nature of human language, it is difficult for any social actor to ignore questions, to refuse requests for information and to refrain from verbal interaction. The police interrogation, to some extent, obeys the normal rules of discourse in which, following the conventions of 'turn-taking', questions lead to answers which lead to questions.[25] There is built into language as a speech-exchange system a series of obligations to speak when we are spoken to, to avoid interruptions until our turn to speak arrives, to avoid speaking when others are speaking and so forth. There are a great variety of other informal expectations for completing conversations, ending stories and completing jokes. The skilled police interrogator employs these rules of discourse to get a suspect to start a 'story' which he is, by the rules of conventional conversations, 'obliged' to complete. Through these responses, the suspect may, largely unconsciously, provide a confession which has been offered voluntarily, but unwittingly. By starting a conversation at a topic which is apparently far removed from the circumstances of the offence, a skilled interrogator can, through a series of questions and answers, lead a suspect to making either a full confession or a variety of incriminating statements.

We can approach conversations as structured in terms of certain sequences of 'utterance pairs', of which 'question-answer' pairs are fundamental. It is possible that any suspect or conversationalist might be able to resist the various social and linguistic constraints which lead the social actor to provide answers to questions. However,[26]

> We would expect that a Q (question) followed either by silence or by talk not formulated as 'an answer' would provide the relevance and grounds for repetition of the Q, or some inference based on the absence of an answer.

Since the police interrogator is in charge of the interrogation (being able to decide upon its place, duration and repetition), refusals to answer questions can always be followed by further questions or by a return to the initial question at a later stage in the interview. More importantly, silence on the part of the suspect is likely to give rise to 'some inference', namely that the suspect is in fact guilty. While there is a legal right to silence, there is a common-sense assumption that an innocent person has nothing to hide. The innocent are expected to talk volubly and voluntarily.

Of course, suspects differ greatly in terms of their skill, experience and sophistication. One might expect that the criminal with experience of previous interrogations and some elementary knowledge of the criminal law would be more practised at covering up his guilt than an innocent suspect at expressing his innocence. There is evidence to suggest, however, criminals appearing at the Crown Courts who have previous criminal records were more likely to confess than criminals without a criminal record.[27] This evidence is, however, complicated by a number of factors. Where the weight of evidence against a criminal is sufficiently great, it may make little difference to the likely outcome of a trial whether or not a confession is secured. Furthermore, there are administrative reasons for obtaining confessions in the case of serious crimes, since guilty suspects who do not confess are also more likely to plead not guilty in court, thereby increasing the administrative demands on the prosecution. Willingness to confess may thus depend more on venue, administrative factors and nature of the offence rather than on the level of criminal sophistication.[28] It is, however, reasonable to assume that the sophisticated criminal is in a better position to make a realistic decision about the advantages and disadvantages of confession in affecting the outcome of the legal process than is the case for either inexperienced criminals or innocent suspects.

In the liberal interpretation of rationality, conscience and confession necessarily play an important part. The freedom of the internal conscience to guide personal actions through the prompting of guilt found its structural requirements in political and social freedom. The struggle between desire and reason, affections and virtue within the individual conscience was the private counterpart to the wider struggle between civilisation and barbarism, between political liberalism and persecution. In the history of punishment, the great virtue of confession, to the liberal mind, was that it was a substitute for legal retribution. Intention and confession, in the moral economy of crime, could replace overt behaviour and physical punishment in a society free from oppression and ignorance. Unfortunately, solutions have to be found to cope with those social groups whose actions appear to threaten the safety and liberty of the majority. The principal solution was in fact administration, that is, the rational organisation of a police force, prison system, educational institutions and the hospital with the aim of reforming, educating and disciplining the deviant, the child and the sick. In the philosophy of Weber and Foucault, the application of rational, calculating science to 'social problems' produces the administered society and the iron cage. The relationship between police science and law provides an illustration of this paradox. While in the liberal view the right to silence may be as important as freedom of speech, the application of scientific procedures to police interrogation practices makes the exercise of the right to silence highly problematic. The law puts restraints on the use of oppression to obtain confessions by formulated norms of admissible evidence so that 'true' confessions have to be voluntary, disinterested and spontaneous. However, the requirements of social order in a society which is perceived to be challenged by illegality puts pressure on law enforcement agencies to obtain admissions of guilt from suspects. The voluntary principle is threatened by oppressive questioning; disinterest, by plea bargains; spontaneity, by sophistication. In addition, there are important features of language itself which compel us to talk regardless of the presence of those central features of liberal psychology – conscience, will and moral sentiment. We are compelled to confess, not by those inner psychological mechanisms suggested by Theodor Reik, but by the very texture and structure of discourse.

Confession remains, however, a sociologically and culturally ambiguous phenomenon. It is certainly possible to treat confession as part of the apparatus of moral repression in Western society. The institutional origins of religious confession in Europe can be traced back to the political struggles of the Church against the Albigenses as part of a campaign to de-paganise the West. The history of confession is tied inextricably to the history of Inquisitions, witch-trials and political coercion. We have, however, attempted to argue that the full repressive potential of the law and state is rarely employed against criminals, deviants and minorities. The law can be seen, not simply as a coercive mechanism, but as a complex system of rituals of inclusion and exclusion. Within this set of rituals, confession was important in the achievement of legal convictions, but it also motivated judges to treat repentant criminals with some degree of mercy. It is clearly difficult to generalise here, since many confessed criminals went straight to the gallows. However, to treat the law as simply repression is to adopt a sociological position which is theoretically too convenient. The consequence is that sanctuary, pardon, mercy and confession are treated as merely subtle forms of repression. The fact is that both the law and social reaction to serious crimes are not invariably uniform in their condemnation of serious offences, especially where detection is followed by remorse and confession. This assertion is not seriously qualified by the recognition that many confessions, especially popular, published confessions, may be highly ritualised affairs. While the police force, both in America and Britain, has adopted scientific practices in acquiring confessions, the courts and legal ideology have retained a residual religious conception of the guilty man who needs to express his guilt in a public manner. Within a wider context than law, there is a widespread belief that confessing is therapeutic from the point of view of the individual and beneficial for society.[29] It has not, however, been our intention to unpack or to resolve these constitutive ambiguities by offering a simple theory to the effect that confession is either a coercive institution or a therapeutic activity. There are no particularly strong reasons against believing both.

In the psychological model of the 'normal' confession, it is the individual burden of guilt working on the conscience which prompts rather than compels the guilty to confess their transgressions of moral rules. The result is a catharsis for the individual character, analogous to Aristotle's theory of tragedy in relation to human emotions. Sociologists are not necessarily required to deny these psychological and common-sense views that talking, expressing emotions, 'getting it off our chest' and confessing have therapeutic consequences for the individual. What is of interest to sociology is that a confession has to be heard. Other parties have to be involved in the making of confessions since our secret, internal admissions of moral failing are, by definition, not confessions. The confession has to be a public declaration of guilt if it is to have its cathartic effects and there's the rub. The admission of guilt may have beneficial psychological consequences for the individual, but it also has a definite public utility for the state and the church. The institutionalisation of confession as a statement of guilt to a person in authority provides a regular flow of information about deviance, crime and heresy. If the thirteenth-century confessional was an important component of the church's moral custody over society, then the application of science to police interrogation practices is an important step in the 'war against crime'. The importance of confession has always been seen in terms of the linkage between the internal conscience and the external social order, since it offers the possibility of external supervision of the interior mentality. The realisation of this possibility by the agencies of social control has, however, created numerous technical difficulties. The institutionalisation of confession, the employment of forceful means and the development of scientific interrogation constantly bring into question the reliability of confessional statements by threatening the criteria of freedom and spontaneity. From the point of view of public order, confessions are desirable, but unreliable. It is for this reason that, in addition to confessions being voluntary, they have to be accompanied by relevant gestures of shame, remorse and self-criticism.

Although it is possible to accept a view of confession as simultaneously therapeutic and repressive, it is equally important to avoid the assumption of an 'oversocialised conception of man'. In sociology, it would be tempting to provide an explanation of social order in terms of the intersection between a compulsion to confess and the rituals of inclusion. The social world would then be maintained by an exchange of personal guilt for institutionalised pardon as a form of social indulgence. Such a world of social harmony is rendered problematic by the artful con and the moral recidivist. While there is a popular belief that confession is therapeutic, there has been, historically speaking, an equally widespread belief that a simple exchange between guilt and pardon is too permissive. The ethical world of liberalism also requires a principle of moral consistency. Thus[30]

> Although a man cannot claim that it is against his moral principles to be cowardly or mean if he regularly does cowardly or mean things, he can do such things occasionally and still justify this claim. His claim is justified if he is prepared to condemn his actions and if he feels remorse.

But can he go on condemning them indefinitely and still justify his claim? In the Protestant history of religion, there is a slippery slope from occasional confession to regular indulgence. Where the inner conscience appears to fail as an instrument of social control, it requires the support of stiffer external agencies – the state and the law – which in themselves are necessary evils. The interior freedom of conscience as the arena of confession thus requires the public supports of authority and social control. It is this ambiguous overlap between individual conscience and public constraint which constitutes the confession as a social institution and which marks its central sociological interest as a cultural practice.

References

Introduction

1 F. Beck and W. Godin, *Russian Purge and the Extraction of Confession*, London, 1951.

2 Robert J. Lifton, ' "Thought reform" of western civilians in Chinese communist prisons', *Psychiatry*, 1956, vol. 19, p. 173.

3 Edgar H. Schein, 'The Chinese indoctrination program for prisoners of war', *Psychiatry*, vol. 19, 1956, pp. 149-72; G. Winokur, ' "Brain washing" – a social phenomenon of our time', *Human Organization*, vol. 13, 1955, pp. 16-18.

4 William Sargant, *Battle for the Mind*, 1959; J.A.C. Brown, *Techniques of Persuasion*, Harmondsworth, 1963.

5 William Sargant, *The Unquiet Mind*, London, 1969, p. 150.

6 Spectrum, 'Electric shock therapist', *Sunday Times*, 22.2.76.

7 Peter Watson, 'The soldiers who became killers', *Sunday Times*, 8.9.74.

8 'The puzzling tale of Lt. Cdr. Narut', *Sunday Times*, 6.7.75.

9 *Ossett Observer*, 29.3.75.

10 Anthony Trollope, *Barchester Towers*, London, 1863, p. 342.

11 Nuttall's *Standard Dictionary*.

12 W. Addis and T. Arnold, *A Catholic Dictionary*, London, 1960, p. 207.

13 Chambers *Twentieth Century Dictionary*.

14 The exceptions include Emmanuel Le Roy Ladurie, *Montaillou*, Harmondsworth, 1980 and Norberto Valentini and Clara di Meglio, *Sex and the Confessional*, London, 1974.

15 Mary Douglas (ed.), *Witchcraft Confessions and Accusations*, London, 1970.

16 Isidore Fishman, *Introduction to Judaism*, London, 1975, p. 83.

17 Michael Gilsenan, *Saint and Sufi in Modern Egypt*, Oxford, 1973, p. 107.

18 J.K. Birge, *The Bektashi Order of Dervishes*, London, 1965, p. 170.

19 E.J. Bicknell, *The Thirty-Nine Articles*, London, 1959, p. 364.

20 Peter Brown, *Augustine of Hippo: A Biography*, London, 1967, p. 175.

21 *Sermons*, 29, 11, 2.

22 Paul Tillich, *The Protestant Era*, London, 1951, p. 153.

23 M.-D. Chenu, *L'Eveil de la Conscience dans la Civilisation Mediévale*, Paris, 1969.

24 ibid., p. 21.

25 ibid., p. 45.

26 Lucien Goldmann, *The Philosophy of the Enlightenment*, London, 1973, p. 18.
27 Max Weber, *The City*, New York, 1958, p. 103.
28 Sigmund Freud, *Two Short Accounts of Psycho-Analysis*, Harmondsworth, 1962, pp. 97-8.
29 Theodor Reik, *Compulsion to Confess*, New York, 1966; Milton W. Horowitz, 'The psychology of confession', *Journal of Criminal Law and Criminology*, vol. 47, 1956, pp. 197-204; J. Aronfreed, *Conduct and Conscience*, New York, 1968.
30 'Royal Commission, on Criminal Procedure, Police Interrogation, Research Studies', no. 1 and no. 2, HMSO, 1960.

Chapter 1 Rituals of social closure

1 Edwin M. Lemert, *Social Pathology*, New York, 1951.
2 Erving Goffman, *Stigma*, Englewood Cliffs, NJ, 1962.
3 Harold Garfinkel, 'Conditions of successful degradation ceremonies', *American Journal of Sociology*, vol. 61, 1956, pp. 420-4.
4 Howard S. Becker, *Outsiders: Studies in the Sociology of Deviance*, New York, 1963, p. 9.
5 Erving Goffman, *Asylums: Essays on the Social Situation of Mental Patients and other inmates*, Garden City, NY, 1961.
6 Madeline Karmel, 'Total institution and self-mortification', in Howard D. Schwartz and Cary S. Kart (eds), *Dominant Issues in Medical Sociology*, Reading, Massachusetts, 1978, pp. 53-61.
7 C. Wright Mills, 'Situated actions and vocabularies of motive', *American Sociological Review*, vol. 5, 1940, pp. 904-13.
8 Marvin B. Scott and Stanford M. Lyman, 'Accounts', *American Sociological Review*, vol. 33, 1968, pp. 46-62.
9 John P. Hewitt and Randall Stokes, 'Disclaimers', *American Sociological Review*, vol. 40, 1975, pp. 1-11.
10 D.M. Sykes and D. Matza, 'Techniques of neutralization', *American Sociological Review*, vol. 22, 1957, pp. 667-9.
11 Garfinkel, op. cit., p. 423.
12 Edward Shils, *Center and Periphery: Essays in Macrosociology*, Chicago, 1975.
13 Louis Althusser, *Lenin, Philosophy and Other Essays*, London, 1971.
14 E.B. Pashukanis, *Law and Marxism: A General Theory*, London, 1978.
15 Kai T. Erikson, 'Notes on the sociology of deviance', in Earl Rubington and Martin S. Weinberg (eds), *Deviance: An Interactionist Perspective*, New York, 1973, p. 26.
16 Garfinkel, op. cit., p. 421.
17 Sasha R. Weitman, 'Intimacies: notes towards a theory of social inclusion and exclusion', *Archives Européennes de Sociologie*, vol. 11, 1970, pp. 348-67 and reprinted in Arnold Birenbaum and Edward Sagarin (eds), *People in Places: The Sociology of the*

Familiar, London, 1973, pp. 217-38.
18 ibid., p. 223.
19 N. Abercrombie, S. Hill and B.S. Turner, *The Dominant Ideology Thesis*, London, 1980.
20 Owsei Temkin, *The Falling Sickness: A History of Epilepsy from the Greeks to the Beginnings of Modern Neurology*, Baltimore and London, 1971.
21 Stanley Rubin, *Medieval English Medicine*, Newton Abbot, Devon, 1974; S.N. Brody, *The Disease of the Soul, leprosy in medieval literature*, Ithaca, NY, 1974.
22 Thomas Szasz, *The Myth of Mental Illness*, New York, 1961; Thomas Szasz, *The Manufacture of Madness*, New York, 1970; Thomas Szasz, *Ideology and Insanity*, New York, 1970; Thomas J. Scheff, *Being Mentally Ill*, London, 1966.
23 Vieda Skultans, *English Madness: Ideas on Insanity 1580-1890*, London, 1979.
24 Max Weber, *Economy and Society*, vol. 1, New York, 1968, p. 342.
25 Frank Parkin, *Marxism and Class Theory: A Bourgeois Critique*, London, 1979.
26 Paul Hirst, *On Law and Ideology*, London, 1979.
27 Pashukanis, op. cit., p. 173.
28 Nicos Poulantzas, *State, Power and Socialism*, London, 1978; Karl Renner, *The Institutions of Private Law and their Social Functions*, London, 1949.
29 David Trubek, 'Max Weber on law and the rise of capitalism', *Wisconsin Law Review*, vol. 3, 1972, pp. 720-53.
30 Franz Neumann, *The Democratic and the Authoritarian State*, New York, 1957.
31 Douglas Hay, Peter Linebaugh, John Rule and E.P. Thompson, *Albion's Fatal Tree: Crime and Society in Eighteenth-Century England*, Harmondsworth, 1977, p. 22.
32 ibid., p. 29.
33 C.H. Rolph, *The Queen's Pardon*, London, 1978.
34 The exceptions include John Bellamy, *Crime and Public Order in England in the Late Middle Ages*, London, 1973; F.E. Inbau and J.E. Reid (eds), *Criminal Interrogation and Confessions*, Baltimore, 1967; Theodor Reik, *Compulsion to Confess: On the Psycho-analysis of Crime and Punishment*, New York, 1966.
35 Immanuel Kant, 'On the failure of all attempted philosophical theodicies', in Michel Despland, *Kant on History and Religion*, Montreal and London, 1973, p. 288.
36 George Orwell, *The Decline of the English Murder and Other Essays*, Harmondsworth, 1965.
37 Edwin Lemert, 'Role enactment, self, and identity in the systematic check forger', in *Human Deviance, Social Problems and Social Control*, Englewood Cliffs, New Jersey, 1967, p. 125.
38 ibid., p. 131.

Chapter 2 Confession and social structure

1 One exception is Norberto Valentini and Clara Di Meglio, *Sex and the Confessional*, London, 1974.
2 Robert Brain, 'Child-witches', in Mary Douglas (ed.), *Witchcraft Confessions and Accusations*, London, 1970.
3 I.M. Lewis, *Ecstatic Religion*, Harmondsworth, 1971.
4 O. Hobart Mowrer, *The Crisis in Psychiatry and Religion*, New York, 1971.
5 Michael Gilsenan, *Saint and Sufi in Modern Egypt*, Oxford, 1973, pp. 107 ff.
6 C.S. Lewis, *Studies in Words*, Cambridge, 1961, p. 197.
7 W. Addis and T. Arnold, *A Catholic Dictionary*, London, 1960, p. 207.
8 For psychological studies of self-accusation, cf., J. Aronfreed, *Conduct and Conscience*, New York, 1968; M.A. Horowitz, 'The psychology of confession', *Journal of Criminal Law and Criminology*, vol. 47, 1956, pp. 197-204; Derek Wright, *The Psychology of Morals*, Harmondsworth, 1971.
9 Ludwig Bieler (ed.), *The Irish Penitentials*, Dublin, 1963, p. 99.
10 F.J. Heggen, *Confession and the Service of Penance*, London and Melbourne, 1967, p. 19.
11 Charles Williams (ed.), *The Letters of Evelyn Underhill*, London, 1945, p. 88.
12 Erik Berggren, *The Psychology of Confession*, Leiden, 1975.
13 Brain, op. cit., p. 176.
14 John Bellamy, *Crime and Public Order in England in the Later Middle Ages*, London, 1973.
15 Etienne Delcambre, 'Witchcraft trials in Lorraine: psychology of the judges', in E.W. Monter (ed.), *European Witchcraft*, New York, 1969, p. 91.
16 Alan Macfarlane, *Witchcraft in Tudor and Stuart England*, London, 1970, p. 19.
17 Delcambre, op. cit., p. 90.
18 The Warickshall case, 168 E.R. 234.
19 Frank Lake, *Clinical Theology*, London, 1966, p. 225.
20 William Sargant, *Battle for the Mind*, London, 1959 and *The Unquiet Mind*, London, 1969; J.A.C. Brown, *Techniques of Persuasion*, Harmondsworth, 1963.
21 Charles de Neuvill, 'Sermons 111', quoted in Bernard Groethuysen, *The Bourgeois: Catholicism vs. Capitalism in Eighteenth-century France*, London, 1968, pp. 233-4.
22 Bronislaw Malinowski, *Magic, Science and Religion and Other Essays*, New York, 1954; A.R. Radcliffe-Brown, *Taboo*, Cambridge, 1939 and *The Anderman Islanders*, New York, 1964.
23 T.L. Doyle and N. Mailloux, 'The problem of scrupulosity in pastoral work', *Proceedings of the Fordham Institute for the Clergy on Problems in Pastoral Psychology*, New York, 1956, pp. 75-85 and pp. 53-65; C.J.O. Corcoran, 'Thomistic analysis and cure of scrupulosity', *American Ecclesiastical Review*, vol. 137, 1957,

pp. 313-29.
24 Wayne M. Weisner and Pius Anthony Riffel, 'Scrupulosity: religion and obsessive compulsive behaviour in children', *American Journal of Psychiatry*, vol. 117, 1960, p. 315.
25 Quoted in John T. Noonan, Jr., *Contraception*, Cambridge, Massachusetts, 1965, p. 375.
26 Robert K. Merton, *Social Theory and Social Structure*, Glencoe, Ill., 1957, p. 44.
27 Thomas N. Tentler, 'The summa for confessors as an instrument of social control', in Charles Trinkaus and Heiko A. Oberman (eds), *The Pursuit of Holiness in Late Medieval and Renaissance Religion*, Leiden, 1974, p. 110.
28 ibid., p. 123.
29 Quoted in Henry Charles Lea, *A History of Auricular Confession and Indulgences in the Latin Church*, vol. 1, London, 1896, p. 250.
30 Abbé A.M. Laurichesse, *Etudes philosophiques et morales sur la confession*, quoted in Theodore Zeldin (ed.), *Conflicts in French Society*, London, 1970, p. 29.
31 Quoted in Keith Thomas, *Religion and the Decline of Magic*, London, 1971, p. 155.
32 ibid., p. 155.
33 Barbara H. Rosenwein and Lester K. Little, 'Social meaning in the monastic and mendicant spiritualities', *Past and Present*, vol. 63, 1974, p. 13.
34 M-D. Chenu, *L'Eveil de la Conscience dans la Civilisation Mediévale*, Paris, 1969.
35 Rosenwein and Little, op. cit., p. 19.
36 ibid., p. 28.
37 ibid., p. 32.
38 Lea, op. cit., p. 290.
39 Lucien Goldmann, *The Philosophy of the Enlightenment*, London, 1973, p. 18.
40 Benjamin Nelson, 'Self-images and systems of spiritual direction', in Samuel Z. Klausner (ed.), *The Quest for Self-Control: Classical Philosophies and Scientific Research*, New York, 1965.
41 Theodor Reik, *Compulsion to Confess: On the Psychoanalysis of Crime and Punishment*, New York, 1966, p. 302.
42 Quoted in Berggren, op. cit., p. 201.
43 Philip Rieff, 'Toward a theory of culture: with special reference to the psychoanalytic case', in T.J. Nossiter, A.H. Hanson and Stein Rokkan (eds), *Imagination and Precision in the Social Sciences*, London, 1972, p. 106.
44 For further discussion, George Steiner, *On Difficulty and Other Essays,* Oxford, 1972.
45 Sigmund Freud, *Two Short Accounts of Psycho-Analysis*, Harmondsworth, 1974, p. 98.
46 Sigmund Freud, *The Complete Psychological Works of Sigmund Freud*, London, 1962, vol. 11, p. 123.
47 Louis Althusser, 'Freud and Lacan', in *Lenin and Philosophy and*

Other Essays, London, 1971.
48 Philip Rieff, *The Triumph of the Therapeutic*, Harmondsworth, 1973, p. 76.
49 Heinrich Meng and Ernst L. Freud (eds), *Psycho-Analysis and Faith*, London, 1963, p. 127.
50 A. Klempt, *Die Sakularisierung der Universalhistorischen Auffassung*, quoted in Larry Shiner, 'The concept of secularization in empirical research', *Journal for the Scientific Study of Religion*, vol. 6, 1967, pp. 207-20.
51 Rieff, 1973, op. cit., p. 87.
52 For a recent summary of British class inequality, John Westergaard and Henrietta Resler, *Class in a Capitalist Society*, London, 1975.
53 August B. Hollingshead and Frederick C. Redlich, 'Social stratification and psychiatric disorders', *American Sociological Review*, vol. 18, 1953, pp. 163-9.
54 Jerome Myers and Leslie Schaffer, 'Social stratification and psychiatric practice: a study of an out-patient clinic', *American Sociological Review*, vol. 19, 1954, p. 310.
55 Erich Fromm, *The Crisis in Psychoanalysis*, Harmondsworth, 1973, p. 101.
56 ibid., p. 58.
57 ibid., p. 49.
58 Peter Homans, *Theology after Freud*, New York, 1970.
59 Samuel Z. Klausner, *Psychiatry and Religion: A Sociological Study of the New Alliance of Ministers and Psychiatrists*, London, 1964.
60 Mowrer, op. cit., p. 107.
61 Bryan Wilson, *Religion in Secular Society*, London, 1966.
62 Max Weber, *The Sociology of Religion*, London, 1963, p. 188.
63 ibid., p. 189.
64 Henry Sidgwick, *History of Ethics*, London, 1967, p. 153.

Chapter 3 On the universality of confession: compulsion, constraint and conscience

1 Benjamin Nelson, *The Idea of Usury: From Tribal Brotherhood to Universal Brotherhood*, Chicago, 1969; 'The medieval canon law of contracts, Renaissance, "Spirit of capitalism" and the Reformation "conscience": a vote for Max Weber', in R.B. Palmer and R. Hamerton-Kelly (eds), *Philomathes: Studies and Essays in the Humanities in Honor of Philip Medan*, The Hague, 1971, pp. 525-49.
2 Benjamin Nelson, 'Conscience and the making of early modern cultures: *The Protestant Ethic* beyond Max Weber', *Social Research*, vol. 36, 1969, p. 19.
3 Bryan S. Turner, *Weber and Islam: A Critical Study*, London, 1974.
4 Solomon Ganzfried, *Code of Jewish Law*, New York, 1961, p. 84. 'On Islamic systems of penance', K. Wagtendonk, *Fasting in the Koran*, Leiden, 1968.

5 Knud Rasmussen, *The People of the Polar North: A Record*, London, 1908; *Intellectual Culture of the Iglulik Eskimos*, Copenhagen, 1930; *The Netsilik Eskimos: Social Life and Spiritual Culture*, Copenhagen, 1931.
6 Mircea Eliade, *Shamanism: Archaic Technique of Ecstasy*, London, 1964, p. 289; Claude Lévi-Strauss, *Structural Anthropology*, London, 1968, p. 181; I.M. Lewis, *Ecstatic Religion: An Anthropological Study of Spirit Possession and Shamanism*, Harmondsworth, 1971, pp. 165 ff.
7 Rasmussen, 1908, op. cit., p. 124.
8 Hans J. Klimkeit, 'Guilt, pollution and purification rites in Vajrayana Buddhism', in *Guilt or Pollution and Rites of Purification*, proceedings of the XIth international congress of the International Association for the History of Religions, vol. 11, 1968, p. 154.
9 Franz Steiner, *Taboo*, London, 1956.
10 J.G. Frazer, *The Golden Bough*, London, 1960, vol. 1, p. 294.
11 Mary Douglas, *Purity and Danger, an analysis of concepts of pollution and taboo*, London, 1966; Mary Douglas, *Natural Symbols*, Harmondsworth, 1973.
12 Pettazzoni's publications are documented and discussed in Jacques Waardenburg, *Classical Approaches to the Study of Religion*, vol. 2, bibliography, The Hague, 1974.
13 Raffaele Pettazzoni, 'Confession of sins: an interpretation', in *Studies in the History of Religions*, Leiden, 1954, p. 52.
14 Basil Clarke, *Mental Disorder in Earlier Britain*, Cardiff, 1975.
15 Francisco Guerra, 'The role of religion in Spanish American medicine', in F.N.L. Poynter (ed.), *Medicine and Culture*, London, 1969, p. 183.
16 Alan Macfarlane, *The Origins of English Individualism*, Oxford, 1978; M-D. Chenu, *L'Eveil de la Conscience dans la Civilisation Mediévale*, Paris, 1969.
17 G.E.H. Palmer, Philip Sherrard and Kallistos Ware (eds), *The Philokalia*, compiled by St Nikodimos of the Holy Mountain and St Makarios of Corinth, London and Boston, 1979, vol. 1, p. 104.
18 Erik Berggren, *The Psychology of Confession*, Leiden, 1975, pp. 11-12.
19 ibid., p. 19.
20 ibid., p. 7.
21 Emmanuel Le Roy Ladurie, *Montaillou*, Harmondsworth, 1980, p. 13.
22 Bernard Hamilton, *Monastic Reform, Catharism and the Crusades, 900-1300*, London, 1979.
23 Yves Renouard, *The Avignon Papacy: 1305-1403*, Hamden, Connecticut, 1970, p. 121.
24 Fernand Braudel, *The Mediterranean and the Mediterranean World in the Age of Philip* II, London, 1972.
25 H.R. Trevor-Roper, *The European Witch-Craze of the 16th and 17th Centuries*, Harmondsworth, 1969, p. 42.
26 Hugh V. McLachlan and J.K. Swales, 'Witchcraft and anti-feminism',

Scottish Journal of Sociology, vol. 4, 1980, pp. 141-66.
27 A. Macfarlane, *Witchcraft in Tudor and Stuart England*, London, 1970; K. Thomas 'The relevance of social anthropology to the historical study of English Witchcraft', in Mary Douglas (ed.), *Witchcraft Confessions and Accusations*, London, 1970, pp. 47-9.
28 Trevor-Roper, op. cit. Various theories of witchcraft are discussed in Max Marwick (ed.), *Witchcraft and Sorcery*, Harmondsworth, 1970.
29 B. Ehrenreich and D. English, *Witches, Midwives and Nurses*, London, 1974.
30 Jean Delumeau, *Catholicism between Luther and Voltaire*, London and Philadelphia, 1977, p. 173.
31 James VI and I, *Daemonologie*, Edinburgh, 1597, pp. 43–4 and quoted in McLachlan and Swales, op. cit., pp. 152-3.
32 Ladurie, op. cit. Theodore Zeldin (ed.), *Conflicts in French Society*, London, 1970.
33 Delumeau, op. cit., p. 170.
34 George Groddeck, *The Meaning of Illness,* London, 1977, p.200.

Chapter 4 Power, knowledge and confession: the work of Michel Foucault

1 Michel Foucault, *The Order of Things: An Archaeology of the Human Sciences*, London, 1970; *The Archaeology of Knowledge*, London, 1972.
2 For discussion and the criticism, cf. Alan Sheridan, *Michel Foucault: The Will to Truth*, London, 1980; Rosalind Coward and John Ellis, *Language and Materialism: Developments in Semiology and the Theory of the Subject*, Boston, London and Henley, 1977; Colin Gordon, 'Other Inquisitions', *Ideology and Consciousness*, no. 6, 1979, pp. 23-46; M. Morris and P. Paton (eds), *Michel Foucault: Power, Truth and Strategy*, Sydney, 1979; B. Brown and M. Cousins, 'The linguistic fault: the case of Foucault's archaeology', *Economy & Society,* vol. 9, 1980, pp. 251-78; Hayden White, 'Michel Foucault', in John Sturrock (ed.), *Structuralism and Since: From Lévi-Strauss to Derrida*, Oxford, 1979, pp. 81-115. For a general discussion of structuralism, Anthony Giddens, 'Structuralism and the theory of the subject' in *Central Problems in Social Theory*, London, 1979, pp. 9-48.
3 On the relationship between Canguilhem and Foucault, cf. the latter's introduction to George Canguilhem, *On the Normal and the Pathological*, Dordrecht, Boston and London, 1978.
4 Foucault, 1972, ibid., pp. 31-9.
5 ibid., p. 51.
6 ibid., pp. 144-5.
7 Gordon, ibid., p. 29.
8 Michel Foucault, *Discipline and Punish: The Birth of the Prison*, London, 1977, p. 18.
9 ibid., p. 29.

10 ibid., p. 61.
11 ibid., p. 39.
12 White, op. cit., p. 105.
13 Michel Foucault (ed.), *I, Pierre Riviere, Having Slaughtered My Mother, My Sister and My Brother: A Case of Parricide in the 19th Century*, New York, 1975, p. 21.
14 ibid., p. 144.
15 ibid., p. 125.
16 ibid., p. 201.
17 Michel Foucault, *The History of Sexuality: An Introduction*, vol.1, London, 1979, p. 21.
18 ibid., p. 59.
19 ibid., pp. 61-2.
20 Arthur Mitzman, *The Iron Cage: An Historical Interpretation of Max Weber* New York, 1970.
21 Michel Foucault, *The Birth of the Clinic: An Archaeology of Medical Perception*, London, 1973, p. xix.
22 Gordon, op. cit., p. 36.
23 Barbara A. Hanawalt, *Crime and Conflict in English Communities 1300-1348*, Cambridge, Massachusetts and London, 1979, p. 268.
24 Michael R. Weisser, *Crime and Punishment in Early Modern Europe*, Hassocks, 1979.
25 Barbara H. Rosenwein and Lester K. Little, 'Social meaning in the monastic and mendicant spiritualities', *Past & Present*, vol. 63, 1973, pp. 4-32.
26 Nicholas Abercrombie, Stephen Hill and Bryan S. Turner, *The Dominant Ideology Thesis*, London, 1980.
27 Foucault, 1979, op. cit., p. 20.
28 George Duby, *Medieval Marriage: Two Models From Twelfth Century France*, Baltimore and London, 1978.
29 G.R. Quaife, *Wanton Wenches and Wayward Wives*, London, 1979.
30 H.J. Habakkuk, 'Marriage settlements in the eighteenth century' *Transactions of the Royal Historical Society*, vol. 32, 1950, pp. 15-30.
31 Frank Parkin, *Marxism and Class Theory: A Bourgeois Critique*, London, 1979.
32 Foucault, 1979, op. cit., pp. 146-7.
33 Owsei Temkin, *Galenism: Rise and Decline of a Medical Philosophy*, Ithaca and London, 1973.
34 Ian MacLean, *The Renaissance Notion of Women*, Cambridge, 1980.

Chapter 5 Confession in popular literature

1 Charles Dickens, 'A Letter to the *Daily News*, 28 February 1846', reproduced in D.D. Cooper, *The Lesson of the Scaffold: The Public Execution Controversy in Victorian England*, London, 1974, p. 80.
2 R. Graves, *They Hanged My Saintly Billy: The Macabre Life and*

Execution of Dr Wm Palmer, London, 1962, p. 265.
3 ibid.
4 H. Douglas, *Burke and Hare: The True Story*, London, 1973.
5 ibid., p. 120.
6 J. Berry, *My Experiences As An Executioner*, Newton Abbot, reprinted 1972, p. 47.
7 Reproduced in R.D. Altick, *Victorian Studies in Scarlet*, London, 1972, p. 99.
8 ibid., p. 100.
9 Quoted in the *Illustrated Guide To Madame Tussaud's*, London, nd, p. 24.
10 Berry, op. cit., pp. 112-13.
11 ibid.
12 Reproduced in J.H. Marchburn, *Murder and Witchcraft in England 1550-1640 As Recounted in Pamphlets, Ballads, Broadsides and Plays*, Oklahoma, 1971.
13 M.S. Hartman, *Victorian Murderesses*, London, 1977.
14 M.E. Grenander, 'The Heritage of Cain: Crime in American Fiction', *Annals of The American Academy of Political and Social Science*, vol. ccccxxii, January 1976, p. 47.
15 J.M. Parrish and J.R. Crossland (eds), *The Fifty Most Amazing Crimes of The Last Hundred Years*, London, 1936, pp. 7-8.
16 E. Lustgarten, *A Century of Murderers*, London, 1975.
17 Reproduced in Hartman, op. cit., p. 282.
18 ibid.
19 Lustgarten, op. cit.
20 Berry, op. cit.
21 L. Henderson, 'The Hangman's Story', in D. Winn (ed.), *Murder Ink: The Mystery Reader's Companion*, Newton Abbot, 1978, pp. 400-1.
22 ibid.
23 R. Whitmore, *Victorian and Edwardian Crime and Punishment From Old Photographs*, London, 1978, p. 128.
24 B. Cobb, *Criminals Confess*, London, 1959, p. 9.
25 H. Douglas Thomson, *Masters of Mystery: A Study of The Detective Story*, London, 1931, pp. 39-40.
26 A.E. Murch, *The Development of the Detective Novel*, London, 1968.
27 W. Bolitho, *Murder For Profit*, London, 1953 (originally published, 1926).
28 Quoted in Douglas Thomson, op. cit.
29 W. Godwin, *Caleb Williams*, London, 1975, p. 315 (originally published 1794).
30 I. Ousby, *Bloodhounds of Heaven: The Detective in English Fiction From Godwin to Doyle*, Cambridge (USA) and London, 1976, p. 42.
31 J. Symons, *Bloody Murder: From The Detective Story To The Crime Novel: A History*, Harmondsworth, 1974.
32 J. Goodman, *Posts-Mortem: The Correspondence of Murder*, Newton Abbot, 1971, p. 119.

33 Symons, op. cit., p. 16.
34 ibid, pp. 183-4.
35 Bolitho, op. cit., p. 43.
36 Cf. Hartman, op. cit.
37 J.G. Cawelti, *Adventure, Mystery, and Romance: Formula Stories as Art and Popular Culture*, Chicago, 1976.
38 C.S. Forester, *Payment Deferred*, London, 1973 (originally published 1926).
39 E. Raymond, *We, The Accused*, London, 1973 (originally published 1935).
40 Forester, op. cit., p. 7.
41 C.S. Forester, *Plain Murder*, London, 1970 (originally published 1930).
42 Forester, 1973, op. cit., pp. 33-4.
43 Raymond, op. cit., p. 505.

Chapter 6 Confessing to murder: critical notes on the sociology of motivation

1 H. de Balzac, *A Murky Business*, Harmondsworth, 1972, p. 154.
2 Contemporary sociology of motivation, particularly in the realm of the sociology of deviance, has taken as its point of departure C. Wright Mills's seminal paper, 'Situated actions and vocabularies of motive', 1940, vol. 5, *American Sociological Review*, pp. 904-13. For a definition of 'motivational accounts' see p. 46 infra. Two valuable empirical explorations may be found in Taylor, 'The significance and interpretation of replies to motivational questions: the case of sex offenders', 1972, vol. 6, *Sociology*, pp. 23-39, and J. Auld, 'Drug use: the mystification of accounts', in *Contemporary Social Problems in Britain* (eds), R.V. Bailey and J. Young, London, 1973, Saxon House, 145-69.
3 J. Loftland, *Deviance and Identity*, Englewood Cliffs, N.J., 1969.
4 We are drawing on David Matza's elaboration of appreciation: 'The growth of a sociological view of deviant phenomena involved, as major phases, the replacement of a correctional stance by an appreciation of the deviant subject, the tacit purging of a conception of pathology by new stress on human diversity, and the erosion of a simple distinction between deviant and conventional phenomena. . .', *Becoming Deviant*, Englewood Cliffs, NJ, 1969, p. 10.
5 Donald Newman's observation about the need for research into the conviction process is particularly relevant: 'Apart from the "fix" and the "third degree", the conviction process has generally been neglected in research as of minor importance in the complicated process of defining "criminals" as the basic unit of research.' Cf. Newman, 'Pleading Guilty for Considerations: A Study of Bargain Justice', *Journal of Criminal Law, Criminology, and Police Science*, 1956, vol. 46, p. 780.
6 The word 'confession' is commonly defined as: 'A making known

or acknowledging of one's fault, wrong, crime, weakness, etc. 1602', *The Oxford Universal Dictionary*, vol. 1, London, 1959.

7 See, for example, Anthony Wilden's essay on Svevo's novel, *The Confessions of Zeno* (1923), where he underscores the inadequate translation of the word *coscienza* (appearing in the original Italian title of the book) into the English 'confessions'. This act, he argues, 'obscures the triple sense of the Italian' meaning conscience, knowledge and consciousness. 'Death, Desire and Repetition: Commentary on Svevo's Confessions of Zeno' in *System and Structure: Essays in Communication and Exchange*, London, 1972, p. 63.

8 See paragraphs 53-69 of the Criminal Law Revision Committee, *Eleventh Report Evidence (General)* (1972: Cmnd. 4991) for a description of the current legal approach to 'Confessions'.

9 L. Radzinowicz, *History of English Criminal Law and Its Administration from 1750, Grappling for Control*, vol. 4, London, 1968, p. 348.

10 See J.D.J. Havard for an examination of the historical development of medico-legal investigative procedures and the alleged relationship of their continuing inadequacies to the pervasive presence of undiscovered murders in our midst. *The Detection of Secret Homicide: A Study of the Medico-Legal System of Investigation of Sudden and Unexplained Deaths*, London, 1960. The point here of course is, as with the general 'dark' or 'hidden number' of crime theory, that confessions to murder are largely limited to police suspects in the first place: or to that other important category of 'cranks' whose outpourings tend to be dismissed. Presumably those who can live quietly with their deed are not burdened by a sense of guilt demanding public expiation.

11 Radzinowicz, op. cit.

12 English murder has always been 'understandable': the situational vocabulary delimiting motives for murder has remained relatively uncomplicated in English criminal history. A range, regardless of the presence of apparent mental disturbance however defined, which has been limited to gain, revenge, elimination, jealousy, lust and conviction. Cf. L. Taylor and I. Taylor, 'Changes in the Motivational Construction of Deviance' (Universities of York and Sheffield, unpublished). See also E. Gibson and S. Klein, *Murder*. London, 1961; E. Gibson and S. Klein, *Murder 1957 to 1968*, London, 1969; A.D. Weatherhead and B.M. Robinson, *Firearms in Crime*, London, 1970; and T. Morris and L. Blom-Cooper, *A Calendar of Murder: Criminal Homicide in England Since 1957*, London, 1964.

13 The classic accessible interrogation manual where 'tactics' and their over-all relations to conventional ideologies distinguishing criminal from non-criminal character are most unambiguously worked out is F.E. Inbau and J.E. Reid (eds), *Criminal Interrogation and Confessions*, Baltimore, 1967. This is an American book. By contrast formal accessible materials outlining interrogation tactics for English policemen are hard to come by. Most discussions detail

wider administrative procedures surrounding this area of criminal investigation. Occasionally public preoccupation with a *cause célèbre* breaches the barriers of reserve; see Ludovic Kennedy on the interrogation of Timothy Evans, posthumously pardoned for murder, in *Ten Rillington Place*, London, 1963.

14 R. Collison, *The Story of Street Literature: Forerunner of the Popular Press*, London, 1973, p. 47.

15 Cf. Taylor and Taylor, op. cit.

16 C. Wilson, *A Casebook of Murder*, London, 1969.

17 G. Orwell, *Decline of the English Murder and Other Essays*, Harmondsworth, 1965, emphasis added.

18 Gibson and Klein, *Murder 1957 to 1968,* op. cit. ' "Abnormal" murder is murder committed by someone "suffering from such abnormality of mind" as "substantially impaired his mental responsibility for his acts and omissions in doing or being a party to the killing".'

19 R. Williams, *The Country and The City*, London, 1973.

20 Inbau and Reid, op. cit. argue from experience that criminal offenders ordinarily will not admit their guilt unless lengthily questioned under conditions of privacy. Critics of police interrogation procedures have frequently drawn attention to the fact that confessions to all kinds of crimes often take place unwitnessed by outsiders in what amount to conditions of secrecy. See, for example, M. King's edited assessment of the Criminal Law Revision Committee's Eleventh Report, *Guilty Until Proved Innocent*, London, 1973.

21 Radzinowicz, op. cit.

22 Commensurate with the general aim of the Committee to modify 'rules which have ceased to be appropriate to modern conditions', where it was felt that the emergent sophistication of modern criminal classes rendered the police mandate of winning the war against crime increasingly arduous, the Committee focused on *the criteria defining confessions as reliable evidence*. The problem is to get confessions efficiently while preserving traditional legal safeguards.

23 P. Gillman, 'Murder on His Mind', *Sunday Times Magazine*, 2 January 1972, pp. 7-17.

24 ibid., p. 16.

25 H. Garfinkel, 'Conditions of Successful Degradation Ceremonies' *American Journal of Sociology*, vol. 61, 1956, pp. 420-4.

26 A useful comparison may be made between the voluntary confession springing from 'the burden of guilt' and Edwin Lemert's classic study of the isolating experiences of certain lone-operating systematic cheque forgers in America. Lemert notes that his analysis

> 'argues strongly that the personal crisis of the systematic forger' [producing a situation where he deliberately engineers his own detection and arrest] 'stems less from a moral dilemma than it does from the erosion of identity. So conceived, his problem resides in a neutral component or dimension of the self, namely

the sense of separateness and relationship to others, which is assumed to have its own consequences for behaviour apart from substantive social value, 'good or bad', assigned to it. In a sense the forger fails because he is able to fend off or evade self-degradative consequences of his actions but in so doing he rejects forms of interaction necessary to convert his rewards into positive, status-specific self-evaluations. In time he reaches a point at which he can no longer define himself in relation to others on any basis. The self becomes amorphous, without boundaries; the identity substructure is lost. Apathy replaces motivation, and in phenomenological terms, 'life' or 'this way of life' is no longer worth living. This is the common prelude to the forger's arrest'.

E.M. Lemert, 'Role Enactment, Self and Identity in The Systematic Cheque Forger', in *Human Deviance, Social Problems and Social Control*, Englewood Cliffs, N.J., pp. 119-34. To this we may add that in spite of Lemert's persuasive analysis it remains problematic whether all isolated undetected offenders undergo these experiences.

27 An example of a multiple confession is discussed in Zimbardo, 'The Psychology of Police Confessions' *Psychology Today*, July 1969, pp. 17-20.

28 The police and the Home Office have persistently refused to give further credence to Peter Alphon's confession that he in fact committed the A6 murder in August 1961 (for which James Hanratty was hanged) in spite of the flimsy circumstantial evidence against him. For Alphon's confession see P. Foot, *Who Killed Hanratty?*, St Albans, 1973.

29 Cf. Ludovic Kennedy's discussion of the confession of Timothy Evans, op. cit.

30 ibid., for the subsequent behaviour of Reginald Halliday Christie, later shown to have carried out the murder for which Evans was hanged.

31 De Salvo was at first disbelieved because his observed personality did not fit the pre-existing psychiatric model of the type of offender likely to be responsible for the mass strangulations. Also, there was no evidence at first to connect him with the killings. G. Frank, *The Boston Strangler*, London, 1967.

32 For example, Hermann Mannheim has written: 'The ideas of reparation and confession are essential elements in both religion and penology', *Comparative Criminology*, vol. 1, London, 1965, p. 37.

33 Baldwin Smith, 'English Treason Trials and Confessions in the Sixteenth Century' (1954) 15 *J. of the History of Ideas* 151-476. For further comments on confessions and loyalty to the State, cf. John Bellamy, *Crime and Public Order in England in the Later Middle Ages*, London, 1973, ch. 6.

34 The Warickshall case, 168 E.R. 234 is discussed in *Criminal Law Revision Committee, Eleventh Report*, op. cit.

35 W. Addis and T. Arnold, *A Catholic Dictionary*, London, 1960, p. 207.
36 E.J. Bicknell (revised by H.J. Carpenter), *A Theological Introduction to the Thirty-nine Articles of the Church of England*, London, 1959, p. 364.
37 J. Berry, *My Experiences As An Executioner*, Newton Abbot, 1972, p. 67.
38 The relationship between guilt, conversion and confession is noted in William Sargant, *Battle for the Mind*, London, 1959; Argyle, 'Seven Psychological Roots of Religion', *Theology*, vol. 67, 1964, pp. 1-7.
39 Besides Inbau and Reid, op. cit., additional commentary can be pursued in Sterling, 'Police Interrogation and the Psychology of Confession', *Journal of Public Law*, vol. 14, 1965, pp. 25-65.
40 *Miranda v. Arizona*, 384 US 436 (1966). A comprehensive discussion of the Miranda decision and its institutionalisation is presented in Medalie, Zeitz and Alexander, 'Custodial Police Interrogation in our Nations's Capital: the Attempt to Implement Miranda', *Michigan Law Review*, vol. 66, 1968, pp. 1347-422.
41 Cf. Blumberg, 'The Practice of Law as Confidence Game: Organisational Co-optation of a Profession', *Law and Society Review*, vol. 1, 1967, pp. 15-39.
42 *Criminal Law Revision Committee, Eleventh Report*, op. cit.
43 Frank Lake, *Clinical Theology*, London, 1966, p. 225.
44 See for example, Inbau and Reid, op. cit.
45 J. Michelet's *Le Prêtre, La Femme et La Famille* is discussed, along with other confessional material, in Theodore Zeldin, 'The Conflict of Moralities: Confession, Sin and Pleasure in The Nineteenth Century', *Conflicts in French Society* (ed.), T. Zeldin, London, 1970.
46 Theodor Reik, *Compulsion to Confess: On the Psychoanalysis of Crime and Punishment*, New York, 1966 John Wiley, p. 302. Further psychoanalytical interpretations of guilt and confession can be found in Horowitz, 'The Psychology of Confession', *Journal of Criminal Law and Criminology*, vol. 47, 1956, pp. 197-204.
47 *Methodist New Connexion Magazine*, October 1867, p. 125.
48 Gordon W. Allport, *The Individual and His Religion*, New York, 1962.
49 *Criminal Law Revision Committee, Eleventh Report*, op. cit.
50 ibid., para. 273
51 Alasdair MacIntyre, *Secularization and Moral Change*, London, 1967.
52 Richard D. Altick, *Victorian Studies in Scarlet: Murders and Manners in the Age of Victoria*, London, 1972.
53 Cf. N. Walker, *Crime and Insanity in England* vol. 1 and vol. 2, Edinburgh, 1968 and 1973.
54 Cf. Taylor and Taylor, op. cit.
55 Much of the contemporary research into interrogation practice in the United States is reviewed and discussed by Edward D. Driver, 'Confessions and the Social Psychology of Coercion', in *Law and*

Order in a Democratic Society (eds), Marvin R. Summers and Thomas E. Barth, Ohio, 1970, pp. 71-90.
56 Cf. Gibson and Klein, 1961 and 1969, op. cit.; Morris and Blom-Cooper, op. cit.
57 In Perry Anderson's view this political stability is partly explained by the fact that the landed aristocracy adopted capitalist means of production and retained control of the English cabinet and parliament. In short, England had a capitalist economic revolution but did not produce a completely dominant bourgeois society. For a number of other historical reasons the British government never came to depend solely on a land army for its political authority. Cf. Perry Anderson, 'The Origins of the Present Crisis', in *Towards Socialism*, London, 1966, pp. 11-52. All of this contributed to the domesticity of English murder. One might also add that the absence of a 'peasant problem' in English social stratification contributed to the strong urban characteristics of crime, particularly murder. On the transformation of the traditional rural society, cf. Barrington Moore, *Social Origins of Dictatorship and Democracy*, Harmondsworth, 1966.
58 Altick, op. cit.
59 Erving Goffman, *Strategic Interaction*, Oxford, 1971, pp. 96-125 in which he is especially concerned with the problem of how it is possible 'for mere avowals to play a role in strategic interaction'.
60 For example, Gerson and Victoroff, 'Experimental Investigation into The Validity of Confessions Obtained Under Sodium Amytal Narcosis', *Journal of Clinical Psychopathology*, vol. 9, 1948, pp. 359–75.
61 M.B. Scott and S.M. Lyman, 'Accounts', *American Sociological Review*, vol. 33, 1968, pp. 46–62.
62 ibid.
63 For various views of coercive methods of obtaining accounts, cf. Winokur, 'Brain-washing – a social phenomenon of our time', *Human Organisation*, vol. 13, 1955, pp. 16–18; Winokur, 'The Germ Warfare Statements; A Synthesis of a Method for the Extortion of False Confessions' *Journal of Neuro-Mental Disorders*, vol. 122, 1955, pp. 65-72; George H. Dession, Laurence Z. Freedman, Richard C. Donnelly and Frederick C. Bellich, 'Drug-induced revelation and criminal investigation', *Yale Law Journal*, vol. 62, 1953, pp. 316-47.
64 The same distinction between pragmatic and normative acceptance of dominant values is made in Mann, 'The Social Cohesion of Liberal Democracy', *American Sociological Review*, vol. 35, 1970, pp. 423-39.
65 Probably one of the most influential papers has been, of course, Sykes and Matza, 'Techniques of Neutralisation: A Theory of Delinquency', *American Sociological Review*, vol. 22, 1957, pp. 664-70.
66 Basso, 1970, 'To Give Up on Words: Silence in Western Apache Culture', (1970) *Southwestern Journal of Anthropology*, revised version in *Language and Social Context* (ed.), Pier Paolo Gigliolo, Harmondsworth, 1972, p. 69.

67 *Criminal Law Revision Committee*, op. cit., para. 17.
68 Griffiths and Ayres, 'A Postscript to the Miranda Project: Interrogation of Draft Protestors', *Yale Law Journal*, vol. 77, 1967, pp. 300-19.

Chapter 7 Confession, guilt and responsibility

1 J.H.H. Gaute and R. Odell, *The Murderer's Who's Who*, London 1979.
2 C. Wilson, *A Casebook of Murder* London, 1971.
3 *Trial, Sentence, and Condemnation of Mary Ann Cotton, The West Auckland Secret Poisoner*, London, 1873.
4 J.P. Martin (ed.), *Violence and The Family*, Chichester, New York, 1978.
5 L. Radzinowicz and J. King, *The Growth of Crime: The International Experience*, Harmondsworth, 1977.
6 E. Gibson and S. Klein, *Murder 1957-68*, 1969; E. Gibson, *Homicide in England and Wales 1967-71*, London, 1975.
7 International examples include P. Bohannan (ed.), *African Homicide and Suicide* London, 1960; H.P. Lundsgaarde, *Murder in Space City: A Cultural Analysis of Houston Homicide Patterns*, New York, 1977; Luckenbill, 'Criminal Homicide as A Situated Transaction', 1977 *Social Problems*, 25; and M.S. Hartman, *Victorian Murderesses: A True History of Thirteen Respectable French and English Women Accused of Unspeakable Crimes*, London, 1977.
8 J. Berry, *My Experiences as An Executioner* Reprinted, Newton Abbot, 1972.
9 J. Goodman, *Bloody Versicles: The Rhymes of Crime*, Newton Abbot, 1971.
10 J. Berry, op. cit.
11 C.S. Lewis, *Studies in Words*, Cambridge, 1961.
12 W. Addis and T. Arnold, *A Catholic Dictionary*, London, 1960.
13 L. Radzinowicz, *History of English Criminal Law and Its Administration From 1750*, London, 1968.
14 H. Dalziel Duncan, *Communication and Social Order*, New York, 1962.
15 J.T. McNeil, *A History of The Cure of Souls*, London, 1952.
16 Thomas N. Tentler. 'The Summa for Confessors as An Instrument of Social Control', in C. Trinkaus and H.A. Oberman (eds), *The Pursuit of Holiness in Late Medieval and Renaissance Religion* (1974).
17 de Penaforte and other confessors are discussed in J.T. McNeil and H.M. Gamer, *Medieval Handbooks of Penance*, London, 1938; and H.C. Lea, *History of Auricular Confessions and Indulgences* 2 vols, London, 1896.
18 Tentler, op. cit.
19 J. Bellamy, *Crime and Public Order in England in the Late Middle Ages*, London, 1973.

20 J. Samaha, *Law and Order in Historical Perspective: The Case of Elizabethan Essex*, New York and London, 1974.
21 J.H. Marchburn, *Murder and Witchcraft in England 1550-1640*. As recounted in *Pamphlets, Ballads, Broadsides and Plays*, London, 1971.
22 R. Collison, *The Story of Street Literature: Forerunner of The Popular Press*, London, 1973.
23 E. Lustgarten, *A Century of Murderers*, London, 1975.
24 Peter Linebaugh, 'The Ordinary of Newgate and His Account', in J.S. Cockburn, (ed.), *Crime in England 1550-1800*, London, 1977.
25 J. Lofland, 'The Dramaturgy of State Executions', in H. Bleakley and J. Lofland, *State Executions Viewed Historically and Sociologically*, London, 1977; D.D. Cooper, *The Lesson of The Scaffold*, London, 1974; M. Foucault, *Discipline and Punish: The Birth of The Prison*, Harmondsworth, 1977.
26 *The Newgate Calendar*, vol. 3, Wilkinson's Edition reprinted, St Albans, 1963.
27 N. Walker, *Crime and Insanity in England, vol. 1*, Edinburgh, 1968.
28 10 Cl + F200; 8 E.R.718.
29 D.R. Watson, 'Some Features of The Elicitation of Confessions in Murder Interrogations', unpublished paper, University of Manchester.
30 E.M. Lemert, 'An Isolation and Closure Theory of Naive Cheque Forgery', in E.M. Lemert, *Human Deviance, Social Problems, and Social Control*, Englewood Cliffs, 1967.
31 *Criminal Law Revision Committee, Eleventh Report: Evidence* (General), London, 1972.
32 For comparative evidence on police interrogations in the United States see F. Inbau and J. Reid, *Criminal Interrogations and Confessions*, Baltimore, 1962.
33 Much of the relevant literature has been outlined in Driver, 'Confessions and the social psychology of coercion', in M.R. Summers and T.E. Barth (eds) *Law and Order in A Democratic Society*, London, 1970.
34 For further elaboration see E. Goffman, *Strategic Interaction*, Oxford, 1969.
35 H. Mannheim, *Comparative Criminology*, vol. 1, London, 1965.
36 Certain aspects of religious therapy and the confessional technique are discussed by F. Lake, *Criminal Theology*, London, 1966.
37 E. Goffman, *Relations in Public: The Microstudies of The Public Order*, London, 1971.
38 Lewis, op. cit.
39 T. Duster, in N. Sanford and L. Comstock (eds), *Sanctions for Evil*, San Francisco, 1971.

Conclusion: oppression and confession

1 J.S. Mill, *Dissertations and Discussions*, vol. 1, 3rd edn, London,

1875, p. 471. For an analysis of Mill's views on democracy, cf. J.H. Burns, 'J.S. Mill and democracy, 1829-1861', *Political Studies*, vol. 5, 1957 and reprinted in J.B. Schneewind (ed.), *Mill: A Collection of Critical Essays*, London, 1969, pp. 280-328. Mill's notion of 'Chinese stationariness' is considered in Bryan S. Turner, 'The concept of social "stationariness": utilitarianism and Marxism', *Science and Society*, vol. 38, 1974, pp. 3-18.

2 These liberal fears are outlined in Sheldon S. Wolin, *Politics and Vision*, London, 1961.

3 W.E.H. Lecky, *The Rise and Influence of Rationalism in Europe*, London, 1910, p. xv.

4 ibid., p. 15.

5 ibid., p. 129.

6 H.R. Trevor-Roper, *The European Witch-Craze of the 16th and 17th Centuries*, Harmondsworth, 1969, p. 22.

7 N. Cohn, *The Pursuit of the Millennium*, New York, 1957.

8 J.A.C. Brown, *Techniques of Persuasion: From Propaganda to Brainwashing*, Harmondsworth, 1963.

9 R.K. Merton, *Science, Technology and Society in 17th century England*, New York, 1970.

10 F.H. Tenbruck, 'Max Weber and the sociology of science: a case reopened', *Zeitschrift für Soziologie*, vol. 3, 1974, p. 315.

11 Jürgen Habermas, *Toward a Rational Society*, London, 1971 and *Knowledge and Human Interests*, London, 1972.

12 Habermas, 1972, op. cit., p. 253.

13 Jürgen Habermas, 'On systematically distorted communication', *Inquiry*, vol. 13, 1970, pp. 205-18.

14 Richard J. Bernstein, *The Restructuring of Social and Political Theory*, London, 1979, p. 222.

15 Michel Foucault, *Discipline and Punishment: The Birth of Prison*, Harmondsworth 1977, p. 27.

16 Alan Sheridan, *Michel Foucault: The Will to Truth*, London, 1980, p. 206.

17 Michel Foucault *The History of Sexuality: An Introduction*, vol. 1, London, 1979, p. 60.

18 Peter Taylor, *Beating the Terrorists? Interrogation in Omagh, Gough and Castlereagh*, Harmondsworth, 1980.

19 A.D. Biderman, 'The image of brainwashing', *Public Opinion Quarterly*, vol. 26, 1962, pp. 547-63.

20 M.G. Wiley and L. Hudik, 'Police-citizen encounters: a field test of exchange theory', *Social Problems*, vol. 22, 1974, pp. 119-27.

21 E.D. Driver 'Confessions and the social psychology of coercion', *Harvard Law Review*, vol. 82, 1968, pp. 42-61.

22 F.E. Inbau and J. Reid, *Criminal Interrogations and Confessions*, Baltimore, 1967.

23 Barrie Irving and Linden Hilgendorf, *Police Interrogation: The Psychological Approach: A Case Study of Current Practice. Royal Commission on Criminal Procedure. Research Studies no. 1 and no. 2,* London, 1980, p. 25.

24 ibid., p. 153.

25 Harvey Sacks, Emanuel A. Schegloff and Gail Jefferson. 'A simplest systematics for the organization of turn-taking for conversation', *Language*, vol. 50, 1974, pp. 696-735.
26 Emanuel A. Schegloff, 'Notes on a conversational practice: formulating place', in David Sudnow (ed.), *Studies in Social Interaction*, New York, 1972, p. 77.
27 J. Baldwin and M. McConville, *Confessions in Crown Court Trials*, London, 1980.
28 David Moxon and Paul Softley, 'Confession, criminal record, venue and plea', *Research Bulletin* (Home Office Research Unit), no. 10, 1980, pp. 14-15.
29 J.C. Flugel, *Man, Morals and Society*, Harmondsworth, 1955, p. 38.
30 P.H. Nowell-Smith, *Ethics*, Harmondsworth, 1954, p. 308.

Name Index

Subject Index